# WORLD
# HISTORY

First published by Parragon in 2011

Parragon
Queen Street House
4 Queen Street
Bath BA1 1HE, UK

Designed and edited by Ignition

The contents of this book are believed
correct at the time of printing.
Nevertheless, the publishers cannot be
held responsible for any errors, omissions
or for changes in the details given in this
book or for the consequences of any
reliance on the information provided by
the same.

ISBN 978-1-4454-1770-7
Printed in China

# WORLD HISTORY

Bath • New York • Singapore • Hong Kong • Cologne • Delhi
Melbourne • Amsterdam • Johannesburg • Auckland • Shenzhen

# Contents

## Chapter 1

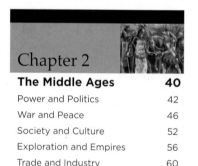

## Chapter 2

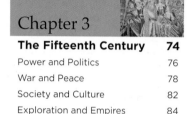

## Chapter 3

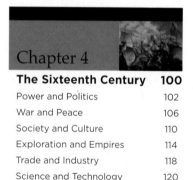

## Chapter 4

# Contents

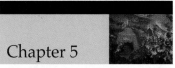

## Chapter 5

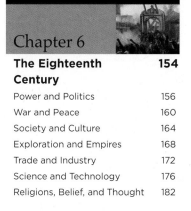

## Chapter 6

## Chapter 7

## Chapter 8

# Introduction

THIS IS AN ACCESSIBLE HISTORY for the close of one millennium and the start of another. In looking back we understand better not only the fascination of the past, but also ourselves, our world, and our possibilities for the future This, then, is an exciting tale of bold coverage. The key thematic perspectives through which each century is seen offer both a comprehensive account of world history and provide a coherent coverage of crucial dynamics of the human past. Individually, they offer important perspectives and, collectively, they build toward a compelling whole in which aspects of all cultures, regions, and periods are covered.

The dominating issues in human history covered here—all as important for our future as for our past—include human relations with the environment; the demographic history of the species; relations between the generations and the sexes—the crucial issues in social structure; the structures of productive society, such as class; the world belief, particularly religion; the ways in which people identify themselves, their families, and their worlds: place, ethnic group, language, religion, each of which is often in a dynamic but also has an unsteady relationship with the others;

*A changing world full of remarkable events.*

*Tea being thrown into the sea by disguised Bostonians in retaliation against British trade restrictions.*

the organization of political society: units of authority and the objectives, relations within and between states; and the march of scientific knowledge, technological capability, and economic development. These issues are all approached through the themes and entries of this book. The issues link greater technological strength that requires more resources

*Three Roman coins.*

and, thus, puts more pressure on the environment. Indeed, in this century, man has altered his environment more than in any other. Yet, this process of change is not new, and an understanding of the ongoing nature of change is important when looking at our own age. Thus, deforestation—the clearing of natural woodland to provide agriculture and settlement—has been going on for centuries.

Change is the issue in history. The past is not a series of static shots, frozen in time—for example, Paris in 1650 or the life of the factory worker in 1850.

*Hitler, Von Keitel, and Jodl during World War II, Germany.*

governments, and religions were the fabric of the past and the cause of altering experiences for its people.

The reality is with us today. Take anyone of 80 years of age. In their life, they have seen what would have been regarded as inconceivable or unlikely when they were born: space rockets and microchips, antibiotics and artificial hips. We take all this for granted, but also know how important it is to understand these changes. History is not just a record of change; it also helps us understand it.

At the start of a new millennium there is hope and uncertainty— a sense of particular balance between past and future. That is a useful image, but much of the thrust of this book rests on the notion that past and future are not rival worlds. Instead, we

*Chain-mail armor, in common usage in the 11th century.*

Such an approach can yield interesting images, but it is essentially rigid. Instead, it is necessary to understand how the past is part of a living process of change, and was and is given energy and meaning, importance, and explanation by this change. Without an understanding of change, we cannot appreciate the "whys" of the past and, thus, of the present: why did they do this in 1700, 1900, 2000? Change also provides the dynamic of history. The effects of, for example, rising or falling populations, economies,

future are not rival worlds. Instead, we see them as part of a continuous process, bound together by the energy of change.

The people of the past knew there would be a future and were affected by this knowledge. If in the sixteenth century Europeans explored the—to them—New World, they did so knowing there were other worlds to explore.

This is part of the excitement of history: purposeful exploration and understanding of others and ourselves. Take, for example, an obvious feature of life: the darkness of night. The modern world can overcome this with electric lighting, but earlier the dark was a world of danger and menace. This was especially true for the traveler literally unable to see his route, as in Benjamin Franklin's quote:

*"Do not anticipate trouble, or worry about what may never happen. Keep in the sunlight."*

To see how we have overcome the abrupt shift from light to darkness, we have to see the fearful world of dark in the past. Look at the pictures from the period. In twilight and at night, space shrank to the shadowy spots lit by flickering lights.

Different readers will draw varied conclusions from history. Some see it as a cause for celebration or optimism; others are more pessimistic. Both interpretations can find support. What is clear, however, is that in assessing how far and why we have done better or worse it is necessary to look back and around us, to consider history as a source of our world, not as something that is past and gone. History is interesting and fun, stimulating and thought provoking. It is also valuable, an important source of knowledge, reflection, and understanding.

*President Barack Obama (born 1961).*

9

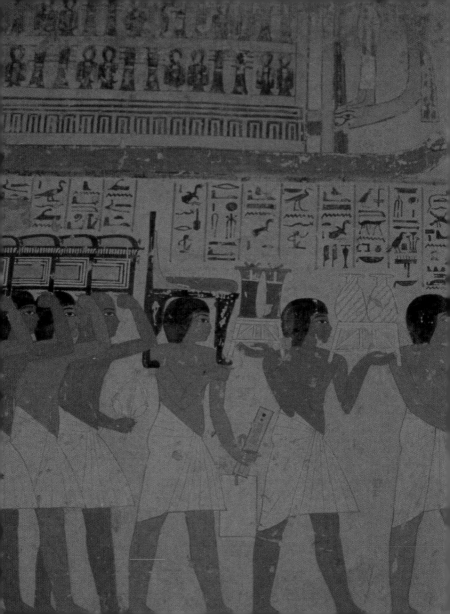

# Chapter 1
## The Ancient World

FROM THE BEGINNINGS of civilization, democracy, early medicine, and science to the transformation of ancient lands into countries and empires as told, recorded, or created by ancient historians, philosophers, kings, and emperors, the Ancient World offers a valuable insight into the world's recorded ancient past.

Opening in the first half of the first millennium BC with the introduction of the Roman Republic and continuing through to the Middle Ages, this chapter reveals the history behind legendary characters and peoples, such as the philosopher Plato, Emperor Constantine, Alexander the Great, the pharaohs, Vikings, ancient intellectuals, and religious leaders.

# Power and Politics

### 509 BC THE REPUBLIC

THE ROMAN REPUBLIC was set up in 509 BC. Because their kings had been dictators, the Romans were determined that no one should gain complete power in the city, so they created a complex system of controls on all officers of state. Power was exercised by two officials, called consuls, who were elected every year. One stayed in Rome and one took command of the army. There were also elected officials in charge of the treasury, the police, and the city itself. The Romans hoped that the rapid change of personnel would stop anyone from seizing total power, but they also realized that in an emergency it might be necessary to allow one man to take charge, so the Republic allowed the appointment of a "Dictator" for a period of up to six months.

### 508 BC DEMOCRACY

DEMOCRACY WAS FIRST developed in Athens, where there was an Assembly that all citizens were entitled to attend and address. After the Reforms of Solon in 594 BC, the Assembly had the right simply to reject or approve legislation. Laws were introduced by the Council, which, after 508 BC, was chosen by lot. Real power, however, was exercised by the nobles through their council, the "Areopagus." They elected the Archons, who ran the city. From 488 BC, the Archons were also chosen by lot. This meant that the nobles lost much of their power. There were other important aspects of democracy. Magistrates were elected by all freemen. Jurors in trials were paid fees, which meant that any citizen could sit, not just the rich. Athenian democracy did not involve equality, but it did accept the right of all citizens to be involved in some form or another in the governing of their city.

*A Roman regent depicted with his wife and son.*

## 400 BC PHILOSOPHERS AND KINGS

THE GREEKS were the first people in Europe to develop a cursive script. Although Egyptian hieroglyphics and

*The Greek philosopher Plato (circa 428–circa 348 BC), one of the earliest exponents of political ideals.*

Babylonian cuneiform were efficient for making lists, writing records, and publishing laws, they did not allow for sophisticated analysis or discussion. Socrates founded a school of philosophy, which was continued by his pupil Plato. Plato's *Republic* was the first treatise on political ideals written in Europe. The Greeks were, therefore, the first Europeans capable of analyzing and explaining political institutions and considering alternatives. Socrates, Plato,

and Aristotle provided an analysis of human behavior, which was not to be equaled until the seventeenth century.

## 336 BC ALEXANDER THE GREAT

ALEXANDER THE GREAT (356–323 BC) was the son of Philip of Macedon and succeeded his father in 336 BC at the age of 20. Philip had crushed the army of the Greek city-states at the Battle of Chaeronea in 338 BC and had forced the states to join the Hellenic League. Only Sparta refused. He then planned to invade Asia, but was murdered before he was able to put his plans into action. After the death of

*Carvings found on sarcophagus of Alexander the Great.*

Philip, the Greek states revolted, but Alexander crushed the rebellion and appointed a governor in Greece before he left for his invasion of Persia. When Alexander died in 322 BC, Athens rebelled again and formed a new Hellenic League. The revolt was once again crushed and the Athenian navy completely destroyed. The Macedonians had changed the face of Greece for good.

## 44 BC THE TRIUMVIRATES AND THE DEATH OF CAESAR

IN THE MIDDLE YEARS of the first century BC, two groups of men fought for control of the Roman Republic. Between 60 and 48 BC, Julius Caesar and Pompey fought a civil war, which became even more violent after the death of Crassus, the third member of the First Triumvirate, in 53 BC. After the Battle of Pharsalus in

*The death of Caesar in a painting by Vincenzo Camuccini.*

48 BC and Pompey's murder in Egypt in the same year, Julius Caesar was the undisputed master of Rome. Increasingly he acted like a king, and it was this behavior that brought about his murder at the hands of a group of Republicans in 44 BC. This act led to the formation of the Second Triumvirate in 43 BC. The members, Mark Antony, Lepidus, and Octavian, hunted down Caesar's murderers, but then fell out among themselves. Finally, Octavian defeated Mark Antony at Actium in 31 BC, after which Mark Antony and his wife Cleopatra committed suicide.

## AD 306 CONSTANTINE

BY THE EARLY THIRD century, it was becoming increasingly obvious that the empire could not be governed by one man. Constantine (reigned 306–337) took the extreme step of dividing the empire in half and building a new capital for the eastern half at Constantinople. For all the strength of its army,

the Roman Empire never developed real political stability. Success depended upon the character of the emperor and on the support of the army. When the empire became increasingly attacked from the outside in the fourth century, the chaos that ensued only encouraged attempts to seize control. These attempts were a major factor in the collapse of the Western Roman Empire by the end of the fifth century. However, Constantine's creation—the Eastern Roman Empire— survived, in one form or another, for over one thousand years.

*Emperor Constantine.*

# War and Peace

### 1027 BC THE WARRING STATES

THE EARLIEST RELIABLE PERIOD in Chinese history, the Chou dynasty, dates from 1027 BC. China was a feudal land, and champions and their retinues fighting small pitched battles dealt with many of the conflicts. As the strength of the Chou declined in the sixth century BC, warfare became a more serious game; chariots remained the important factor, but foot soldiers were fast becoming the dominant force on the battlefield. When the Chou dynasty fell in 249, the Qin took control, and it had become essential to present a united front against incursions from outside the empire. As the Qin had fought for years against the nomads in the north, it was natural that they should adopt the horse as their main means of warfare.

### 669 BC THE HOPLITES

THE FIRST TRUE HOPLITE force was created by the Argives in Greece and used at the Battle of Hysiae in 669 BC. These close-order formations of heavy infantry consisted of men armed with a long

*King Leonidas I of Sparta at Thermopylae, 480 BC.*

*The naval battle in the harbor of Syracuse, where Sparta defeated the Athenians during the Second Peloponnesian War.*

thrusting spear, sword, helmet, breastplate, greaves, and a 3-foot (1-m) round shield. They confronted the enemy with a solid line of alternating shields and spears; the continuity of the line was all-important, and each man depended on his neighbor. At Plataea (479 BC), the Spartans fought eight deep, the rear ranks filling in at the front as men fell. Steadiness and weight of numbers in the right place were the key to victories on the field. Tactics were still somewhat limited and sieges rare.

### 431 BC THE PELOPONNESIAN WAR

THE DELIAN LEAGUE (478 BC) was formed by the Greeks with the aim of driving the Persians out of the Aegean Sea. The Athenians took control and absorbed a total of 150 states into their empire. The Spartans reacted violently to this action and in 431 BC, the Peloponnesian War broke out. For the next 27 years, the Greek states would be at war with the Spartans. The Athenians ruled the seas while the Spartans were dominant on land. The Spartans won the Battle of Mantinea (418 BC), forcing the Athenians to risk all. They invaded Sicily in 415 BC in the hope of cutting off Spartan trade and supplies, but in 413 BC the fleet was lost at Syracuse. Athens hung on until 405 BC, losing another fleet at Aegospotami; they surrendered the following year.

## 322 BC HELLENISTIC WARFARE

ALEXANDER THE GREAT died in 322 BC without naming a successor and, deprived of personality, the empire fell apart. Despite his warlike life, he had hoped that the lands would be melded together, but all his governors claimed territories. Chief among them were Antigonus I, Antipater, Demetrius I (or Poliorcetes), Lysimachus, Perdiccas, Ptolemy I, and Seleucus I. This period is known as Diadochi (successors) and was marked by the extensive use of the phalanx (pike blocks of infantry),

Persian cavalry, siege equipment, elephants, and camels. This generation is taken to end with Seleucus's death in 281 BC. Pyrrhus, the King of Epirus, continued the Hellenistic style of warfare, beating the Romans in 280 BC by using elephants, but was decisively defeated by their infantry at Beneventum in 275 BC.

## 59 BC JULIUS CAESAR

AT THE AGE OF 41, Julius Caesar was thrust into prominence when, in 59 BC, he became Governor of Illyricum, Cisalpine,

*Classical painting showing Emperor Julius Caesar.*

and Transalpine Gaul. He checked the threat of the Helvetii in 58 BC and advanced north of the old Roman frontier to clear Alsace of the German tribes. In the spring of 57 BC, he defeated a massive 300,000-strong Belgae army on the Aisne, and by 56 BC, had added nearly all of Gaul to the empire. He landed in Britain in 55 BC but had to turn his attention elsewhere. The Gauls, under Vercingetorix, rebelled in 52 BC, and at the siege of Alesia, they were crushed for many years. He faced Pompey in a civil war that lasted until 45 BC, but Brutus and Cassius murdered him in the following year.

## AD 476 THE FALL OF ROME

THERE WAS A LULL in warfare after AD 410. The Vandals had settled in North Africa, the Burgundians and Franks in France, and the Visigoths had moved on to Spain and Gaul. A graver danger for all lay ahead. By the middle of the fifth century, under Attila, the Huns descended on the Western world. The Chinese had repelled them between 207 BC and AD 39, so they had turned west. Attila came to power in 433, and after invading the Balkans in 440–447, he crossed the Rhine and faced the Visigoths and Romans at Champagne. Attila was

*Attila, the King of the Huns, whose attacks in Italy contributed to the fall of Rome.*

defeated, but in 451 he invaded northern Italy. They were turned back, but Rome was not saved. Odovacar, commander of the Roman army, was a barbarian and he seized the capital (AD 476).

**19**

# Society and Culture

### PREHISTORY HUMANS EVOLVE

ABOUT 20 MILLION years ago, somewhere in Africa, apelike creatures that anthropologists call proconsul came down out of the trees and began to live on the ground, searching for their food on the broad savannas. In time, they adapted to this new life, began to walk upright, used tools, made fire, and eventually began to reason and talk. Now markedly different from their ape like ancestors, they had become hominids, the first creatures to be noticeably humanlike. There was a long way to go, of course, before the hominids evolved into *Homo sapiens*, our own species. However, the way was now open for gradual development toward organized bands of hunter-gatherers and cave-dwelling families, essentially very little different in basic aspects from families of today.

### PREHISTORY EARLY TECHNOLOGY

THE PRACTICAL DEMANDS of prehistoric life led to a range of technological discoveries. Chipping or flaking flints to produce sharp edges was succeeded by a more clever method—using stones to grind them. Levers and wedges were developed for lifting heavy objects, as was rope, made from the braided fur or hair of animals. Making fire by striking

*Man began to forge a hunter-gatherer lifestyle in prehistoric times.*

flint on stone was a much more convenient method than waiting for lightning to set the forests ablaze, and the supply of long-distance weapons for hunting was extended to bows and arrows, boomerangs, and slings for throwing large stones. The greatest prehistoric discovery of all was made when the rolling qualities of large, round stones inspired the making of the first wheel.

## 900 BC THE FIRST MILITARY STATE

THE ASSYRIANS, who came on the scene around 900 BC, were the first people to form a military state. In conquering their extensive empire, the Assyrian army used mighty siege machines, some made of iron, to batter down walls and shower opponents with missiles. The Assyrians, however, were not all warlike. They were careful to preserve the libraries they found in cities they captured. Assyrian astronomers made observations of the moon and recorded them on circular clay disks. The knowledge the Assyrians amassed was considerable. In 1929, the library of Ashurbanipal, who became king *circa* 626 BC, was discovered at his capital of Nineveh. It contained over 20,000 clay tablets, inscribed with information on mathematics, botany, chemistry, medicine, and history.

## 776 BC THE FIRST OLYMPIC GAMES

EVERY FOUR YEARS, the Greek city-states, so often at loggerheads, set aside their differences to take part in the Olympic Games. Held on Mount Olympus, in east-central Greece, the Games attracted athletes from all over Greece and wars were suspended while they continued. Contestants competed naked in javelin-throwing, boxing, wrestling, and chariot racing. The winners received branches of wild olive. Inaugurated some time before 776 BC, when records began, the Games were held until, in AD 394, they were abolished by the Romans—by then the masters of Greece. It was not surprising that these foreign conquerors should take this step, since the basic idea behind the Games was to unify the Greeks, even if only for a short time.

*Mount Olympus in Greece—home of the original Olympic Games.*

### 214 BC THE GREAT WALL OF CHINA

THE QIN DYNASTY ended nearly two centuries of violent conflict and created the first strong, centralized empire in China. In 214 BC Emperor Shihuangdi ordered that a great wall, eventually some 1,450 miles (2,350 km) long, be built in the north to keep out aggressive Mongol and Turkish nomads. The 25-foot (7.6-m) high wall, later extended by the Han dynasty (202 BC –AD 220), was made of earth and stone faced with brick and featured a series of watchtowers. Today, it is the earth's only artificial construction visible from space. Although internal Chinese politics remained perennially in flux, this mighty defense line stood for over 1,400 years before the nomads—the much more powerful Mongols—managed to break through.

### 149 BC THE ROMAN EMPIRE

THE EARLY ROMANS hated kings and ejected their last, tyrannical monarch, Tarquinius Superbus, in 509 BC. Some five centuries later, however, the Romans accepted their first emperor, Augustus, because a strong individual was needed to cure the Roman Republic, which was then blighted by anarchy. The Roman Empire itself began much earlier, after

*The Great Wall of China, built to defend the empire against invading Mongols and Turks.*

*The Egyptian pyramids count among the Ancient World's greatest feats of engineering.*

149 BC, when the Romans smashed the Carthaginians of North Africa and took over their territories. In time, the empire stretched from Britannia in the north to the deserts of Saudi Arabia in the south. Within its strongly guarded borders, Pax Romana (the Roman Peace) prevailed, allowing Roman subjects the security to travel and trade, a life that provided comparative luxury for the rich and comforts unique in the ancient world.

## 100 BC THE SEVEN WONDERS OF THE ANCIENT WORLD

TOURISM IS NOT a modern phenomenon. Tourists, armed with guidebooks, traveled the ancient world to visit great cities and impressive monuments, buy souvenirs, and return home to enthuse about the wonders they had seen. The most comprehensive "package" tour took in the Seven Wonders of the Ancient World: the pyramids of Egypt; the "hanging" gardens of Semiramis at Babylon; the statue of Zeus at Olympia, the temple of Artemis, and the mausoleum at Halicarnassus (all three in Greece); the Colossus of Rhodes; and the pharos, or lighthouse, at Alexandria in Egypt. It is doubtful if large numbers of people could afford the time and expense of visiting all seven, but it seems that tourist guides did a lively trade nevertheless.

# Exploration and Empires

### 2600 BC THE EARLIEST EXPLORATIONS

ONCE AN EARLY urban society became aware of the existence of other lands producing valuable products, it was also possible to trade with them. In 2600 BC, the Egyptian pharaoh Huni sent a fleet of at least 40 ships north along the Mediterranean coast to the town of Byblos, in modern

*Egyptian seagoing ship, circa 2500 BC, made from cedar wood, which was probably imported from Byblos.*

Lebanon. This expedition brought back shiploads of lumber, a commodity in comparatively short supply in the parched lands of the Nile valley. The Egyptians also explored south, along the Nile and the Red Sea. Somewhere here was a land they called Punt, where a

supply of incense was available. During the third millennium BC, two major expeditions are known to have taken place. One was during the reign of the pharaoh Sahure, and the other led by an Egyptian named Hennu.

### 2371 BC IMPERIALISM IN THE ANCIENT NEAR EAST

IN MESOPOTAMIA, the most dramatic change occurred during the time of Sargon the Great (2371 BC). Where previous victors had allowed the governments of defeated cities to continue to rule, only demanding payment of tribute, Sargon did away with enemy-ruling dynasties and placed his conquests under the control of governors appointed by him. This ensured a loyal subordinate who could administer the internal affairs of a city-state with a free hand, while still supplying the dominant ruler with the means to support an army capable of enforcing his authority. The effect of

*Mask depicting the head of Mesopotamian ruler Sargon the Great.*

a group of Phoenician sailors to voyage around Libya. During the third year, they sailed through the Strait of Gibraltar and back into the Mediterranean. Herodotus did not believe this account because, when the Phoenicians took a westward heading, the sun was unexpectedly on their right, in the northern quadrant of the sky—which is exactly where it would be if one were sailing west around the Cape of Good Hope.

### AD 50s VOYAGES TO INDIA

THE EMPERORS of Rome occasionally commissioned expeditions, but they were generally uninterested in exploration. During the first century AD, however, a Greek merchant named Hippalus discovered a secret that Arab traders with India had jealously guarded for centuries—that the monsoon winds of the Indian Ocean reversed themselves. He was the first European to sail across the Indian Ocean instead of the slow process of following the coast. Mediterranean merchants and geographers knew of a land beyond India, and a geographer writing in the second century described several places in Southeast Asia, including Malaya and possibly Hanoi, but the details of distance and location are very vague.

the Mesopotamian practice of ruling conquered territories through governors meant that if an empire fell, the bulk of it transferred its allegiance to the victor.

### 610 BC THE CIRCUMNAVIGATION OF AFRICA

ONE OF THE EARLIEST expeditions ever ordered by a government expressly to achieve greater geographical knowledge was made during the reign of the pharaoh Necho (*circa* 610–594 BC). Necho instructed

## AD 97 EXPLORATION IN THE FAR EAST

CHINA ITSELF, in the second century AD, was the location of another great empire. While it had knowledge of Southeast Asia and India, its information about the lands beyond the Central Asian desert was as sketchy as that of the ancient Romans about East Asia. In AD 97, a Chinese general named Ban Chao reached the shores about the Caspian Sea. He sent a subordinate of his, named Gan Ying, further west, and he reached the Black Sea. Here, he came into contact with the Roman Empire, which he called Da Qin. This was described as a land of great wealth, but the length of the journey further westward was too daunting for Gan Ying, and both he and Ban Chao returned to China.

## AD 600s THE GREAT CONQUESTS BEGIN

BETWEEN AD 634 AND 638, Arab armies defeated both the Byzantine heirs of Rome and the Persian Empire. They had gained domination over the whole of the Middle East when, in 639, they invaded Egypt. By the end of 645, all the land in Egypt had become part of the Islamic world. The pace of conquest now slowed, but its movement nevertheless

*The fall of Carthage at the hands of the Arabs.*

seemed inexorable. In 672, a Muslim fleet began a five-year blockade of the great city of Constantinople, but they lacked sufficiently advanced siege-warfare technology to tackle the mighty walls of the Byzantine capital. Arab-led armies marched west across North Africa, and Carthage fell to them in 698.

## AD 600s RISE OF SCANDINAVIA

THE COLLAPSE OF the Roman Empire paradoxically allowed the foundations of the European supremacy of the eighteenth and nineteenth centuries to be laid. The lack of a central bureaucratic authority permitted individual initiatives on the part of different societies. The Scandinavian region of Denmark, Norway, and Sweden, at the end of the eighth century AD, suddenly produced an aggressive seafaring culture that is collectively known as the Vikings. The technological basis for this lay in the excellent ocean-going craft that the Vikings built. The best example that has survived is the Gokstad ship, now housed in the Viking Ship Museum in Oslo, Norway.

*Viking sailors belonged to an aggressive, seafaring culture.*

# Trade and Industry

### 4000 BC THE FIRST TOOLMAKERS

SOME OF THE first people to make implements were the flint and ax makers of the Neolithic period (or New Stone

*Early flint tools and weapons.*

Age, *circa* 4000–1000 BC). Flint is a hard stone found in layers of chalk. It can be broken, or "knapped," into sharp-edge flakes that make good cutting tools. An example of a flint mine is Grimes Graves in Norfolk, England. Here, people used antlers as picks to chip out the flint. In the mine shafts, they worked by the light of candles made with grease and a wick. When the flint was brought to the surface it was broken up and shaped into ax heads, arrowheads, knives, and scrapers. Around 3500 BC, flint was used as barter for animal skins, pottery, and food.

### 2590 BC TRIUMPHS OF THE ANCIENT EGYPTIANS

BETWEEN 2630 AND 1640 BC, the pharaohs, or kings, of Egypt had gigantic stone pyramids made to serve as their tombs. The largest remaining pyramid, at Giza (*circa* 2590 BC), took 84,000 workers 20 years to build. Although the enormous blocks of stone used in construction were placed and measured with amazing

*Illustration of a man standing next to a T-shape sun dial, ancient Egypt.*

accuracy, the simplest tools were used—levers, pulleys, rollers, and human muscle. Pictures and models found in the tombs show what Egyptian life was like. One picture shows a simple boat made of bundles of reeds bound together and covered with pitch. Later, rowing or sailing ships were used for trading in the Mediterranean region. The Egyptians developed an accurate calendar of 365 days. To measure time, they used sun dials and water clocks.

### 1700 BC EARLIEST ROAD BUILDING

THE ASSYRIANS and Persians (*circa* 1700–500 BC) controlled great political and military empires. Their success was largely attributable to economic and technological advances. Systematic road building, for example, permitted goods to be concentrated in sufficient supply to keep large numbers of men in the field under arms all year round. Wheeled vehicles using these roads could not only supply the troops but could also keep them moving quickly, cheaply, and over long distances. Traders received legal protection and merchants were exempt from military service. Key cities inhabited by merchants and artisans paid a money tribute in return for extensive rights of self-government. The imperial government and field armies both policed the roads to allow passengers unhampered, safe passage. Thus, inter-regional traders and the armies entered into an alliance of mutual support.

### 600 BC MODERN MONEY

THE WORLD'S FIRST metallic money appeared around 2000 BC. Before that time cattle had been used for currency, and, indeed, in some parts of the world they still are. The word "pecuniary" comes from the Latin word for "cattle"— *pecu*. The first money was made of bronze ingots shaped to resemble cattle. Unlike later coins, which had a fixed value, the value of these coins was determined by weight. Around 800 BC, bean-shape ingots were

*Example of early metallic coin, discovered at Sutton Hoo, England.*

introduced. The first coins of the modern type—round and flat, with a value and images or inscriptions marked on the surface—appeared in Lydia, Asia Minor (now Turkey), *circa* 600 BC. They were made in copper and silver. From then on, commodities, land, taxes, and services could be valued in terms of money.

## AD 23 TRIUMPH OF THE RED EYEBROWS

UNDER EMPEROR WUDI (141–87 BC) the Han dynasty in China (206 BC–AD 220) expanded south of the Yangtze River (now the Chang), absorbing land as far afield as the borders of modern China. To recoup the costs of their campaigns, the rulers imposed tax increases and state monopolies over key production items, such as iron and salt, eventually causing the currency to become debased. The population soon outgrew the supply of land. In the first century AD, great provincial families were exempt from taxes while the peasants had to pay more. The reforming ruler Wang Mang nationalized the tax-exempt estates, redistributed them among the peasantry, expanded state monopolies, and abolished slavery. Maintenance of the water systems, however, was neglected. In a peasant uprising in AD 23, led by the "Red Eyebrows," Wang Mang was killed.

## AD 300 THE MAYAN EMPIRE FLOURISHES

THE MAYA ARRIVED in the Yucatán peninsula, Mexico, from Central America about 1500 BC. The early Maya were slash-and-burn farmers, working plots called *milpa*, a crop-growing system used throughout Mesoamerica. At the height of its greatness, *circa* AD 300–900, the Mayan Empire included more than 40 well-populated cities thriving on trade. Many of these cities had buildings such as large stone pyramids, plazas, temples, and palaces, together with an enormous stairway that led to an observatory. From these observatories, astronomers

*A tributary stream of Yangtze River, (now the Chang), China.*

*The magnificent pyramid of Papantla in Mexico.*

and mathematicians would take sightings and measurements of the stars, skies, and planets; this makes astronomy one of the world's oldest sciences. Mayan farming included complex irrigation and terracing methods, which were very advanced for their time. Their principal food crop was maize. They also grew cotton and had highly perfected the techniques of spinning, dyeing, and weaving cotton. The Maya domesticated the dog and the turkey but had no draft animals. They were the only ancient American people to develop an accurate calendar.

# Science and Technology

### 1000 BC MATH AND GEOMETRY

WHILE THE GREEKS were pondering philosophically over science and technology, the Romans were far more concerned with putting theory into practice. Their technology, particularly related to engineering and architecture, benefited greatly from the application

*The old Appian Way, one of the finest surviving examples of Roman roads.*

of geometrical and mathematical formulae, which optimized the use of materials and processes available to them. Mathematics was important for making accurate calculations of criteria such as angles, areas, quantities, dimensions, and

proportions. Geometry played an equally vital role in determining appropriate structural shapes for maximizing strength against economy of materials, as well as imposing a general aesthetic discipline, including symmetry. Strict mathematical principles also governed the design of engines and machines used by the Romans for warfare and construction to ensure that they performed their tasks properly and safely.

### 1000 BC ROADS AND BRIDGES

TO BUILD AND maintain an empire, it was essential to be able to maintain communications between different regions and the central government. The Romans, realizing this, went to enormous lengths to construct an infrastructure of roads and bridges that could be relied upon to send troops and supplies to trouble spots as quickly as possible and quell any uprising against the state. Roman roads consisted of closely fitting stone slabs set on a foundation of hard core made from sand, gravel, and masonry rubble, and lined with stone curbs. The land was surveyed to keep the road as level as possible and to find the straightest route from one location to the next. Some sections of Roman roads even had a cambered surface with drainage ditches to deal with heavy rainfall. When it came to spanning rivers and valleys, Roman engineers solved the problem with expertly constructed bridges, viaducts, and aqueducts, which featured use of the arch. This was an invention of the Romans and enabled them to build strong, yet relatively lightweight structures, requiring less effort and materials.

## 1000 BC THE RISE OF THE WHEEL AND AXLE

AS HUMANS BEGAN building settlements and early civilizations started to appear, aided by Bronze Age technology, there came an increased need for an efficient way to transport bulky goods from one place to another. Pressures of trade, industry, and warfare provided the necessity that mothered the invention of the wheel and axle. Various wheeled vehicles, such as carts, wagons, and chariots, pulled by oxen or horses, were adopted rapidly because of the advantages they offered. The wheel and axle proved to be of vital importance, because it usefully opened the door for more effective communications between human populations and provided a far more efficient means for transporting people, equipment, and goods. The net result was an infrastructure within, and between, early civilizations.

*A Roman warrior leaves his family and villa, being driven in a chariot drawn by four horses.*

## 550 BC UNIVERSAL CURRENCY

SCHIST IS A FLINTLIKE black stone that can be used to indicate the purity of gold when rubbed on its surface by displaying marks in a range of possible colors. Following this discovery, Croesus, ruler of Lydia, was prompted to introduce the first standardized, imperial gold coinage, which was called the stater, in 550 BC. The idea was immediately popular and other civilizations around the Mediterranean followed suit. Coinage had the effect of unifying and defining the parameters of the European civilized world, which had previously comprised fairly disparate populations. The reason was that people from different cultures were able to place their collective trust in the

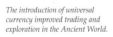

*The introduction of universal currency improved trading and exploration in the Ancient World.*

quality of the metal being minted. This resulted in more diverse and flexible trade, which eventually extended to Asia and encouraged a flow of ideas and information as well as goods.

## 250 BC MAPPING THE ANCIENT WORLD

A GREEK GEOGRAPHER and mathematician called Eratosthenes (*circa* 276–194 BC) was the first mapmaker to apply a mechanism to maps that made them practical for navigation. He

*Eratosthenes, one of the earliest geographers.*

included lines of longitude and latitude so that a grid was created, which meant that different locations were referenced in relation to one another according to real space. It was also possible to determine a position at sea or on land on the map according to the predictable movements of the stars throughout the year. Based on his astronomical observations, Eratosthenes was even able to make a surprisingly accurate calculation of the world's circumference, at a time when the world was generally considered to be flat. During the Iron Age, instead of being navigational aids, maps were useful tools for understanding the overall layout of the known world in the context of empires and enemies.

## AD 100s GALEN AND MEDICINE

ANATOMY AND PHYSIOLOGY became areas of detailed study for the Greeks because they had a curiosity about how things work, and components of the body seemed to have clearly defined roles. Of course, this was essentially true when it came to muscles and bones and so on, but they had no appreciation of the scientific complexity with which life was maintained, so they came up with other, less scientific explanations. The most noted physician and anatomist of the

*Greek physician Claudius Galen, whose theory of "humors" formed the basics of medicine for centuries.*

era, Galen (*circa* AD 129–200) asserted that they must be mysterious energies called humors, which gave and maintained life in the body in the form of natural, vital, and animal spirits. His idea dominated European medicine for some 1,500 years, until science eventually proved him wrong.

# Religions, Belief, and Thought

### 1500 BC THE VEDAS AND THE VEDIC AGE

THE EARLIEST HINDU SCRIPTURES are the four Vedas, and the earliest of these is the *Rig-Veda* ("song of wisdom"), 1500–1000 BC, consisting of 1,000 hymns that were mainly for the Aryan priests (Brahmins) to use during rituals. The hymns are directed toward nature gods, such as Agni, god of fire, and Indra, the sky god, and some of these may have been used by Brahmins before their arrival in India. This was followed by the other three Vedas ("books of wisdom"), the *Sama-Veda*, *Yajur-Veda*, and *Atharva-Veda* and, around 800 BC, by the Brahmana scriptures.

### 995 BC KING DAVID BUILDS JERUSALEM

DAVID, ISRAEL'S GREATEST KING, was originally a shepherd and musician from Bethlehem and is best known for his allegorical defeat of the Philistine giant Goliath—he probably became the leader of a small Hebrew army that defeated a larger Philistine one. He was elected King of the Hebrews, united the various Jewish tribes, and, in 995 BC, captured the small town of Jerusalem, which he rebuilt as his capital. Thereafter it has been known as the City of David. The

*David (1010–970 BC) is anointed King of ancient Israel.*

Ark of the Covenant was moved to the new city, making it the religious center of the nation. He was also responsible, according to tradition, for the creation of many of the Psalms—although many appear to have been written at a later date.

## 850 BC HOMER, THE GREEK GODS, AND TROJAN WARS

THE *ILIAD* AND THE *ODYSSEY*, attributed to the blind poet Homer (*circa* 850 BC), are the earliest and greatest Greek epic poems and provide a detailed picture of early Greek religion. This could be described as an anthropomorphic polytheism derived from earlier nature gods. The many gods who live on Mount Olympus, are ruled over by Zeus, the powerful thunder god. Other gods include Apollo, the sun god; Demeter, the goddess of harvests; and Neptune, god of the sea. All have different human personalities—they can plot against one another and be influenced through prayers and sacrifices. There was no central dogma, theology, or revelation, although later philosophies made use of the ancient myths.

## 551 BC CONFUCIUS

CHINA'S GREAT SAGE, K'ung-fu-tze ("the Master K'ung"), is generally known in the West by his Latinized name "Confucius." Born in 551 BC, he came from an aristocratic but poor family in the state of Lu. At this time, China was in a state of chaos and had divided into many warring states. Much of Confucius' teachings, more accurately described as moral and political instead of religious,

were directed toward restoring a more ancient kind of social order. To Confucius, this was a matter of restoring to the earth the perfect order of heaven, *T'ien ming*. This could be done through virtuous living and the correct practice of the ancient rituals.

*Chinese philosopher Confucius.*

## 399 BC PLATO AND THE DEATH OF SOCRATES

PLATO'S TEACHER SOCRATES was put to death for his teachings in 399 BC. This event is recorded in Plato's *Dialogues*. He argues that knowledge can only exist if there are eternal things to which knowledge can refer, and as material things change, they must, therefore be only expressions of unchanging "Forms"—such as the Good, the True, and the Beautiful. In his *Republic,* he depicts a state based on his ideals and ruled by philosophers. This was the inspiration for many other visions, such as the *Utopia* of Thomas More.

### 367 BC ARISTOTLE'S STUDIES

ARISTOTLE STUDIED at Plato's academy from 367 BC and became a teacher to Alexander the Great. Although he believed in and developed many of Plato's ideas, he rejected the theory of "Forms," arguing that material things were the primary reality and that any properties that they had, such as color or taste, were just aspects or properties of that matter. His rigorous use of logic and rejection of all unnecessary hypotheses resulted in him being seen as the founder of logical theory. His thought covered almost every subject from politics to literature, logic to psychology, and ethics to science.

### 7 BC THE LIFE OF CHRIST

BORN TO A POOR FAMILY in Galilee around 7 BC, the son of a carpenter, Jesus showed an avid interest in religious matters from a very early age. His cousin, John the Baptist, was at that time a radical and ascetic preacher, who was highly critical of the Jewish establishment. Under John the Baptist's influence, Jesus underwent the ritual of baptism, which symbolized a rebirth and the cleansing of the spirit. After a long retreat into the wilderness, Jesus became a wandering preacher, and over time he attracted a large following. He rejected the pursuit of wealth and, being a man of peace, he also disagreed with the

*Jesus Christ blessing the little children.*

use of violence, proclaiming that these sins would prevent us from entering the kingdom of heaven. This message is most explicit in his Sermon on the Mount. It was his message that we can all, like him, become sons of God that led to the persecution of Jesus by the priesthood. The traditional teaching of the Church is that, after his crucifixion, Jesus rose from the dead, but many early Christians and the Jews and Muslims (for whom he is a great prophet) did not share this belief.

*Laotze, Chinese philosopher and founder of Taoism.*

## AD 50 DECLINE OF TAOIST THOUGHT

FROM AROUND THE FIRST century AD, there was a decline in philosophical and contemplative Taoism in China. What had previously been the pursuit of a natural and spontaneous way of life had become the pursuit of an eternal life—or *Hsien*. This began to see the use of magic potions and the practice of forms of sexual yoga. Contemplation of the ineffable "order of nature" was gradually replaced by the worship of countless household gods and the practices of divination, alchemy, astrology, and magic. This form of Taoism is known as "Hsien" Taoism, and it would go on to flourish under the influences of Chan Tao Ling and Chang Lu.

## AD 300s THE DESERT FATHERS

THE MONASTIC LIFE and the practice of contemplative prayer originated with the lives of the "desert fathers"— saints and hermits who lived alone and in small communities in the deserts of Syria and North Africa, especially around Alexandria. St. Antony of Egypt (AD 251–356), a pupil of St. Paul of Thebes, is referred to as the father of Christian monasticism. He created a loose community of hermits whose simple lives were based upon work and prayer (*laborare et orare*). Other important saints include Athanasius (AD 298–373) and the colorful St. Simeon Stylites (AD 387–459) of Syria, who is said to have lived for 36 years on top of a tall pillar to escape his many followers.

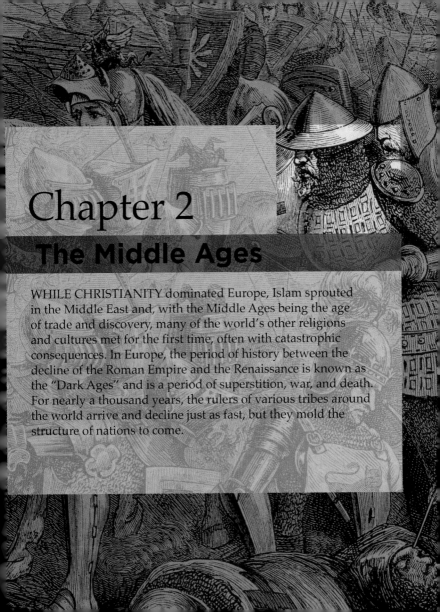

# Chapter 2
## The Middle Ages

WHILE CHRISTIANITY dominated Europe, Islam sprouted in the Middle East and, with the Middle Ages being the age of trade and discovery, many of the world's other religions and cultures met for the first time, often with catastrophic consequences. In Europe, the period of history between the decline of the Roman Empire and the Renaissance is known as the "Dark Ages" and is a period of superstition, war, and death. For nearly a thousand years, the rulers of various tribes around the world arrive and decline just as fast, but they mold the structure of nations to come.

# Power and Politics

## AD 622 THE HEGIRA ("FLIGHT")

ARABIA AT THE BEGINNING of the seventh century was wild, pagan, and unsafe when in AD 612 the Prophet

*The Qu'ran, the Holy Book of the Islamic faith.*

Muhammad began to preach in Mecca. He gained few followers and in 622 was forced to flee from Mecca to Medina. Here, the impact of the teachings of the Prophet Muhammad was immediate. After the Hegira, he organized an alliance of the tribes in Medina and attacked and captured Mecca in 630. By the time of the Prophet Muhammad's death in 632, most of Arabia was Muslim. The Prophet Muhammad's teachings were based on the "Five Pillars" of Islam, and it was the belief and hope that they offered, that attracted so many followers and made Islam such a powerful force.

## AD 750 THE RISE OF BAGHDAD

BAGHDAD BECAME the center of the Islamic Empire in the years after AD 750. The Umayyads were replaced after civil wars by the Abbasids, who built Baghdad. It was a round city surrounded by a wall with four gates. Each gate was defended by 1,000 men. This shows the power and importance of the caliph, who lived in the center of the city in an enormous palace. The most famous of the Abbasid caliphs was Harun al-Rashid. He had an inventory of all the objects in the palace drawn up and it included 4,000 different sets of clothing. The Abbasids also encouraged learning and medicine. Libraries were set up throughout the empire and there were hospitals in every city.

## 1066 WILLIAM OF NORMANDY

WHEN WILLIAM, Duke of Normandy, became King of England in 1066 he took control of all land. Faced with the problem of ruling and controlling a large country, William imposed feudalism upon England. His main aim was to ensure that he had military forces at his disposal and that the dangerous areas of the country were under control. His most important barons were given estates throughout the country. His own half brother Odo, Bishop of Bayeux, held many areas of Kent, the site of a likely invasion. When the kingdom of France emerged, a similar process was followed. In origin, kings were only the most powerful and successful barons. Their position depended upon their ability to handle and control their own subjects.

### 1100s BARON KNIGHTS

WHEN BARONS came to perform military service, they had to be accompanied by the correct number of properly equipped knights. Different kings set different standards of equipment for their knights, but horse, spear, sword, helmet, and hauberk (armor) were common. Barons solved the problem of providing knights by passing on their land to tenants, who had to perform knight service when required. Knights were professional soldiers; they did little else but prepare and practice for war. The vast number of knights, with little to do, was one factor in the development of crusades from the late twelfth century onward. To try to ensure that knights performed military service when needed, barons forced them to go through the same ritual of homage and swearing allegiance.

*Illuminated manuscript depicting baron knights.*

## 1215 MAGNA CARTA

KING JOHN (reigned 1199–1216) of England was faced by enormous debts as a result of his brother's, Richard I, continual campaigns on the Third Crusade and in France. This forced him to increase taxes. John's attempts to recapture the English possessions in

France failed when he was defeated at the Battle of Bouvines by Philip II of France. Finally, John's barons forced him to accept the Magna Carta at Runnymede in 1215. In theory, this guaranteed the rights of freemen, but, in fact, the most important clauses were attempts to limit the king's power and protect the rights of the barons. John probably intended to disregard the Magna Carta as soon as he felt strong enough, but he died the following year and left the throne to his young son, who became Henry III.

*King John signing the Magna Carta at Runnymede, England, 1215.*

## 1264 SIMON DE MONTFORT

MEDIEVAL KINGS were expected to lead their barons into battle and win victories. Henry III, the son of John, was only nine years of age when he became king in 1216. When he took control of the kingdom, he was a poor military leader. In 1264, there was a revolt against him led by Simon de Montfort, who captured Henry III. Simon de Montfort then summoned "Parliament," to which he invited both the barons, or "Lords" as they came to be called, and also, for the first time, representatives of the Commons. Two knights were summoned from every shire, or county, and two burgesses from every town. This is regarded as the first real evidence of the existence of

Parliament, although the name had been used since the 1240s. In 1965, Parliament celebrated its 900th anniversary.

## 1300s PEASANTS

PEASANTS WERE the lowest level in medieval society. There were villeins, who owned some land; cottars, who owned a cottage; and others, who owned virtually nothing. What they all had in common was the obligation to work for, and pay taxes to, their lord, whether he was a knight, a baron, or even the king. Work meant tilling their lord's fields for several days every week. Taxes meant handing over a proportion of their produce to their lord or to the Church and also paying to use their lord's mill to grind their wheat. In addition, they could neither leave the village nor marry without his permission.

1327–77) embarked on his campaigns against France, which became known as the Hundred Years' War. In the 1350s, the Commons and Lords began to meet as distinct bodies at the same time, and the post of Speaker, someone who would put forward the views of the Commons after their debates, was created. Royal officials also stopped attending meetings

*King Edward III with Guy, Earl of Flanders.*

## 1340s EDWARD III AND PARLIAMENT

PARLIAMENT BEGAN to grant money to the king in the 1340s. This became more important as Edward III (reigned of the Lords, which meant that the house was now made up exclusively of bishops and barons. By the end of Edward's reign, the two houses had developed into something similar to their modern form.

45

# War and Peace

### AD 717 THE SIEGE OF CONSTANTINOPLE

THE ARAB GENERAL MASLAMA attacked the city of Constantinople in August AD 717. Having been repulsed by the city's catapults, he organized a blockade. The Arab fleet, under Suleiman, was ordered to intercept any Byzantine shipping and to block the Bosphorus and entry into the Black Sea. As an Arab fleet passed the harbor, the Byzantines struck with their warships, sinking over 20 ships. In the spring, the Arabs were reinforced, but again the Byzantines struck and sunk many vessels. By August 718, believing that the Franks were en route to raise the siege, the caliph gave up, with few of his troops making it home. Leo, the Byzantine emperor, pursued the Arabs, but his victory in 739 at Acroinon in Phrygia finally forced the Arabs out of Asia Minor.

*Holy Roman emperor Charlemagne.*

### AD 768 CHARLEMAGNE

CHARLEMAGNE WAS Charles the Hammer's grandson and became king in AD 768. Between 768–814, Charlemagne fought against the Saxons, Lombards, Spanish Muslims, Avars, Frisians, Bretons, and Byzantines. His empire covered the major part of western Europe and the Pope crowned him Emperor in Rome in 800. It was his wars against the Muslims in Spain for which he will be most remembered, but his introduction of the feudal system allowed him to maintain a strong cavalry force, which was vital in defending the enormous borders and striking out at his enemies. After his death in 814, the empire became fragmented under the pressure of the combined raids from the Arabs, Magyars, and, later, the Vikings in the ninth and tenth centuries, the last proving the most dangerous.

## AD 866 CHARLES THE BALD AND ALFRED THE GREAT

BY THE END of the ninth century, both the Franks and the English had learned to cope with the Vikings. The Franks could now raise a large force of cavalry vital for being able to catch and fight the fast-moving Vikings. In AD 866, Charles the Bald completed a series of fortifications along the Seine and the Loire. In England, Alfred the Great had built up a strong force of heavy infantry and an impressive fleet to counter the Vikings. When Canute became king of England (reigned 1016–35) after the death of Ethelred's son, Edmund Ironside (1016), he won acceptance from the English nobility to whom he promised, and gave, strong government. He forged strong links with the Viking successors, the Normans, and other Scandinavian civilizations.

*A fleet of Danish longboats suffers defeat by King Alfred the Great's navy at Swanage in Dorset, England.*

*The coronation of Edward the Confessor (1003–66) at Winchester Cathedral, England.*

### 1066 NORMANS AND SAXONS

HAROLD II WAS the last Anglo-Saxon king of England. Harold succeeded his father Godwin (died 1053) to the powerful Earldom of Wessex and was named heir to the English throne by Edward the Confessor when Edward was on his deathbed in January 1066. However, the throne was immediately challenged by William of Normandy and by the Norwegian king, Harold III. Harold III allied himself with Tostig, the brother of the English Harold, and invaded northern England. Harold II stopped this attack at Stamford Bridge in Yorkshire on September 25, 1066, but he had to make a forced march south to confront the Norman invaders, who landed in England on September 28. He was ill prepared for the decisive encounter at Hastings, where he was defeated.

### 1071 THE RISE OF THE OTTOMANS

THE SELJUK TURK VICTORY over the Byzantines at Manzikert in 1071 opened the way for a Turkish invasion of Asia

*A crusader and Muslim warrior in hand-to-hand combat.*

Minor. The Turks had been interested in settling in Arabia, but the attractive land of Anatolia was too good an option to ignore. Inspired by their faith as Ghazis (warriors of the Muslim faith), they attacked the ruins of the Byzantine Empire. Osman (reigned 1281–1326) fearlessly led the Ottomans in the early days followed by Orkhan (reigned 1326–62); Europe was in no condition to repel them. When the crusaders sacked Constantinople in 1204, the Ottomans quickly annexed Anatolia. The Europeans failed to support Byzantium because they knew that a superior military force faced them. The poor performance of the crusaders was confirmed by a string of defeats against the Turks.

## 1250 THE DEVELOPMENT OF ARMOR

ARMOR DEVELOPED rapidly during the twelfth and thirteenth centuries; conical helmets gave way to pot helms, with visors added around 1300. Long mail tunics became lighter, more supple, and better fitting, with a quilted surcoat adding to the protection of the rider. By 1250, metal caps were being added to elbows and knees for greater protection, soon to be replaced with a cuirass, which covered the whole of the upper body. Light cavalry

reemerged for skirmishing and scouting. The main fighting was still the task of the man-at-arms, flung at the enemy in a series of mass charges. Simon de Montfort used this tactic at Lewes, in south England, against Henry III in 1264 and Charles of Anjou used the same methods at Benevento against Manfred in 1266.

*Thirteenth-century knight in armor.*

## 1274 THE MONGOL INVASIONS

YORITOMO EMERGED as a strong leader of the Japanese in 1185, establishing a strong central government, while maintaining the feudalism and fighting character of the nation's people. Japan was well prepared for the first Mongol invasion in 1274. For a whole day, the Japanese held the Mongols at their landing point on Kyushu until a storm forced the Mongols to retire to Korea. Since the Japanese had underestimated the fighting skills and numbers of the Mongols, it was inevitable that they would be back. The Japanese did not waste the seven years' respite—they built a stone wall along the shore of Hakozaki Bay from which they would defend their country. The Mongols reappeared off the coast in 1281, but were unable to breach the defenses. They never returned.

## 1300s GUNPOWDER AND FIREARMS

ROGER BACON (*circa* 1214–92), an English monk, was the first to record the manufacturing process and composition of gunpowder in 1260. It would be another 50 years before anyone took the concept seriously. A gun was fired at Metz in 1324 and Edward III probably used cannons against the Scots at Berwick in 1327. The

*Roger Bacon (circa 1214–92) English monk, scientist, philosopher, mathematician.*

French also used cannons against the English at Quesnoy in 1340 and Edward repaid the compliment at Calais in 1346. Another new firearm was being developed, the ribaudequin, which consisted of several tubes mounted on a wagon that could be fired at the same time. It was a primitive rocket battery. Edward ordered 100 of these to be made in 1345. By the mid-fourteenth century, firearms were coming into regular use, but they had not yet made an impact on warfare.

## 1327 THE HUNDRED YEARS' WAR

THE HUNDRED YEARS' WAR began as a result of Edward III's claim to the French throne in 1327 and a series of territorial and trade disputes between the two nations. England won a comprehensive naval victory off Sluys in 1340, but it was not until 1346 that Edward felt strong enough to face the French in a decisive battle. Edward landed in France and headed for Calais with 15,000 men. He was immediately pursued by Philip VI with at least 40,000 troops, including 29,000 mounted knights. Taking up a position overlooking a valley, Edward turned to face them. The French advanced to within 150 yards (137 m) and the skies were filled with English arrows. Wave after wave were slaughtered. The French lost 10,000 to England's 200 men.

*Edward III (1312–77) and his army, showing how armor had developed by the 14th century.*

# Society and Culture

### AD 618 TRAVELERS AND TRADERS IN CHINA

SINCE THE EARLIEST TIMES, the Chinese had shown little interest in exploration. Uncharacteristically, however, the Tang emperors of China (AD 618–907) were very receptive to foreign ideas and imports. Subsequently, Arabian, Persian, and Japanese merchants brought spices to the country, which soon found their way into Chinese food. Persian cakes and sweetmeats also became a special delicacy. Before long, tales of the gold, jewels, and other luxuries whetted the appetites of European merchants, for whom spices, vital for preserving meat, were of as much interest as the luxuries. The trade became rich, although Islamic powers blocked the route at times. After the Europeans entered the Indian Ocean, sea links from Europe to China developed in the sixteenth century.

### AD 700s CITIES OF ISLAM

EARLY ON IN THE MUSLIMS' campaign of conversion, they attacked and captured towns such as Damascus (AD 635) and Aleppo (AD 638); in time, they were turned into magnificent

*Detail of a mosaic from the Umayyad mosque in the old town of Damascus in Syria.*

cities, with elegant mosques, minarets, gardens, fountains, and houses decorated with elaborate mosaics. Such beautiful structures became, and still remain, particular features of many Muslim cities, and the lives of culture and luxury enjoyed by their rulers in the Middle Ages became legendary. One of the most prominent of Islam's cities was Baghdad, now the capital of Iraq, which was founded in AD 762 by the Muslim caliph (civil religious leader) Abu Jafar al-Mansur. Baghdad later became a center of culture and learning. The most famous of all caliphs in Baghdad, Harun al-Rashid (AD 766–809) was himself a great scholar and possessed a library of some 600,000 books.

## AD 800s HOW THE FEUDAL SYSTEM WORKED

THE FEUDAL SYSTEM in England was a pyramid. At its apex was the king, whose vassals, the nobility, owed him fealty and the duty of providing forces for his wars. These were recruited from the mass of ordinary people who, in their turn, were the nobles' vassals. Oaths of fealty were solemn, binding contracts, sworn before God. Breaking them was, therefore, blasphemy, an awesome crime in an age of superstition. However, in return for fealty, and the labor of their humble vassals, the nobles owed them protection; if necessary, physical protection within the walls of their castles. Most feudal estates consisted of these castles, together with a church and tracts of land. Outside, any land was common land, there for the use of all.

## AD 800 AN INTERVAL OF PEACE

WHEN CHARLEMAGNE was crowned Holy Roman Emperor on Christmas Day, AD 800, Europe was able to contemplate a return of law and order and protection from attack that it had not known since the end of the western Roman Empire. The respite, however, was a brief one. Charlemagne died in 814, and with that, Europe was once more vulnerable to assaults by Vikings from Scandinavia, Magyars from Hungary, and those fiercest of Christendom's foes, the Arabs. The areas of Europe that were most at risk were in France, Germany, Italy, and northern Spain, where feudalism was imposed as a system of mutual self-defense. czarist Russia, too, adopted the system, and it persisted there for a thousand years, until the feudal serfs were freed in 1861.

*Charlemagne (747–814) crowned Holy Roman Emperor by Pope Leo III in AD 800.*

*The Toltec god Quetzalcoatl.*

### AD 930 THE TOLTECS, WARRIORS AND CONQUERORS

THE TOLTECS seem to have lived for war and conquest. They seized power in Yucatán in Central America in about AD 930 and occupied Chichen Itzá, doubtless with all the ferocity for which they were notorious. Not long afterward, they founded their own capital city of Tollan (Tula). At Tollan, known as the "city of reeds," the Toltecs built temples with roofs supported by giant statues. They created massive sculptures of warriors and decorated their pyramids with carvings of Quetzalcoatl. Quetzalcoatl it appears was the real-life Topiltzin Ce Acatl, who founded Tollan. In 999, however, he was forced into exile and fled east across the Atlantic. A legend soon arose that one day, Quetzalcoatl would return, punish his enemies, and reclaim his kingdom.

### 1095 MUSLIMS AND CRUSADERS: A CLASH OF CULTURES

POPE URBAN II appealed in 1095 for an army to "take the Cross" and rescue the Holy Land from the Muslims, who had been looting and destroying churches and killing Christians. However, the Crusades, which lasted from 1096 until the last crusader presence was expunged in 1303, gave Christians a different picture from the one they had expected. Many were impressed by Muslim culture, the dedication, and sense of honor of the Muslim knights whom they fought and the practicality of many Muslim ideas, in the castle building, clothing for the desert heat, and hygiene. They took much of what they had learned back with them when they returned home.

### 1324 RICHES IN AFRICA

IN AFRICA, great fortunes were being made in trading kingdoms, such as Ghana, known as the Land of Gold. Ostrich feathers, leather, kola nuts, ivory, and solid gold weapons were traded across the Sahara. In 1324, one Muslim king, Mansa Musa of Mali, made a pilgrimage to Mecca accompanied by 500 attendants carrying golden staffs and 80 camels laden with 10 tons of gold dust, which he distributed among the poor as his journey progressed. Much later, in the nineteenth century, rich kingdoms in Africa, such as Benin, ruined by the slave trade, and Oyo, destroyed by civil war, were to fall. However, as long as it lasted, the prosperity of medieval Africa was, both literally and metaphorically, a "golden age."

## 1348 THE BLACK DEATH

THREE SHIPS ARRIVED at Genoa, Italy, in 1348, infected with a deadly disease—bubonic plague. The Genoese drove the ships away, but it was already too late. The Black Death, as the plague was later called, spread throughout Europe and, by 1350, had killed one-quarter of its population. Another of its casualties was the feudal system. With the workforce drastically reduced, those villeins who survived were able to demand higher wages and greater independence, thus undercutting the power that the lords had once held over them. However, the Black Death was not the only cause. Wealthy merchants in the towns, who had never been included in the feudal system, also contributed to its breakup. So did the development of guns and gunpowder, which made the nobles' castles more impregnable.

*Stewart del.*  THE BLACK RAT.  *Lauvière sc.*

*Rats were commonly believed to have carried the plague into Europe.*

# Exploration and Empires

*Pope Urban II (1040–99, pope in 1088–99) chairing the Ecumenical Council of Clermont and preaching the crusade.*

## 1095 THE CRUSADES

A COUNCIL OF the Catholic Church met in 1095, in Clermont. Pope Urban II then called on Christians throughout Europe to fight a holy war to recover Jerusalem. The Christian kings of Spain had begun to use religion as an excuse for waging war against their Muslim neighbors. In northern France, the younger sons of the landed gentry wanted land. The idea of a pilgrimage to the sites of relics in order to gain the remission of sins had become very popular. The First Crusade was a great success. In the spring of 1097, a huge army drawn from western Europe had assembled outside Constantinople. It marched across Asia Minor and into Syria. The great city of Antioch was captured in 1098, and Jerusalem in the following year.

## 1187 JERUSALEM CONQUERED

THE CHRISTIAN STATES of the Middle East became known as Outre-mer (French for "overseas"). Because the bulk of the crusaders came from France or from parts of Italy and Germany strongly influenced by the kingdom of France, Outre-mer was effectively a French colony in the Middle East. It maintained a precarious existence for some two hundred years. Its survival depended on the ability to receive periodic reinforcements from Europe, in the shape of new crusades, and Muslim disunity. When the Muslim world was united, however, the kingdom suffered. In 1187, a combined Syrian-Egyptian army conquered Jerusalem, and confined the Christian kingdom to the cities of the coast. The final blow came in 1291, when the stronghold of Acre was captured in a bloody assault.

## 1206 THE MONGOLS UNITE

TO THE NORTH OF CHINA, in Mongolia and eastern Siberia, an anarchic world of nomadic and seminomadic clans was in a perpetual state of intrigue and warfare. This was partly stimulated by gold that was shipped north by the Chinese emperors. Toward the end of the twelfth century, however, things

*The Mongol conqueror Genghis Khan (circa 1162–1227).*

began to change as a young man named Temujin rose to become "khan," or "ruler," of one of these groups—the Mongols. He skillfully manipulated the political situation so that in 1206 all of the nomadic groups—the Naiman Turks, the Keraits, and the Tartars—acknowledged his supremacy. He took the name Genghis Khan, and went on to become one of the most infamous warrior leaders in history.

## 1251 PAPAL EMISSARIES

THE FACT THAT THE MONGOLS attacked the Muslim world as well was of great interest to European rulers. Pope Innocent IV sent a Franciscan friar, Giovanni de Plano Carpini, offering an alliance. Giovanni's account of his travel has survived. His report warned the pope that the Mongols were just after conquest and would be unreliable allies. A second emissary, the friar William de Rubruquis, traveled to the court of the Great Khan in 1251. He describes how there were embassies from the Byzantine emperor, the caliph of Damascus, the king of Delhi in India, the sultan of the Seljuk Turks, and Russian princes. In between these European visits, the Mongols sent their own embassy to King St. Louis IX of France, who was on Crusade in Cyprus.

## 1271 THE POLO FAMILY

THE MONGOL EMPIRE had made the caravan routes across Central Asia as safe as they had been in the first and second centuries. Merchants began moving east, for the products of the Far East—silks and spices—were luxury items in Europe. A pair of Venetian brothers, Niccolò and Maffeo Polo, reached Bokhara in Central Asia and then traveled on to Peking before returning briefly to Venice. They then set out once more for the empire of the Great Khan, taking with them their son and nephew Marco, in 1271. The journey lasted three-and-a-half years, and the Great Khan, Kublai, allowed Marco to remain at his court until 1292, when all three Polos began the three-year journey back to Venice.

*Maffeo Polo and his brother Niccolò taking leave of Baldwin II of Courtenay, Emperor of Constantinople.*

## 1300s EARLY MISSIONARIES TO CHINA

WHILE THE NAMES of the merchants who ventured east from Italy are largely unknown to history, several missionaries who carried the Christian Gospel to India and China have left more detailed records. One of the best known is Giovanni of Monte Corvino, who became the first Christian archbishop of Peking, and who sent letters back to Italy in 1305 and 1306. He built a church in Peking and converted some 150 boys to Christianity, teaching them both Greek and Latin. The second letter led to three Franciscan friars being sent to China. One of them, Andrew of Perugia, became bishop in Ts'uenchow on the southeast coast. Giovanni of Monte Corvino died in 1328, and the Khan's own court asked for a successor to be sent to China.

### 1334 IBN BATTUTAH

THE MAIN MUSLIM travel narrative from the fourteenth century was written by Ibn Battutah, a Moroccan. He left Tangier and crossed the Islamic world to Aden, whence he took a ship down the east coast of Africa. He then went north to visit Russia and the great city of Constantinople, before turning east along the Silk Road. In 1334, he went to Delhi in India, and stayed there for eight years before joining an embassy from the sultan to the emperor of China. Ibn Battutah's ship was wrecked on the Malabar coast of southern India, however, and his trip to China was delayed. Instead, he went to the Maldives, and then claims to have made a voyage via Sri Lanka and the Malay archipelago to China.

### 1368 BREAKING THE BONDS

THE GOLDEN AGE of medieval exploration came to an end in the second half of the fourteenth century. One cause was the great plague in Europe, which significantly reduced the population of many of the richest parts of the Continent. The plague itself was a product of the contact between the different societies of Eurasia, spread along the Silk Road by flea-infested rats. Another cause was the rise of new,

*Tamerlane (1336–1405), also known as Timur the Lame.*

militantly Islamic societies in Central Asia and Asia Minor. Timur the Lame, a new conqueror worthy of comparison with Genghis Khan, swept across the Middle East and into India. His savage empire was strictly Islamic and inhospitable to Christian travelers. Finally, in China itself, the cosmopolitan Yuan dynasty founded by Genghis Khan was overthrown by the Ming family in 1368.

# Trade and Industry

### AD 600s CHINA IN THE MIDDLE AGES

THE TANG DYNASTY (AD 618–907) marked the beginnings of significant economic development. Paddy fields were extended to yield enough rice to maintain an expanding, urban population of craftspeople and officials. Trade was often in foreign hands, especially those of Uighurs and Arabs. According to Confucian doctrine, merchants were social parasites. Nevertheless, external and internal trade grew. The land-owning gentry remained the dominant class, served by others, leaving them free to pursue such gentlemanly activities as painting and poetry. In the eleventh and twelfth centuries, China built up a massive iron industry using coal for fuel. Regional specialization permitted the expansion of trade, and seagoing ships developed overseas commerce. Trade was now undertaken on an unprecedented scale. Trading was not entirely respectable, however, and once a merchant had made his fortune, he generally bought land and changed to a more civilized occupation. Tradition and state control triumphed, preventing a thorough industrial and social revolution.

*Modern paddy fields in China.*

*Asante people figures, from the kingdom of Ghana.*

## AD 750 THE KINGDOM OF GHANA

THE KINGDOM OF GHANA was the first of several West African empires to grow rich on trade. The kingdom, founded before AD 750, was favorably positioned on river plains and its alluvial gold was carried north on the trans-Saharan routes in exchange for salt, textiles, weaponry, copper goods, and horses. Imports came from as far afield as Egypt, Germany, and Italy. The Ghanaian state included slaves among its exports, and charged taxes at relay stations along the trade routes. West Africa was a key source of gold until the metal was discovered in the Americas in the fifteenth century. The kingdom reached the height of its prosperity about the tenth century, when it extended from Timbuktu (now in Mali) to the Atlantic Ocean, and its capital had a population of 30,000.

## AD 1000 DEVELOPMENTS IN EUROPE

AROUND THE YEAR 1000, German cultivators invented a new type of heavy mold-board plow, capable of draining wet, low-lying lands and strong enough to work the heavy, clay soil that covered much of northern Europe, where the light scratch plows known in the Mediterranean and the Middle East were useless. Most of the villages of western Europe were under the control of a professional fighting man equipped with a horse, a lance, and armor. Other developments were the construction of windmills and water mills (not new inventions but of much improved design), and the horse collar and horseshoes, which allowed for horses to be used as work animals instead of oxen. Trading settlements also grew up at this time. The eleventh century in Europe was, in fact, a very productive time.

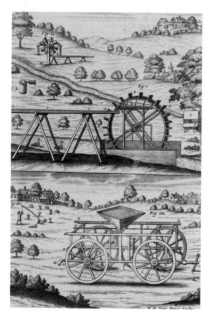

*Water mills were used in early industries for driving machinery and grinding corn.*

## 1086 WATER MILLS

LONG BEFORE WINDMILLS were built, in Britain, water mills were used to drive machinery. At the time of the Doomsday survey in 1086, there were more than 5,600 water mills. At first, they were used for grinding corn, but later water wheels drove various kinds of machinery. They could move a hammer up and down in scour and tighten the weave in cloth to make it thicker; this process was called "fulling" the cloth. Hammers were also used in early iron foundries to shape the iron and to grind dyes. There were three types of wheel, called undershot, overshot, and breast. They differed in the point at which water struck them—from underneath, on top, or half way up.

## 1100s THE FEUDAL MANOR SYSTEM

THE FEUDAL PERIOD in Europe began soon after the fall of the Roman Empire and reached its height around 1100. The feudal society (from "fief," an inherited estate) was a self-contained community, often comprising the home of the fief owner (sometimes called "lord"), a parish church, and one or more villages. The manor occupied 900–2,000 acres (350–800 ha) of arable land, and owned other land as well. A large manor might have a mill for grinding grain, an oven for baking bread, a wine- or oil-press, fish ponds, orchards, and gardens. Food, linen, and woolen textiles, and garments and leather were produced. The arable land was cultivated under a three-field system: one field was sown in fall, another in spring, and the third left fallow (see page 66). A four-year cycle of rotation of fallow land came into use around the eighth century, involving three periods of plowing in the year.

## 1200s THE SILK ROUTE REVIVAL

THE SILK ROUTE was a series of land routes, altogether more than 3,750 miles (6,000 km) long that connected the eastern Mediterranean with East Asia. The first routes opened about 100 BC, when Emperor Wudi of the Han dynasty subdued large areas of Central Asia through conquest and alliance. Various routes ran from the Chinese capital Chang'an (now Xi'an, Shaanxi province) across northern China to the Mediterranean ports of Antioch and Alexandria. The Silk Route fell into disuse with the rise of militarized and belligerent Islamic states and the fragmentation of the Roman Empire. It was revived under the Mongol Empire in the thirteenth century, when Marco Polo traveled the route to China, taking three years. Shipments of Chinese silk traveled westward along the Silk Route, while metals, glass, and coins went in the reverse direction.

*Illustrated map depicting the journey of the Venetian merchant Marco Polo (1254–1324) along the Silk Route to China.*

*Mongol warlords were a dominant force in Europe and India from the tenth century.*

## 1240 MONGOL RULE

THE TURKISH ADVANCE into Europe and India, starting about AD 900, was temporarily halted in the thirteenth century by a Mongol whirlwind. Genghis Khan created a huge military alliance between the peoples of the Asian steppes and then raided in every direction. Mongol dominance lasted only about 150 years before the Turks mounted a new offensive. From this arose the Ottoman Empire, headed by a sultan. The sultan required not only a standing army, the famous janissary corps, but also several thousand slaves. At first, most of these were war captives; additional numbers were purchased from commercial slave dealers or obtained by conscription. One legacy of Mongol rule in the north (1240–1480) was the subcontracting of tax collection, first to corporations of Central Asian merchants and then to Russian princes, who created an enduring bureaucracy of tax gatherers.

## 1300s FIREARM TECHNOLOGY

THE CHINESE WERE the first people to make firearms, including cannon. This technology traveled to Europe in the fourteenth century, giving the users a great advantage over opponents armed with only swords. The barrels of early guns were made of iron strips fastened with iron hoops, or of cast brass and bronze. Later, bell-making foundries learned how to cast cannon barrels and later still musket and handgun barrels from iron. The new technology had an impact on architecture and ship design. Forts were built in a star shape, which would help to deflect cannon balls and with their own emplacements for cannon. The acme of shipbuilding in this era was the galleon, which had guns on both flanks showing through gun ports.

## 1345 THE AZTECS AND THE INCAS

THE AZTECS founded their city of Tenochtitlán on swampy islands in Lake Texcoco (Mexico) in 1345. Canoes plied the lake and canals and the produce grown on the "floating gardens," or *chinampas*, were taken to market. Food and clothing, pottery utensils, tobacco pipes, and cigarettes were sold, along with luxury items—gold, silver, jade, and feathers. Slaves, displayed in wooden cages, were also for sale. The Aztecs used fixed units of value, such as jade necklaces, for barter. The Incas of South America were the other most important contemporary American civilization. Most Inca commoners worked under a communal system in which they had to farm fields designated for the gods and the emperor, as well as their own. Inca cities had efficient drainage and water-supply systems.

*Wall and entrance gate of the Aztec city of Tenochtitlán.*

# Science and Technology

### AD 500s THE USE OF THE ASTROLABE

BY THE NINTH CENTURY, the Arab inventiveness had perfected the astrolabe, a device that was first conceived by Ptolemy (*circa* AD 100–170), a scientist from Alexandria. It was a device by which the position of the stars could be used to determine a position at sea or on land by knowing the date, and vice versa. Although it had obvious limitations, it became the most important instrument for navigation for several hundred years— partly because sailors usually remained within familiar waters and only traveled during a season of congenial weather, between May and September. By the late twelfth century, the Arabs had knowledge of the loadstone compass, possibly invented in China. Suddenly, it was possible to navigate without being able to see the sun or the stars, so confidence in navigating uncharted waters grew.

*An astrolabe.*

### AD 500s ROTATION FARMING

THE IMPROVEMENTS made to farming, with the introduction of the mold-board plow, resulted in surplus production, and the net effect meant more leisure time, or rather, time to learn the art of warfare. Nevertheless, people still suffered from malnutrition due to lack of food variety, and productivity peaked off as the soil became exhausted of nutrients. There was a no-win situation until a new system of farming was introduced, which made it self-sustaining. The solution was the three-field rotation pattern. Fields were used for two years in succession and then left for a year. The first crop was used as a green fertilizer as well as a food source, and the second was grain, which tended to drain the goodness from the earth, thus requiring that the field lie fallow for 12 months to recover. Fields were grouped in threes so that each was subject to a different phase in any one year.

## AD 751 PAPERMAKING

A CHINESE TEAM set up a factory for making paper in AD 751 in Samarkand, east of the Caspian Sea. From there, the Arabs brought the technology to Spain. By the end of the eleventh century, water-powered paper mills were operating in Italy. It was old linen that supplied the principal raw material, flax fiber. This was soaked and pulped, ready to be lifted in uniform layers with mesh screens made from drawn wires. The drained pulp was then placed between layers of cloth to form a pile, which was then squeezed under a press to remove as

*Throughout the Middle Ages, many thousands of manuscripts worldwide were written and illuminated.*

much water as possible before hanging each leaf to dry. Paper was far cheaper than alternatives, such as parchment, so it quickly grew in popularity. The net result was an increase in literacy as people became more interested in being able to read and contribute to the information that was being circulated.

## AD 765 THE REDISCOVERY OF EARLY SCIENCE

WHEN FANATICAL CHRISTIANS, and then Muslims, sacked Alexandria at the beginning of the Middle Ages, a vast library of manuscripts was lost, which contained information about every kind of scientific discovery and theory. Amazingly, in AD 765, a Byzantine monastery in Persia was discovered to contain copies of many of the lost works. They were translated from Greek into Arabic in Baghdad and duplicate copies eventually found their way to Muslim-held Spain. By the mid-thirteenth century, Spain had come under Christian control and the manuscripts were translated into Latin. Copies found their way to all parts of Europe, where they were the subject of intense interest, particularly because of the astronomical information, which had a direct practical application to navigation.

*The Japanese shogun, Yoritomo, with armed guards.*

## 1044 GUNPOWDER AND SWORD

IN THE EARLY eleventh century, the Chinese chanced on the formula for gunpowder. The first recipe for making saltpeter, the main constituent, was first recorded in 1044 by Wu Ching Tsao Yao. The potential for gunpowder as a firearms propellant was only fully realized when it got into the hands of the warring Europeans. It gained its familiar name when it was used in the first cannons, which were little more than upturned bells from which large stone balls could be fired. Initially, the early cannons were more feared for their display of noise and smoke instead of their accuracy, but before long cannon shot was ripping through soldiers and castle ramparts alike.

In the late thirteenth century, Mongols had made repeated attempts to invade Japan. Thanks to a curved sword made from expertly tempered steel, the Japanese won against the odds. In 1274, the Mongols made their last assault but, hindered by a storm, the Japanese samurai were able to make an offensive move, getting close enough to massacre the Mongols while they fumbled with their own inferior weapons.

## 1066 STIRRUP AND LONGBOW

WARFARE PLAYED a significant role in asserting control over regions of Europe during the Middle Ages. There were two significant developments in warfare technology around the time of the Battle of Hastings in England in 1066. Warhorses were important for gaining an advantage over heavily armed opposing infantrymen. This advantage was quickly lost, however, if the cavalryman was dislodged from his horse by losing his balance or being pulled off. The solution was the stirrup. This simple invention made all the difference, giving the rider a secure foothold while striking his lance or wielding his sword. The crossbow was a weapon favored by Continental troops because it fired bolts at high velocity and could penetrate chain mail and armor. The British, however, had the Welsh longbow, which had a decisive advantage over the crossbow. A well-trained archer could send eight arrows in the time it took to load and fire just one bolt.

*Warhorses provided a significant advantage over enemies during the Middle Ages.*

## 1100s EUROPE GETS CAST IRON

EUROPEANS AT LAST mastered a technique for producing cast iron in the 1100s, some 1,500 years after the Chinese. This was by means of a blast furnace, so-called because of the blasts of air required to achieve temperatures high enough to melt the iron. Water and sometimes wind power were used to operate the bellows and for crushing up the iron ore to increase its surface area. Blast furnaces gradually grew in capacity to meet the demand for the new cast iron, which had wider applications than wrought

iron, but two distinct problems arose as a result. Charcoal began to run short as Europe's trees were increasingly felled, and slag impurities prevented as much as 50 percent of the iron from being run off for casting. The introduction of coke and lime into the smelting process solved both of these problems, but not until several centuries to come.

## A REGULATED EXISTENCE

THE END OF the Middle Ages saw town clocks being introduced all over Europe. The concept of arriving for and leaving from work at certain times was just one example of the effect clocks had, particularly in towns and cities where increased efficiency was the underlying motive for introducing clocks. By the middle of the fifteenth century, the steel spring had been introduced for powering clock mechanisms, replacing the weight drive. Smaller clocks could now be made, but springs lose their energy gradually as they unwind, so a device called a fusee had to be incorporated. It was a tapered or conical drive wheel that compensated for the loss of energy. In 1581, Galileo Galilei noticed the phenomenon of the pendulum. A hundred years later, the pendulum would set a new benchmark in time-keeping accuracy.

# Religions, Belief, and Thought

## AD 500s NESTORIAN CHRISTIANITY

THE CHRISTIANS OF JERUSALEM, following the destruction of the Jewish Temple in AD 70, fled mainly to Syria. Here, Nestorius (AD 381–451) created the Syriac, or "Nestorian," church, which taught (like Arius) that Jesus was not himself God but was a human made divine by God. After reaching Chaldea (Mesopotamia), Nestorian Christianity spread rapidly to Central Asia, China, and India. By the third century, a Christian sect, based on the teachings of St. Thomas, was active in South India. Meanwhile, the hermits of Egypt gave birth to the Coptic Church, whose teachings soon spread to Ethiopia, where it has been the dominant faith for 17 centuries. Many of these churches survive to this day.

## AD 500s CHAN AND ZEN

THE CHAN SCHOOL was traditionally brought to China by the sixth-century Indian monk, Bodhidharma, and was systematized by Hui Neng (the "6th Patriarch") in the Tang dynasty. The name derives from *Dhyana*, Sanskrit for meditation, and the central practice is the direct realization of reality through meditation. Chan was influenced by the

*Different schools of Buddhism have appeared throughout Japan and China since the sixth century.*

*Diamond Sutra* and also by the teachings of Taoism and the Hua Yen School. Hui Neng's Southern School taught that enlightenment was instantaneous, whereas Shen Xiu's Northern School taught that it was gradual. In Japan, Chan was called Zen. This came from the Southern School and took two forms—the

Soto Zen, taught by Dogen (1200–53), emphasized *zazen* meditation, whereas the Rinzai Zen, taught by Hakuin Ekaku (1686–1769), used *koans*, unanswerable riddles, to force the mind out of the delusory world of words.

## AD 570 THE PROPHET MUHAMMAD

MUHAMMAD, the prophet of Allah, was born in Arabia in AD 570, and married a wealthy widow, Khadija.

*Archangel Gabriel, who appeared to the prophet Muhammad.*

In 610, he received his first revelations from Archangel Gabriel while living in a cave undergoing a solitary retreat. To Muslims, Muhammad was the Final Prophet, the last in the line descending from Abraham and Moses, and his message was to have faith in the One True God. His first converts were his wife Khadija and his cousin, Ali. He experienced grave opposition from polytheists in Mecca, who used the Kaaba (the shrine toward which all Muslims must pray) for the worship of idols, but eventually he captured Mecca and rapidly began to spread his faith.

## AD 622 FLIGHT TO MEDINA AND CAPTURE OF MECCA

MUHAMMAD'S TEACHINGS in Mecca led to hostility from the population—who were polytheists—and he, therefore, fled in AD 622 to Yathrib (later Medina), which had a sympathetic Jewish population, in an event known as the Hegira, or "flight." This event is used as the starting point of the Muslim calendar. Over the next eight years, he led raids on the camel caravans to Mecca, destroying the Meccan economy and enriching that of Medina. In 630, he captured Mecca and cleared the idols from the Kaaba. He returned to Medina, where he died two years later.

## AD 700s VAJRAYANA: TIBETAN BUDDHISM

BY TRADITION, BUDDHISM was introduced to Tibet by the eighth-century Indian monk Padmasambhava, who founded the Nyingma tradition and introduced Dzogchen meditation. Atisha (AD 982–1034), another Indian monk, was responsible for the second wave of Buddhism, resulting in the Kadampa order. The Tibetan scholar and householder, Marpa, founded the Sakya order. His disciple, the poet and ascetic monk Milarepa (1040–1123), is seen as the founder of the Kagyu order. The various schools of Tibetan Buddhism were synthesized and united by Tsongkhapa (1357–1418) to create the Celugpa tradition.

*Padmasambhava statue Samdruptse, Sikkim India.*

## 1000 MUSLIM INVASIONS

THE EXPANSION OF ISLAM had little impact on India until the invasions by Mahmud, a king of Ghazni, a province in Afghanistan. Between 1000 and 1026, he led annual campaigns to capture Indian territories, such as the Punjab, and seize the wealth of Hindu temples in the holy towns of Mathura, Thanesar, Kannauj, and Somnath, in the hope that the population would convert to Islam. At Somnath, over 50,000 died in defense of the temple. This and the next two centuries were a "dark age" for Hinduism as repeated Islamic invasions from the northwest, by Afghans and Turks, devastated the country. With the loss of the temples and academic centers, philosophy and religious thought declined, to be replaced by a vast jumble of superstitions.

## 1181 ST. FRANCIS OF ASSISI

ST. FRANCIS, the patron saint of ecology and founder of the Franciscan Order of Friars, has been called the Second Christ, and he did more to reestablish the simple teachings and way of life of Jesus than anyone since St. Antony of Egypt. He was born into a family of wealthy merchants in 1181, but following several religious experiences, he abandoned this way of life and gave away all his possessions to

*St. Francis of Assisi, founder of the Franciscan Order of Friars.*

Muslims had generally allowed Christians to visit and worship in the city. Each crusade ended either with temporary success or in complete chaos. The Fourth Crusade never reached Jerusalem and the soldiers, impatient to attack something, plundered the Christian City of Constantinople. The Children 's Crusade of 1212 resulted in 20,000 children being sold as slaves. In response to the crusades, the Muslims abandoned their policy of appeasement and for several centuries slowly conquered Christian territory. They advanced as far as the Danube, conquering Constantinople in 1453.

become a wandering friar. His reverence for nature, as expressed in his *Canticle of the Sun*, is similar to that found in Celtic Christianity. When large numbers began to follow him, he created simple rules; these included complete poverty, abstinence from meat, and service to the poor. Today, his Order is one of the largest in the Catholic and Anglican churches.

## 1212 THE CHILDREN'S CRUSADE

IT IS ONE OF THE IRONIES of history that over four centuries of war were dedicated to promoting the teachings of the prophet of peace. There were eight crusades to free the Holy City of Jerusalem from Muslim control—although

## 1274 EAST AND WEST DIVIDE

THE DIVISION of the Western Roman Catholic and Eastern Orthodox churches was a gradual process. The cause was probably the division of the Roman Empire into two, centered on Rome and on Constantinople. This led to dispute over the status of the Pope, the Bishop of Rome. Theologically, this division was reinforced by dispute over the "filioqui clause," a technical theological point that was probably given importance for political reasons. By the time that Thomas Aquinas' treatise, *Against the Errors of the Greeks,* was published in 1274, the division had become irreconcilable.

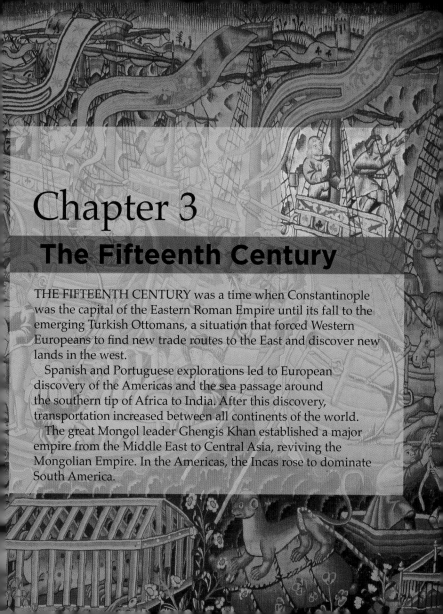

# Chapter 3
## The Fifteenth Century

THE FIFTEENTH CENTURY was a time when Constantinople was the capital of the Eastern Roman Empire until its fall to the emerging Turkish Ottomans, a situation that forced Western Europeans to find new trade routes to the East and discover new lands in the west.

Spanish and Portuguese explorations led to European discovery of the Americas and the sea passage around the southern tip of Africa to India. After this discovery, transportation increased between all continents of the world.

The great Mongol leader Ghengis Khan established a major empire from the Middle East to Central Asia, reviving the Mongolian Empire. In the Americas, the Incas rose to dominate South America.

# Power and Politics

## 1453 THE RISE OF THE OTTOMANS

IN THE FOURTEENTH CENTURY, the Ottoman Turks conquered the Islamic Empire and began to advance into Europe. Mehmet II (reigned 1451–81) captured Constantinople in 1453 and then invaded the Balkans. For the next 200 years, the Turks constantly tried to invade eastern Europe. Belgrade was eventually captured in 1521 and Vienna was besieged in 1526 and again in 1683. The city was only saved by the arrival of the Polish army commanded by John III Sobieski. The Ottoman sultans ruled a huge empire in the Middle East, North Africa, and the Balkans. Their capital was Constantinople, but the empire was divided into provinces, each ruled by a governor. The extreme wealth of the empire inevitably led to increasing corruption and conflict, and in the nineteenth century some provincial governors, such as Mehmet Ali in Egypt, began to try to break away from central control.

*Entry of the Turks of Mehmet II into Constantinople, 1453.*

## 1471 END OF FEUDALISM

A CONSEQUENCE of feudalism in England was that the barons came to see the king as little better than themselves. If the king was weak or unsuccessful, it was very tempting for the powerful barons to try to overthrow him. When King Henry V of England died in 1422, his nine-month-old son, Henry VI, was unable to rule immediately. When he was eventually mature enough to take control of the throne, he was a poor ruler and failed to hold onto the English empire in France. His continued failures encouraged his enemies, the Yorkists, to try to seize power. Eventually, Henry was captured in 1461 and held prisoner in the Tower of London. He was almost certainly murdered in 1471. This was the final chapter of feudalism. Kings realized that they needed some greater degree of certainty in their control of the country and could not afford to allow powerful barons to challenge them.

### 1485 HENRY VII

HENRY VII BECAME KING of England in 1485. His immediate aim was to pacify England after the Wars of the Roses—the royal houses of Lancaster and York, fighting for some 30 years to establish who should be king. His methods were simple and, at times, brutally harsh. Any possible rivals to the throne were arrested and executed. The noble families, which had fought for the throne, were forced to give up their private armies. This brought an end, once and for all, to the feudal system. Henry also built up a strong treasury, which gave him a high degree of independence. On the one

*Henry VII, the first Tudor king of England.*

occasion that he went to war in 1492, again with France, he signed an armistice almost immediately. The French agreed to pay him £50,000, a figure that more than covered his war costs. Henry VII set in motion a pattern that later monarchs followed, but few ever demonstrated his ability to manage their resources as effectively as he.

# War and Peace

*The Jahaz Mahal, or Ship Palace, in the Royal Enclave, Mandu, Madhya Pradesh, India.*

### 1406 INDIAN HILL FORTS

INDIAN HILL FORTS were as good as anything built in Europe in the fifteenth century. A typical example of this is Mandu in Gujarat, built by Howshang Shah Gori (1406–35). Its powerful walls, bastions, and gates stand 1,000 feet (305 m) above the plain, with sheer sides to the south. The Indians were forced to accept the arrival of the Portuguese, the French, the Dutch, and the British, but it was the latter that would expel the others and finally bring India into their own empire. In 1757, at Plassey, Clive with fewer than 3,000 men defeated the Indians under Suraj-ud-Dowah, leading to the establishment of the British in the wealthy region of Bengal. Nevertheless, there was still much fighting before the British dominated all of India.

## 1415 HARFLEUR AND AGINCOURT

THE ENGLISH SPENT the latter half of the fourteenth century sending forces into France in vain attempts to search for the elusive French army. A peace treaty was finally signed in 1396, but it did not last very long. Henry V, eager to press his claim to the French throne, took advantage of French indecision and renewed the war in 1415. He captured Harfleur and marched on Calais. A huge French army was lured out in pursuit of his army of less than 6,000. The armies met at Agincourt, where the French showed that they had ignored the lessons of previous encounters with the English. In a little more than half an hour, Henry's archers slaughtered 6,000 of the 25,000-strong French army.

## 1452 THE USE OF CANNON

WHEN URBAN, a Hungarian engineer was turned away by Constantine, the Byzantine emperor, in 1452, he was employed by Mehmet II to construct a cannon 27 feet (8.2 m) long with a range of 1 mile (1.6 km). The Ottomans had already realized the importance of cannons and by 1364 had begun mass production. They had used field artillery at Kosovo in 1389. Mehmet arrived with his 100,000 men, a huge siege train, and kept up a ceaseless bombardment of the city of Kosovo for six weeks. Within a week, the outer wall had been breached in several places, and when the Ottomans placed more cannon on a pontoon across the Golden Horn, none of the city was safe from their bombardment. On two occasions, Mehmet thought that the bombardment had done enough, but was repulsed each time. On the third attempt, the city fell.

*England's Henry V among his troops at Agincourt during the Hundred Years' War.*

## 1479 FERDINAND AND ISABELLA

BY A CHANCE of dynastic fortune—the accession of Isabella I to the throne of Castile in 1474 and of her husband Ferdinand II to the throne of Aragon in 1479—the two most important kingdoms of Spain were now joined. The "Catholic kings" were exceptionally gifted rulers. Isabella was famed for her abilities in internal politics and Ferdinand was renown for his skillfulness in foreign policy maneuvering. Upon the couple's new alliance, Ferdinand quickly turned his attention to the conquest of Naples and to disputes with neighboring France over the control of Italy. In 1502, Ferdinand conquered Granada, thus completing the reconquest of Spain from the Muslim Arabs. Isabella died in 1504, and upon Ferdinand's death in 1516, both of their crowns were united and went to their grandson Charles I.

*Ferdinand and Isabella seeing Christopher Columbus off from the dock at Palos, 1492.*

*Charles VIII of France, during his invasion of Italy in 1495.*

Threatened by a coalition of Italian states allied with Emperor Maximilian I and King Ferdinand II of Aragon, Charles soon withdrew. A period of intermittent warfare followed, during which the Spanish general Gonzalo Fernandez de Cordoba conquered Naples (1503–4), bringing southern Italy under Spanish control, whereas France dominated the northern half of the peninsula.

### 1495 GONZALO DE CORDOBA IN ITALY

SPANISH GENERAL Gonzalo Fernandez de Cordoba was known as el Gran Capitan. He fought in the wars to drive the Muslims from Spain and helped negotiate the surrender of the Moorish kingdom of Granada (1492). He was sent to Italy with an army (1495), where he soon forced the French to withdraw. His brilliant victories at Cerignola and at Garigliano brought all of Naples under Spanish rule. He is credited with the introduction of the harquebusier, men armed with the latest handguns. Each had a bullet pouch; match, ramrod, and powder in tubes hung on a bandolier. They also had a sword and helmet. He realized that these troops were perfectly capable of stopping the assault of any enemy thrown at them.

### 1494 ITALIAN WARS (HABSBURG-VALOIS WARS)

AFTER THE PEACE OF LODI (1454), a precarious balance of power had been maintained among the chief Italian states: Florence, Milan, Naples, the papacy, and Venice. This equilibrium was upset when Ludovico Sforza of Milan appealed to France for aid against a secret league of Florence and Naples. The French king Charles VIII descended into Italy with his army (1494), expelled the Florentine ruler Piero de' Medici, and entered Naples in February 1495.

# Society and Culture

### 1400s SLAVERY

SLAVERY HAS BEEN called "the greatest crime in the world." It is also a very old one; it is probably as old as civilization itself. There were slaves in ancient Judea, where Jewish law decreed that they should be released after a certain time. Ancient Rome teemed with slaves: nearly 21 million throughout Italy by about AD 50. Throughout the fifteenth century, Arabs traded in slaves across the Sahara. However, a crime becomes a crime only when people become sufficiently shocked by it to call it so, and it was not until much later that an increasing level of dismay arose over the transportation of Africans across the Atlantic to work as slaves in the European colonies, established there in the previous three centuries.

### 1450 THE LEGACY OF ANCIENT GREECE

IN ABOUT 1450, at the start of the Renaissance, the ancient Greeks and ancient Romans (who had long ago emulated the Greeks) provided the models for this revival of art, architecture, and learning. Doctors began to look back to the Greek physicians Hippocrates

(460–377 BC) and Galen (*circa* AD 129–200), and philosophers to Aristotle (384–322 BC). Aristotle's theories on the motion of heavenly bodies were studied and

*The Greek physician Hippocrates (460–377 BC), who became known as the "father of medicine."*

*Aristotle (384–322 BC), Greek philosopher and teacher to the young Alexander the Great.*

adopted by astronomers. The colonnaded buildings of ancient Greece would again influence architects and mathematicians would consult the works of Euclid (330–260 BC). Renaissance artists and sculptors portrayed Greek mythical characters and other classical subjects. The ideas of Galen and Aristotle's theories of astronomy have been superseded, but the Renaissance began a long period, which still continues today, when Greek ideas, including their democracy, retained—and still retain to this day—an enduring influence on society.

### 1453 LIFE UNDER TURKISH OTTOMAN RULE

WHILE EUROPE was moving toward a more enlightened and humanitarian concept of life, no such freedom existed in the Ottoman Empire, which was established after 1453, with the Muslim Turks' capture of Constantinople. While the Ottoman sultan had numerous Christian and Jewish subjects in the Balkans, Cyprus, Poland, the Crimea, and in Russia, these groups were often persecuted or, at best, treated very much as second-class citizens. They were organized into minority communities, and known as *rai'yah*, or "the shepherded people," their lives, their property, and even their livelihoods depended entirely on the will of the sultan. They were not allowed to ride horses or carry weapons and they were barred from the Ottoman army and civil service. None of these rules applied to the majority of Muslims, subjects of the empire.

# Exploration and Empires

### 1403 A TURNING POINT

THE THIRD MING EMPEROR, Yongle (reigned 1402–24) was an unusual Chinese ruler in that, for a time at least, he considered the possibility of expanding south-eastward. He had assembled a huge fleet of 62 ships, which he sent into the Indian Ocean under Admiral Cheng Ho. Cheng Ho eventually made seven voyages around the Indian Ocean visiting India, Sri Lanka, and even the coast of East Africa at Mogadishu. He also sailed into the Red Sea and anchored in the Arabian port of Jedda, the traditional route for pilgrims to the holiest Muslim shrine at Mecca. After Cheng-Ho's death in 1434, and given the general preference of the Ming rulers for a self-sufficient economy, the great days of Chinese exploration came to an end. The tentative opening to the world had been closed off.

### 1420 SAILING INTO THE UNKNOWN

DURING THIS TIME, it was commonly believed among seafarers that to sail beyond Morocco would lead to waters boiled by liquid flames from the sun and that to sail west would lead to dangerous swamps. To prepare crews for these hazards and to overcome their fears, Henry the Navigator (1394–1460) established a maritime center that would equip sailors with knowledge, instruments, and vessels. Storms drove Henry's first expedition in 1420 to the Madeira islands. The islands were eventually colonized by Portugal,

*Mecca surrounded by the Mountains of Arafa.*

*Portuguese explorer Henry the Navigator (1394–1460).*

principality in Russia in support of the rights of the Russian Orthodox Church and in dealings with the Tatars. Under Ivan III, the first of its rulers to call himself czar (Russian for Caesar), the territorial expansion of Muscovy moved rapidly. The great trading city of Novgorod, with its vast lands to the north, was annexed in 1478. Other states to the northwest of Muscovy were also added. By the end of the reign of Vasilii III, in 1533, Muscovy was sufficiently powerful to be treated as an equal by the Hapsburg dynasty.

who introduced new crops and livestock. The islands of the Azores, reached in 1431, became a base for subsequent expeditions. By Henry's death (1460), his ships had sailed one-third of the way down the African coast to present-day Sierra Leone. These ships stopped along the coast and sailed into river mouths to trade with African kingdoms, many of which had grown rich through trading with the Arabs.

## 1480 MUSCOVY EMERGES

IN 1480, MOSCOW DEFEATED an attempt to reassert the right to tribute made by the heirs of the Mongols, the Tatar khan of the Great Horde. Moscow had long been the most important

*Ivan III (1440–1505), ruler of Russia and Grand Duke of Moscow from 1462 to 1505.*

## 1487 THE ROUTE TO EAST AFRICA

JOHN II OF PORTUGAL revived interest in exploration, leading to a series of voyages culminating in the first European sailing around the southern tip of Africa. Bartholomeu Diaz left Portugal in 1487 with three vessels and sailed along the African coast until blown into open seas by

*Bartholomeu Diaz, the Portuguese sailor who discovered the Cape of Good Hope in 1487.*

storms. After sailing south for 13 days, Diaz turned east, failed to sight land, so turned north and sighted mountains, which was East Africa. A mutiny forced him to return home, sailing around Africa's southern tip. John II later called this the Cape of Good Hope. Diaz's critical discovery was not exploited because disputes over the Portuguese crown and hostility with Spain focused attention on domestic affairs. Despite this delay, Spain had not found a route to Asia, so explorations continued under Manuel I (1469–1521).

## 1492 SAILING TO THE NEW WORLD

COLUMBUS' FIRST EXPEDITION embarked in September 1492 with three ships carrying 100 men. In October, they first landed on Watling Island and proceeded to sail around the Bahamas, Cuba, and Hispaniola to find Asia, unaware of the significance of the discovery. Columbus was convinced that these were Asiatic islands leading to China. Relations with the indigenous peoples (mistakenly called Indians) deteriorated after the Spanish continually demanded provisions and thefts occurred. His second voyage carried 1,200 people, tools, seeds, and animals to begin colonizing the largest and most accessible Caribbean islands. Columbus' 1498 voyage

*Christopher Columbus (1451–1506) landing at Watling Island in 1492.*

found mainland Venezuela and the 1502 voyage found Central America. Columbus lost support as the elusive route to the East, and the anticipated riches, failed to materialize. Columbus died in 1506 convinced that the discovery of mainland Asia was imminent.

### 1492 SPAIN'S EMPIRE

THE SPANISH CROWN exercised tight control over its fifteenth-century empire and its trade. All conquistadores gave a proportion of their profits to the royal treasury and crown representatives often followed their expeditions. All land was owned by the crown, but the *encomienda* system granted colonists control over particular areas (and all its indigenous inhabitants). In return, the colonists helped the crown defend the empire and support missionary work within it. The crown also appointed colonial viceroys and legislators but was still the ultimate decision maker. From 1503, a "house of trade" in Seville, Spain, oversaw colonial trade and travel. All colonial exports were brought to Spain by royal "treasure fleets" and taxes were imposed on imports.

## 1493 DIVIDING THE WORLD

POPE ALEXANDER VI (1431–1503) had used his spiritual authority in 1493 to divide the world along a meridian west of Cape Verde islands between Portugal and Spain, in an attempt to distribute the new colonies and to avoid conflict. Spain received the western hemisphere

*Pope Alexander VI (1431–1503) split the world between Spain and Portugal.*

and Portugal the eastern hemisphere, but disputes over the precise boundary line soon arose. After the Reformation, Protestant rulers would come to challenge the spiritual powers of Rome and begin competing for overseas empires. Although Spain continued to spend vast amounts controlling the colonies and defending the empire, it became weaker internally and consequently vulnerable to challenges from the rising European powers. Spain's control over its overseas possessions weakened as the problems of communication and local efforts to assume greater autonomy across its vast empire grew.

## 1493 THE LURE OF INDIA

AT THE CENTER of all this traveling lay the Indian subcontinent. China, the Islamic world, and Europe were all drawn toward it. Places such as Calicut, Cambay, and the Coromandel coast were major cosmopolitan commercial centers, with Arab traders, Chinese merchants, and spice dealers from the Malay archipelago all conducting transactions in Indian markets. In 1493, , Hieronimo de Santos Stepahon and Hieronimo Adorno, Genoese merchants traveled across Egypt and into the Indian Ocean. They reached Calicut and pressed on further east to

Sumatra, but the hardships of the journey killed Adorno. Santos Stepahon only reached Tripoli in the Lebanon before writing his story in 1499. What happened to him afterward is unknown.

## 1497 CROSSING THE INDIAN OCEAN

VASCO DA GAMA (1469–1524) finally made the voyage by sea to India with four ships that sailed around the Cape of Good Hope in 1497. Explorations of Mozambique, Malindi, and Mombasa revealed abundant trade with Indians and Arabs. Frictions between the Christian explorers and African Muslims led to clashes, but da Gama secured a pilot who guided them to Calicut, an Indian commercial center, in May 1498. Da Gama had discovered a passage to Asia by finding the best Atlantic winds for sailing around the Cape of Good Hope, and had crossed to India in three weeks. Trading fleets emerged to carry cargo between India and Lisbon, which became a major commercial center.

*Tapestry showing Vasco da Gama's (1469–1524) arrival in India.*

# Trade and Industry

*Portrait of Amerigo Vespucci (1451–1512).*

## 1400s EUROPEAN NAVIGATORS

IN THE FIFTEENTH century, the European navigators sailed, usually at the command of their rulers, in search of gain. Fortunes were to be made from trade—in ivory from Africa, gold from Brazil, porcelain from China, and tea and spices from India and Ceylon (spices were particularly sought after because they hid the taste of rotting food before the days of refrigeration). Among the early explorers were: Amerigo Vespucci (Italian), who sailed to the Caribbean and South America; Vasco da Gama (Portuguese), who pioneered the eastern sea route to India; Christopher Columbus (Italian), who made four voyages to the Caribbean; and Ferdinand Magellan (Portuguese), who led the first expedition around the world.

## 1400s THE NATIVE PEOPLES OF CENTRAL AND SOUTH AMERICA

FROM A CENTER in the high Andes, the Incas developed a strictly centralized empire, which expanded to its greatest extent in the fifteenth century. The empire was linked together by a network of roads, of which the two main ones, running along the coast and inland, were each 2,240 miles (3,600 km) long. Potatoes and maize were the chief crops and llamas were an important resource. Practically every man was a farmer, producing his own food and clothing, which was made of llama wool and cotton. A relay service carried messages in the form of *quipu* (knotted cords) at a rate of 150 miles (240 km) per day. Inca communication networks greatly facilitated their conquest by the Spanish.

*The fabrication of palm oil at Whydah, on the west coast of Africa.*

## 1400 THE KINGDOM OF BENIN

THE AFRICAN KINGDOM of Benin flourished from 1400 for three centuries in the area of what is today Nigeria. The oba, or king, performed ceremonies to ensure significant events, such as the arrival of rains and the success of harvests. Considered as one of the most important festivals was the *agwe*, the feast of new yams, which took place at harvest time in November. During the start of the festival, a number of unfortunate slaves and animals would be sacrificed, and these gruesome rituals would then be followed by singing, dancing, and "magic" acts. Twice a year, the villages had to send a tax to the oba, consisting of yams, palm oil, pepper, and kola nuts. Only the oba alone was allowed to trade with foreigners, who began to visit Benin in the 1840s. Benin sold kola nuts to north Africans and palm oil (used for making soap), ivory, pepper, and slaves to European traders.

# Chapter 3 — **The Fifteenth Century**

## 1405 THE VOYAGES OF CHENG HO

SOON AFTER 1400, the Chinese emperor selected a court eunuch named Cheng Ho to be commander in chief of missions to the Western oceans to consolidate Chinese supremacy in trade and the art of seafaring. In the course of his seven voyages (1405–33)—on the first he commanded 62 ships and 27,800 men—Cheng visited Malacca, Ceylon, Calicut, Sumatra, India, Hormuz on the Persian Gulf, and the east coast of Africa. In 1424, the new Ming emperor forbade the building of seagoing vessels and suspended naval expeditions abroad. It was believed that imperial resources should not be squandered on distant enterprises but mustered in defense against nomads. In the wake of Cheng's voyages, Chinese emigration increased, resulting in Chinese colonization, notably in Southeast Asia, and the accompanying tributary trade, which lasted until the nineteenth century.

## 1430s THE RISE OF JAPANESE SEA POWER

CHINESE IMPROVEMENTS in naval design penetrated Japanese society after about 1300: the compass, adjustable centerboards, keels, cloth sail, and generally larger, more serviceable ships.

*Japanese warriors took up piracy in the fifteenth century.*

Sea voyaging was now practicable along the Japanese coasts, across to China and Southeast Asia and to the nearer Pacific islands. Fishing soon developed into an important industry, and when the Chinese withdrew from the seas in the 1430s, Japan rapidly became the foremost naval nation in the region. Samurai (warriors), who had too little or no land, took up piracy and quickly became the scourge of the China coast. They brought back rich booty to their home ports, where the interchange between merchants and warriors became intense and important and gave rise to a warlike, self-reliant middle class.

## 1488 PORTUGUESE NAVAL ARTS AND INVENTIONS

BARTOLOMEU DIAZ sailed south and into history, in 1488, when he discovered the Cape of Good Hope at the southernmost tip of the African continent. However, it would be another nine years before Vasco da Gama, another Portuguese sea captain, rounded the Cape, and in 1499 he and his crew became the first Europeans to complete a round trip to India. Both of these adventurous sea captain explorers had the royal blessing of Henry of Portugal (died 1460), nicknamed the "Navigator." It was Henry who would prepare the way for the great voyages of discovery that would go on to open up the entire habitable world to European exploitation. Henry's motive was to circumvent and eventually overwhelm the realm of Islam. So enthused was Henry for this mission, he commissioned astronomers and mathematicians to compile accurate tables of the sun's declination at known latitudes to help his navigators precisely determine their positions while at sea. Thanks to these innovations, da Gama spent a total of 97 days out of sight of land, yet managed to steer an accurate course to the cape, an area notorious for its rough waters. It was during this period that the Portuguese also took the lead in shipbuilding, constructing stronger vessels with stouter hulls, more masts, and several sails.

*Portuguese explorer Vasco da Gama (1469–1524) during a storm at Cape of Good Hope off South Africa.*

# Science and Technology

### 1450s MOVABLE TYPE PRINTING

IT WAS THE INVENTIVE GENIUS of a German goldsmith called Johannes Gutenberg (*circa* 1400–68) that ushered in the age of printing. During the late 1450s, he devised a system for using individual type characters, cast in molds from an alloy of lead, tin, and antimony, which were interchangeable within a frame. The phonetic nature of writing in Europe, with its relatively few characters, gave it

*Printing press of 1498, from a book printed in that year.*

a distinct advantage over other writing, such as Chinese, which comprised thousands of different characters and had been the language originally used to develop printing. It was quick and easy to assemble whole pages of type that could all be used time and time again for other jobs. As a result, printing took off rapidly. Within 30 years most of the western European countries had several printing works, and by the early sixteenth century, most classical manuscripts were made available in print. The first newspaper appeared on sale in 1609 in Germany, where it had all started.

### 1473 THE BIRTH OF COPERNICUS

THE REINSTATEMENT OF SCIENTIFIC inquiry led to an acceleration of progress, and it became the driving force in world culture. As a result, theories began to surface that contradicted popular opinion, but were postulated simply because the scientific evidence suggested them to be tenable. Nicolaus Copernicus (1473–1543), a Polish astronomer, was the first to suggest that the earth was not the center of the universe in post-medieval times. This came as a shock to European culture. His observations

*Polish astronomer Nicolaus Copernicus revolutionized thought about the earth's position in the universe.*

refuted the theory on the basis that the results of observation and experiment should override the preconceptions of traditional lore, and that the results of his own studies had suggested scientifically based processes at work. He consequently established the practice of seeking external agents as explanations for disease and infection, making important progress in this area. By 1543, Vesalius, another great physician, had published his *On the Structure of the Human Body*, which opened the way for microscopic studies in the following centuries.

showed the earth to be rotating around the sun, which he in turn, mistakenly took to be the center of the universe, but nonetheless, the solar-system hypothesis had been born. Christian beliefs were dominant at this time, so any idea that refuted the notion that the universe was centered around humanity was not well received. Copernicus' major treatise—*The Revolutions of the Celestial Spheres*—was not published until the year of his death.

### 1493 THE BIRTH OF PARACELSUS

A SWISS PHYSICIAN named Paracelsus (1493–1541) was the first scientist to challenge of Galen's ideas about humors controlling the body and mind. He

*Paracelsus (1493–1541) was the first to question Galen's theories on science and medicine.*

# Religions, Belief, and Thought

## 1440 THE BIRTH OF KABIR

KABIR WAS BORN in 1440 in the Hindu holy city of Benares. His father was a Muslim and his mother is believed to have been a Hindu. He sought to reconcile the mystical forms of Hinduism and Islam through worship of Rama / Allah as the one God and rejected the polytheism of popular Hinduism. He is known as the "saint poet" and for being a teacher of Guru Nanak (1469–1539), the founder of the Sikh religion. His teachings helped to reduce conflict between Hindus and Muslims.

*Krishna (left), one of the avatars of the Hindu god Vishnu.*

## 1450s THE BEGINNINGS OF RENAISSANCE PHILOSOPHY

WESTERN THOUGHT was in decline by the end of the Middle Ages. It was confined to the monasteries and rigidly controlled by the Church. The teachings of the scholastics were otherworldly and were learned by rote in Latin. Corruption was rife and the popes had more interest in politics than spiritual practice. The liberal-intellectual revival that brought learning out of the cloisters was known as the Renaissance. This began in the city of Florence and slowly spread to northern Europe and England. It was sparked by two events—the introduction of printing in 1451 and the arrival of Greek scholars and classical texts following their expulsion from Constantinople by the Muslims in 1453. Study of Plato and other classical writers inspired humanist philosophies, which were centered upon man and the world.

## 1472 WANG YANG MING AND THE SCHOOL OF MIND

WANG YANG MING was a leading Neo-Confucian scholar and became the principal thinker in the School of Mind. This school challenged the older

*Confucianism is still widely practiced throughout Japan and Korea.*

teachings of Chu Hsi and the School of Principles. Wang Yang Ming taught that the human mind was a perfect reflection of the Mind of Heaven and that humans should discover the Mind of Heaven only through study of the workings of their own minds. The school, therefore encouraged self-cultivation through introspection and meditation during daily activity and incorporated many Buddhist and Taoist ideas on meditation. These teachings were to spread rapidly to Korea and Japan.

## 1480s THE DECAY OF THE CATHOLIC CHURCH

THE CORRUPTION AND DECAY of the medieval Catholic Church and monasticism, which had its roots in the 1480s, had myriad consequences. It led to the humanist revival of the Renaissance, to the political breakaway of the Anglican Church in England under Henry VIII, and to the more fundamentalist and puritanical response of the Protestants under Martin Luther and John Calvin. This wide-ranging dissatisfaction eventually forced the Catholic Church to reform and, from around 1550, there was a spiritual and institutional revival that would come to be known as the Counter-Reformation.

## 1482 MARSILIO FICINO'S *THEOLOGICA PLATONICA*

MARSILIO FICINO (1433–99) played an important role during the Renaissance in reviving the theories of Plato. He established a Platonic Academy near Florence, Italy, for the purposes of studying the philosophies of the ancient Greeks. His commentaries and translations of Plato (from Greek to Latin), which he produced at his academy, include *Theologica Platonica* (1482). In these works, he explores Plato's religious thoughts, his theory of the immortality of souls, and his observations on platonic love. His particular interest was in integrating the thoughts of Plotinus (*circa* AD 205–270) and the Neo-Platonists with Christianity, as Ficino felt that these teachings existed in all religions.

## 1485 THE BIRTH OF LORD CHAITANYA

CHAITANYA WAS BORN in Bengal in 1485 and became the founder of a Vaishnava sect, which is named after him. His teaching was that of passionate devotion, *bhakti*, directed toward Krishna, the latest avatar of Vishnu. His teachings follow on from the tradition of Ramanuja. The practice he taught was of devotion and remembrance through continual chanting of the mantra, Hare Krishna (Praise Krishna). Devotees of this society live lives that are extremely simple, but which are also full of festivals and celebrations. The traditional Hindu teaching of *ahimsa* (nonviolence) is still given great emphasis. Other Hindu teachings, in particular to adhere to a strictly vegetarian and healthy diet and the care of cows, which are sacred to Krishna, are also still observed.

## 1489 GIOVANNI PICO DELLA MIRANDOLA'S *HEPTAPLUS*

COUNT GIOVANNI Pico della Mirandola (1463–94) was a Renaissance philosopher who studied at the University of Bologna before becoming a wandering scholar, visiting many universities throughout Italy and France. He later settled in Rome and created an extensive, and probably one of the greatest, libraries of his time. He was inspired by the writings of the philosopher Plato and especially those of Plotinus and the Neo-Platonists. These teachings are explored in his *Oration on the Dignity of Man*, which presents man as a microcosm reflecting the order of the universe. In 1489, he published the *Heptaplus*, in which he gives a mystical explanation of the origins of the cosmos.

*The Italian Renaissance philosopher, Giovanni Pico della Mirandola (1463–94).*

## 1492 DESIDERIUS ERASMUS AND HUMANIST CHRISTIANITY

ERASMUS WAS the central figure in the development of liberal, humanist Christianity during the Renaissance. Born in Rotterdam, Erasmus became a priest

*Desiderius Erasmus (circa 1466–1536), Christian humanist leader.*

in 1492. He criticized the corrupt state of monastic life and scholarship, especially the stale dogmatism of the teachings of Aquinas, Ockham, and Scotus—all ideologies derived from Aristotle. Instead, he advocated a return to the study of original texts, such as the original Greek New Testament and the writings of Plato. His views were published in his satirical *The Praise of Folly* in 1509. Unfortunately, his moderate criticisms were attacked as heresy by both the Catholic Church and their new opponents, the evangelical Protestant authorities.

### 1492 EXPULSION FROM SPAIN
MANY OF THE JEWS who had dispersed from Israel settled throughout Europe, where oppression by Christian governments occurred on a regular basis. Anti-Semitism grew during the Middle Ages and, in many cities, Jews were forced to live in separate enclaves. A dramatic example of this occurred in Spain in 1492 when the Moors (Moroccan Muslims), who ruled the south (Andalusia), were defeated. When they were in power, the Moors had promoted religious tolerance between the faiths. When they were defeated, all non-Christians, both Muslims and Jews, were expelled or sentenced to death by the Spanish Inquisition.

*The synagogue built in 1315 in Córdoba, Andalusia, Spain.*

# Chapter 4
## The Sixteenth Century

THIS WAS A PERIOD when, Spain and Portugal colonized South America and opened up oceanic trade routes around the world. The Portuguese became the masters of Asian and African Indian Ocean trade, while the Spanish opened trade across the Pacific Ocean, linking the Americas with Asia.

In Europe, the Protestant Reformation threatened the authority of the Pope and the Roman Catholic Church and European politics became dominated by religious conflicts, laying the groundwork for the Thirty Years' War.

Under the rule of Suleiman the Magnificent, the Ottoman Empire grew in Europe, while dealing with a resurgent Persia.

In India, the Mogul emperor Akbar the Great tried to reconcile the major religions by founding a new religion.

# Power and Politics

### 1500s THE RISE OF SPAIN

FERDINAND OF ARAGON (reigned 1479–1516) and Isabella of Castile (reigned 1474–1504) were the king and queen who united Spain at the end of the fifteenth century. Throughout the sixteenth century, Spain became the most powerful force in Europe. The power of the nobles, especially in Castile, was reduced and a centralized government set up. The Moors were driven from Granada, their last stronghold, in 1492.

*Holy Roman emperor Charles V (1500–58).*

Ferdinand and Isabella also opened up a new field of power struggle when they sent Christopher Columbus to the New World in 1492. Their grandson, Charles I (1500–58), who became the Holy Roman emperor Charles V, played a key role in developing a new order in Europe. He set up a centralized administration for the whole empire and founded the Hapsburg family dynasty, which was to rule the Holy Roman Empire and later Austria until the end of World War I.

### 1519 THE SPANISH EMPIRE

THE DESIRE FOR WEALTH and power brought the Spanish Empire into conflict with the civilizations of Central America. The Aztec civilization had evolved over a period of one thousand years and, in 1519, had a capital city of perhaps 200,000 people. The Aztecs were ruled by a king who was elected and who appointed provincial governors. There was an effective system of law courts and a large army. Altogether the empire had about five million inhabitants. The Aztecs had developed the principles of architecture and engineering, and by the sixteenth century, were on the verge of developing a cursive script. In 1519, the Aztec Empire

*In the conquest of Mexico, the Spaniards retreated on July 1, 1520.*

elder sister Mary become very unpopular after she married Philip II of Spain and then tried to reimpose Catholicism on England. Elizabeth was determined to reestablish the authority of the crown. Traditionally, the monarch in England was referred to as "Your Grace." This was the same title as was used for a duke and an archbishop. Elizabeth forced her courtiers, as they now became called, to address her as "Your Majesty." This implied that there was something different and remote about royalty. This set a pattern, which all other monarchs were to follow.

*Elizabeth I (1553–1603) reestablished Protestantism and the authority of monarch in England.*

was savagely attacked by the Spanish under Cortés and was destroyed within two years. Tenochtitlán, the capital, was completely obliterated.

### 1558 THE VIRGIN QUEEN

ELIZABETH I (1553–1603) became Queen of England in 1558. She was 25 years old. During her lifetime, she had seen her father, Henry VIII, grow old and increasingly unhappy, her brother Edward VI die at the age of 15, and her

*Philip II of Spain (1527–98).*

## 1568 THE DUTCH REVOLT

IN THE SIXTEENTH CENTURY, the Netherlands were part of the Holy Roman Empire. Philip II of Spain planned to introduce the Inquisition into the Netherlands, where many people were Protestant, and this led to a revolt in 1568 by the Dutch. It was the first of a series of wars between Catholics and Protestants, which were to continue for almost a century. Philip tried to crush the revolt by force. He sent 20,000 troops and executed the leaders of the revolt. He managed to regain control of the southern provinces, but the north held out and eventually became independent as the United Provinces, often known as the Netherlands, or Holland, after the largest province.

## 1578 ORGANIZING THE MOGUL EMPIRE

THE MOGUL EMPIRE was founded by Babar (reigned 1526–30), but the organization of the empire was the work of Akbar (reigned 1556–1605). He took control of all land and arranged for it to be administered directly by the crown. He also set up a state civil service that would carry out his orders. Non-Muslims within the empire were treated as equals and were not subject to any special laws or taxes. In 1578, Akbar allowed public

*Emperor Akbar (reigned 1556–1605) being entertained by his foster brother Azim Khan at Dipalpur, Punjab, 1571.*

*The expulsion of the Huguenots from France is one example of the conflict between Catholics and Protestants that occurred throughout Europe at this time.*

debates on religion involving all faiths, including Christians. Akhbar strengthened the empire by conquering Gujarat and Bengal to the west and thereafter began the conquest of the Deccan to the south. This was the first time that a large part of India had been unified.

## 1598 PROTESTANTS GET RIGHTS

FROM 1562 TO 1598, there was a series of eight wars between Catholics and Protestants (called Huguenots) in France. The Huguenots were concentrated in the southwest of France, but Paris and the northeast remained Catholic. Henry of Navarre became King Henry IV in 1589. He was a Huguenot, but converted to Catholicism to ensure that the Catholics would accept him. In 1598, he issued the Edict of Nantes, which gave Huguenots equal political rights with Catholics and allowed the Protestant religion to be practiced in some parts of France, but not in Paris and some other cities. It was the first example, however, of acceptance of Protestantism in a major Catholic country.

# War and Peace

### 1500s KEEPING ENEMIES CLOSE

VENICE SEEMED to pose the next threat, and in response France, the Hapsburg Empire, the papacy, and Spain formed the League of Cambrai (1508). Following its victory at Agnadello (1509), the League conquered all of Venice's mainland possessions. In 1512, the Hapsburgs restored the Medici to Florence and in 1515 were defeated by the French at the Battle of Marignano. By the Treaty of Noyon (1516), France received Milan but renounced its claim to Naples. During the 1520s, France and the Hapsburg Empire continued to fight over Lombardy. The French defeat at Pavia (1525) doomed French influence in Italy. The League of Cognac (1526) allied France, Florence, Milan, Venice, and the papacy against the Hapsburgs, but Spanish pikemen quickly conquered Milan and, in May 1527, sacked Rome.

### 1519 THE CONQUESTS OF MEXICO AND PERU

CHARLES I (1500–58) had hardly set foot in his new kingdoms when he was elected Holy Roman emperor Charles V and departed for Germany. For the next two centuries, the fate of Spain was tied to that

*The Battle of the Platform at Tenochtitlán.*

of the Hapsburg dynasty. Charles spent most of his life defending his scattered domains against his enemies. The conquest of Mexico (1519–21) by Hernán Cortés (1488–1549) and the conquest of Peru (1531–33) by Francisco Pizarro (*circa* 1475–1541) resulted in the influx of gold and silver, making Spain the greatest European power of the age. Charles abdicated in 1555–56, leaving Spain to his son, Philip II, and his German dominions to his brother, later Holy Roman emperor Ferdinand I.

**1522 SULEIMAN TAKES RHODES**

WHEN CONSTANTINOPLE was taken by the Ottomans, they also captured one of the world's greatest shipbuilding centers. The Turkish fleet expanded greatly, with notable victories against the Venetians (1463–79), leading to the occupation of Albania in 1478. In 1480, Mehmet failed in his attempt to take Rhodes from the Knights of St. John, but when Suleiman the Magnificent landed on the island in 1522, it was clear that they meant to stay. The town was surrounded by a wall 30 feet (9 m) high and 40 feet (12 m) thick. Four assaults were beaten off in September, but in December the defenders had had enough and they departed to Malta, but this, too, was besieged in 1565.

*Suleiman the Magnificent (1495–1566) as a young man.*

**1538 PHILIP II AND BARBAROSSA**

BY THE MID-SIXTEENTH CENTURY, Spain had become the dominant European sea power in the Mediterranean, but western expansion plans were a key part of Suleiman's policies. With his chief allies, the Barbary Corsairs, they quickly built up a fleet and defeated a Christian force off the Albanian coast in 1538. The Ottomans now had sea supremacy east of Italy. Dragut captured Tripoli in 1559 for the Corsairs, but the Turkish attempt to capture Malta in 1565 failed. Philip II of Spain had massively increased his fleets, and after Suleiman died in 1566, the tide changed in favor of the Christians.

*The naval battle of Lepanto between the Italy League and the Turks in 1571.*

### 1571 LEPANTO

WHEN THE CHRISTIAN FLEET, under Don John of Austria, assembled at Messina in September 1571, it could boast 200 galleys, 6 galliasses, 24 large transports, and 50 other craft. There were 50,000 seamen, most still shackled to their rowing positions and 30,000 fighting men. Against them, the Ottoman fleet, under Ali Pasha, mustered 250 galleys, 40 galliots, and 20 other craft, with some 25,000 fighting men. The fleets spotted one another off the coast of Lepanto near the Gulf of Corinth on October 7. The Turkish center and right were destroyed, with a loss of around 200 ships and 30,000 men. This was the last time that oar-driven ships were used in a naval battle. Lepanto ended Ottoman naval supremacy in the Mediterranean.

### 1578 DUTCH WAR OF INDEPENDENCE

RELIGIOUS AND POLITICAL factors fueled a revolt in the Netherlands in 1578. The revolt actually began in the southern provinces in 1566. In 1567, the Duke of Alba was sent to quell the uprising, but the revolt spread under the leadership of William I of Orange (William the Silent). Under the treaty, called the Pacification of Ghent (1576), all the provinces united to drive out the Spanish. Beginning in 1578, the Spanish governor Alessandro Farnese won back the southern provinces by political concessions. The northern provinces of Holland formed the Union of Utrecht (1579) and declared themselves a republic in 1581. The Dutch were aided by the war between Spain and England, which forced the Spanish to fight on two fronts and made England a valuable Dutch ally.

## 1588 THE SPANISH ARMADA

THE ARMADA was a great Spanish fleet assembled in 1588 as part of the attempt by Philip II to invade England. The plan was to send a fleet of 130 ships commanded by the Duke of Medina Sidonia to cover an invasion force from Flanders under Alessandro Farnese. Lacking adequate ships or his own, and blockaded by Dutch rebels, Farnese could not embark his troops. The Armada fought its way through the English Channel but, on August 8, English fire ships drove the Armada out of its Calais anchorage. The Spanish regrouped and fought another action off Gravelines, but they were now out of ammunition. Realizing that the situation was lost, Medina Sidonia sailed north around Scotland and Ireland and returned to Spain. He suffered heavy losses because of disease and shipwreck.

*The ill-fated Armada fleet, part of Philip II of Spain's plan to invade England.*

# Society and Culture

*Slave trading was one of the most profitable businesses in the 16th century.*

## 1500s TRADING IN SLAVES

BY THEIR OWN ACCOUNTS, the sixteenth-century slavers were not evil men. They did not, in fact, regard Africans as properly human at all, since they were, in their eyes, uncivilized heathens. In any case, slavery was one of the most profitable trades in the sixteenth century, The sufferings of the slaves began when they were captured by raiding parties sent out by kings or chiefs of rival tribes. Sometimes the raiders ventured far inland for their "booty," snaring unwary Africans in the forest or kidnapping them from their villages. The raiders took men, women, and children—anyone who looked strong enough to stand the rigors of what lay ahead. Afterward, a column of slaves might be marched, yoked and chained for 1,000 miles (1,600 km) before they reached the coast. Many collapsed from exhaustion on the way and many died. Those who reached the coast were sold or traded for cloth, ornaments, and other manufactured goods not available in Africa, which the slave traders had brought specially from Europe.

## 1500s SAILORS AND GEOGRAPHERS

MUSLIM SEAMEN and navigators had a great deal to teach Europeans, even long after the crusades were over. European vessels, for instance, routinely used square sails until they discovered how the Muslim triangular lateen sails made better and faster use of the wind at sea. Muslim maps were preferred for those venturing out of sight of land, since they had a more accurate view of the earth. In the early sixteenth century, the Muslim mapmaker Pir Muhyi al Din Ra'is drew a chart of the South Atlantic Ocean showing West Africa and South America.

## 1519 THE CITY OF THE AZTECS

THE THIN AIR and freezing cold conditions made the Spaniards' journey through the mountains a grueling one, but on November 8, 1519, Cortés and his conquistadores entered Tenochtitlán, the Aztecs' capital city, to be greeted by the gorgeously garbed Montezuma, the Great Speaker. Montezuma was worshipped by his people and treated like a god. Tenochtitlán was a revelation to the Spaniards, with its massive palace and sacrificial towers, its metals, which decorated statues and images of the Aztec gods, and its sheer size and complexity. However, the Aztecs, too, were due for a revelation. They had never before seen

*The encounter between Hernán Cortés and Montezuma II.*

soldiers mounted on horseback and thought soldier and horse were a single animal, gods perhaps. Another thing the Aztecs had never seen was the Spanish gun. Harquebuses and muskets were amazing novelties that they would soon see breathe fire and bring destruction and devastation to the Aztecs and help bring them to their eventual downfall.

## 1521 THE DOWNFALL OF THE AZTEC EMPIRE

ONCE THE AZTECS realized the Spaniards' aggressive intent, they drove them out of Tenochtitlán. However, soon the Spaniards returned, this time aided by vast numbers of the Aztec Empire's long-misused subjects. After a ferocious struggle, which reduced Tenochtitlán to ruins, the city fell on August 13, 1521. What followed was the total destruction of Aztec society—the end of human sacrifice, which disgusted the Spaniards, forcible conversion to Christianity, the breakup of the Aztec *calpulli* (clans), and the enslavement of the people. The allies who had helped the Spaniards to their triumph—Tepanecs, Mixtecs, Totonacs, Zapotecs, and Mayas—received the same treatment. Mexico became New Spain, and part of the Spanish American Empire, which lasted 300 years.

*The conqueror of Peru, Francisco Pizarro (circa 1475–1541 ) battles with the ill-prepared Incas led by the last Inca king of Peru, Atahualpa.*

## 1532 THE CONQUEST OF THE INCAS

HISTORY REPEATED ITSELF, although with extraordinary variations, in the South American Andes, where, in 1532, Spaniards under Francisco Pizarro (*circa* 1475–1541) reached Tahuantinsuyu and imprisoned the Sapa Inca Atahualpa. These Spaniards, too, had come for gold and Atahualpa, realizing it, made them an amazing offer: whole rooms full of gold and silver in exchange for his freedom. The Spaniards could hardly refuse, but they soon realized, and feared, Atahualpa's near-mesmeric power when, without demur, his subjects filled the rooms as ordered. Atahualpa could just as easily have commanded the Spaniards' slaughter, but they moved first, contriving a murder charge and executing him on August 29, 1532. At that, the Incas, supine as always before authority, awaited the orders of their new, Spanish masters.

## 1550s DISEASES

MEDICAL KNOWLEDGE in Europe in the sixteenth century did not yet encompass the causes of disease or, in the case of fatal infections, their proper cure. Yet, within the new Spanish American Empire, realization dawned before long of the disaster that the conquerors had brought with them. When Orellana voyaged the Amazon, he noted how many people there were on its banks. Native America was clearly crowded, but not after thousands of people began to die from smallpox and other European diseases to which they had no resistance. Spanish priests who tended the sick realized what had happened, but disease worked both ways. Spaniards began to die, in their turn, of strange fevers and infections that Spanish physicians had never seen before.

## 1550s MEDICINE AND MERCY

IN MEDIEVAL MEDICINE, the cure for an illness had often been worse than the disease. For instance, bleeding patients to expel evil "humors" weakened and often killed them. Although this savage approach to medical care did not disappear, more intelligent methods began to appear in the mid-sixteenth century. There was a determined quest to understand disease and the processes of human anatomy. The Italian Girolamo Fracastoro (*circa* 1478–1553) did important work on how contagion spread. Another Italian, Andreas Vesalius (1514–64), investigated the workings of the human body. In Britain, in 1628, William Harvey (1578–1657) discovered the circulation of the blood. The French army surgeon Ambroise Paré (*circa* 1509–90) dressed wounds with soothing balms, instead of cauterizing them, and prevented profuse bleeding in amputations by tying off the blood vessels.

## 1550s SCIENCE AND INVENTION

SCIENTISTS, TOO, WERE seeking better methods that would lighten workloads, improve working conditions, and promote efficiency. The German Georg Bauer or "Agricola" (1494–1555), investigated mining technology and described diseases that affected miners. Such work had added importance because of the increasing use of coal that replaced the wood formerly used to fuel fires. Later, in 1712, Thomas Newcomen (1663–1729) invented the "atmospheric engine," designed to pump water from mines and so reduce the danger of flooding, which would otherwise overtake the men, and frequently children, working underground. He was preceded by Thomas Savery (*circa* 1650–1715), inventor of the water-driven steam engine in 1696. In manufacturing

*Georg Bauer, "Agricola," made pioneering investigations into mining diseases.*

industry, new techniques in glassmaking were introduced and the first frame knitting machine was invented by William Lee (*circa* 1550–1610).

# Exploration and Empires

### 1519 DISCOVERING A NEW CONTINENT

AFTER FAILING to find sufficient riches in the Caribbean, explorers began to search the interiors of the Americas in the hope of greater reward. These were named after the Italian Amerigo Vespucci, who had traveled to the New World between 1497 and 1504. Conquistadores (military adventurers) launched privately funded expeditions to these areas, and settlements were established from 1509. Vasco Nunez de Balbosa's 1519 journey across the Isthmus of Panama between North and South America to the Pacific Ocean was one of the most significant expeditions. Until then, Europeans did know this "Great South Sea" existed and that Asia must be beyond this new continent.

### 1520 THE EXPANSION OF THE OTTOMAN EMPIRE

AN ENERGETIC young sultan became Ottoman emperor in 1520. Suleiman, who was called "the Magnificent," extended Ottoman power deep into Europe and across the Mediterranean. His victories over Hungary in 1526 led to a failed attempt to capture Vienna in 1529. In 1538, an Ottoman expedition

*Siege of Vienna by Suleiman the Magnificent, in 1529.*

even threatened the Portuguese trading post of Diu in India. Suleiman's empire, however, had reached its limits. The Hapsburg dynasty in Spain managed to stall the Ottoman offensive in the Mediterranean during the 1540s. The failure of the siege of Malta in 1565, and the defeat of the Turkish fleet at Lepanto in 1571, five years after Suleiman's death, ended the immediate Turkish menace toward Europe.

### 1540s EXPLORING THE AMAZON

CONQUISTADORES such as Gonzalo, Pizarro and Francisco de Orellana, continued overland expeditions in

South America. They finally crossed the
continent during an expedition to find the
legendary golden kingdom of El Dorado.
After being carried by a current down
the Napo River, a branch of the Amazon,
the expedition traveled almost 3,000
miles (5,000 km) down the Amazon to
the Atlantic Ocean. Orellana named the
Amazon after the legendary Greek female
fighters because he had encountered
warrior women during the expedition.
Indigenous cultures were often destroyed
by the introduction of the language,
architecture, customs, and religion of
Spain. Colonists married indigenous
nobility, who liaised between the Spanish
and the local population.

## 1542 FRANCIS XAVIER SPREADS THE FAITH

PORTUGAL MARKED each "discovery"
with a *padráos*—a cross built on a stone
pillar. This represented the arrival of
the new power and its faith. Christian
missionaries responsible for religious
conversion soon followed. Diogo Cão
crossed the equator in 1482 with four
Franciscans and left them in the Congo
in an attempt to convert the natives to
Christianity. This practice was repeated
along the entire route to Asia. Jesuit
Francis Xavier (1506–51), who arrived in
Goa in 1542, moved through Southeast
Asia to Japan on a ten-year ministry to
achieve Portugal's spiritual ambitions.

*St. Francis Xavier (1506–51) and his entourage in a detail of the right-hand section of a folding screen depicting the arrival of the Portuguese in Japan, Kano School.*

*Czar Ivan the Terrible on horseback in front of his army.*

### 1558 WARS IN THE WEST

IVAN THE TERRIBLE turned his army west in 1558 when he invaded the state of Livonia. This was to be the beginning of a long series of wars involving the powers of the region that only very gradually extended the border of Muscovy westward. The struggle was with the Baltic powers of Sweden and the united kingdom of Poland-Lithuania. At the time of Ivan's death in 1584, however, there was little to show for these wars.

The most important gain was the port of Narva on the Baltic, but this was lost to Sweden in 1617, after a chaotic period known as the "Time of Troubles," which saw a Polish army occupy Moscow itself.

### 1568 ENGLISH PIRACY

ENGLISH TRADERS wanted to participate in the newly found and valuable commerce with the Spanish colonies in the New World. However, the Spanish government was not prepared to share this lucrative trade and sought

*Sir Francis Drake (circa 1540–96), who practiced piracy in Spanish waters during his voyages.*

to maintain a monopoly, so that any exchange would only take place in Spain. As a result, an undeclared maritime war broke out between England and Spain in 1568. Initially, the conflict was confined to the waters of the Atlantic Ocean, but in 1576 one Englishman, Sir Francis Drake (*circa* 1540–96), began planning a voyage to the Pacific. Drake was an accomplished sea captain, privateer, navigator, slave trader and politician, and went on to become Vice Admiral. However, on this voyage his plan was piracy. He left Plymouth in England, in 1577, sailed around South America, pillaging Spanish ports along the coast on the way, and reached the Spice Islands in November 1579. He took on a cargo of cloves and continued eastward, returning to Plymouth in September 1580. Drake's voyage proved so profitable that it produced several imitators.

## 1592 JAMES LANCASTER

THE EXTENSIVE KNOWLEDGE from all over the world that Drake brought back to England from his extensive voyages of exploration would probably have been exploited more energetically were it not for the demands of a war with Spain. The defeat of the Spanish Armada in 1588 required virtually every seagoing warship that the English ports could

*The great Mogul receiving Sir John Mildenhall, Queen Elizabeth's ambassador.*

muster. A sustained assault by the English on the Portuguese spice trade was delayed until 1592, when James Lancaster (*circa* 1554–1618) reached Penang in the Malay peninsula. From there, he sailed the Straits of Malacca and attacked every Portuguese ship he came across before sailing for home. Unfortunately for Lancaster, upon reaching Bermuda part of his crew mutinied and made off with his ship. Lancaster's voyage itself was a failure, but the knowledge he gained contributed to the foundation of the Honourable East India Company in 1600.

# Trade and Industry

### 1500s PAPER MONEY

MONEY WAS INVENTED in different countries around the same time: 2000 BC. Paper was first introduced as money in China, probably as early as the seventh century. Being rare, paper was precious. Paper money was widely used during the Ming dynasty, 1368–1644. Not until the sixteenth century did Europeans discover the value of paper money. A merchant would store his money with a goldsmith, against a receipt promising to pay back the money. The merchant could use the receipt to buy goods from another trader, who would then use it to reclaim the money from the goldsmith. In due course, the receipts were used instead of coins. Goldsmiths soon formed organizations called banks to issue notes worth fixed amounts. The first European bank to print its own paper money was the Stockholm Bank, Sweden, in 1661.

### 1500s EUROPEAN EXPANSION

FROM THE EARLY sixteenth century, the Europeans became world superpowers. Their discoveries took them all over the world, where they established trading companies and laid claim to territory. They exported many things: finished goods,

notions of law and governance, enterprise and inventiveness, and diseases. Among their imports were tobacco, foodstuffs, coffee and tea, and manufactured goods, such as cloth, gold, and silver. Although European influence did not predominate everywhere in the world—for example, in Africa—it was only a matter of time before European requirements made inroads into other civilizations. Trade, commerce, and finance began to be subjected to principles and controls superimposed from above.

*The ancient port of Antwerp.*

### 1500s FINDING THE MARK

WITH THE INTRODUCTION of gunpowder, the developments in firearms were rapid. Soon it became possible to attack from great distances. Reaching a distant target could no longer depend on trial and error, so a new science of ballistics was

*Siege of a fortified castle in the 16th century.*

developed. Ballistics involved geometry and physics in calculating the required trajectory of a projectile. The calculations were based on a number of key factors, so that the incline and azimuth (vertical and horizontal) angles of the gun barrel were correct. They are direction, distance, elevation, wind interference, and velocity of projectile. A number of devices for making the measurements were invented and developed during the sixteenth century. They also found useful service in surveying land for more accurate mapmaking.

### 1500s CONSEQUENCES OF EUROPEAN DISCOVERIES

EUROPEAN NAVAL SUPREMACY had three major consequences. The flow of massive quantities of silver and gold from the Americas made prices rise—by four times in Spain—adversely affecting buyers on fixed incomes while profiting sellers. A second consequence was the spread of American food crops, such as corn and potato. New food crops increased local food supplies and swelled the population, not least in West Africa, the source of the millions of slaves who were taken to America in the seventeenth and eighteenth centuries. The third major impact was the spread of disease. In the Spanish New World, the population in 1500 was about 50 million; by about 1650, it had shrunk to four million.

### 1500s MERCANTILISM

WITH THE ESTABLISHMENT of empires and colonies by European countries, each empire tried to acquire as much wealth as possible for as little outlay as possible. This form of trade, known as mercantilism, embodied the belief that foreign exports are preferable to both internal trade and imports and that governmental interference in the national economy toward such ends is justified. The earliest mercantilist efforts were directed toward eliminating internal trade barriers, which had been in place since the Middle Ages. Governments helped industries to grow because they were a promising source of taxation. Colonies were exploited as sources of raw materials and prevented from trading with other nations.

# Science and Technology

## 1500s GLASS AND COAL

GLASS FOR MAKING windows was in increasingly high demand by the end of the sixteenth century in Europe. Broad and crown glass were the two main types used, which were still made using glass-blowing techniques. The enormous growth in the industry had led to a shortage of charcoal because forests had yielded all of their timber. At the turn of the seventeenth century, things had got so desperate that alternatives were being sought. Coal was a familiar domestic fuel but too dirty for glass smelting, until a new underfed furnace was invented that kept the glass free from soot and smuts. This was hailed as such an important event that the use of charcoal for making glass was banned. The coal mining industry took off in one quantum leap. Soon it was the driving force behind copper, brass, and lead production and only a few years away from powering the Industrial Revolution.

## 1539 CARTOGRAPHY

WHILE MANY MAPMAKERS were developing ways to portray the lands and oceans of the world on to flat maps, others were directing their attentions toward detailed mapping of more familiar territory. In 1539, Richard Benese, the man who defined the area of an acre, issued a comprehensive volume of instruction on surveying and the use of associated tools and instruments. He had set a precedent, which marked the way for modern cartography. In 1592, the first fully surveyed map of England was published by Saxton, showing villages, market

*Coal mining increased in importance during the 16th century, when coal began to be used in glassmaking.*

towns, and rivers; 1592 also saw the first surveyed map to include the courses of all principal roads. By the mid-seventeenth century, precise distances were being added to maps, meticulously recorded using foot wheels. The first world atlas became available in France in 1658.

## 1551 MAKING MEASUREMENTS: THE THEODOLITE

EDMUND GUNTER (1580–1626) was the man who made detailed mapping possible by inventing his Gunter's chain. It was a simple device, comprising a series of 22 yard (20 m) sticks linked together. The chain could take the dimensions of areas of land, which could be used to calculate larger areas by triangulation.

The theodolite, invented in 1551, was a military ballistics instrument that was used in conjunction with Gunter's chain for measuring the relative elevations of locations. By contrast, Pierre Vernier (*circa* 1580–1637) of France, invented a device for taking very accurate width and thickness measurements of small objects. It was called the Vernier, after its inventor.

## 1580s MAPPING THE GLOBE

FOLLOWING THE GREAT voyages of discovery, the world had been charted to show a considerable number of land masses and oceans spread out fairly evenly over a spherical surface. The curvature of the earth's surface presented itself as a practical problem when it came to drawing maps onto flat pieces of paper. A Flemish mapmaker named Gerardus Mercator (1512–94) hit on the idea of inventing a cylindrical projection to solve the problem partially. Mercator's projection displayed the lines of longitude and latitude (parallels and meridians)

*Flemish cartographer, Gerardus Mercator (1512–94), introduced the idea of a cylindrical plan to map the globe.*

as a grid, which became immediately popular because it meant that courses could be plotted in straight lines with a pair of compasses. All map projections distort reality, however they work, and the flaw in Mercator's was that exaggerations in width occurred moving away from the equator north and south, until the poles were stretched to equal the length of the equator itself.

# Religions, Belief, and Thought

## 1500s COUNTER-REFORMATION AND CATHOLIC MYSTICS

THE RECOVERY of the Catholic faith was aided by the emergence of several spiritual thinkers, including three Spanish saints: St. Teresa, St. John, and St. Ignatius Loyola, the founder of the Jesuit Order. St. Teresa of Avila (1515–82), the Carmelite mystic, is famous for her ecstatic visions, and St. John of the Cross (1542–91), who was inspired by her, wrote of his own mystic experience of abandoning self in *The Dark Night of the Soul*. Ignatius Loyola (1491–1556) was a Spanish theologian and military leader. After serious injury he adopted a religious life and studied spiritual practices—as described in his *Spiritual Exercises*. His highly intellectual Jesuit Order, of which he was the general, was organized along military lines, with the objective of rooting out Protestant heresy and restoring the true faith.

## 1513 MACHIAVELLI'S PRINCE

NICCOLÒ MACHIAVELLI (1469–1527) was responsible for a revolution in political thought as a result of the publication of his *Il Principe* (*The Prince*) in 1513. In common with other Renaissance thinkers, his views are secular; they

*Niccolò Machiavelli was an Italian philosopher and is considered one of the main founders of modern political science.*

center on man and the world and they are inspired by Classical literature. His advice to the Italian city-states and their princes was so much based not upon religious principles, such as the divine right of kings, but simply upon doing whatever worked. This empirical and pragmatic approach can be seen as a precursor to the Scientific Revolution. He looks at past events, such as the lives of Romulus, Theseus, and Brutus, as described in Livy's *Histories*, for lessons about the most effective ways for a state to maintain its power.

## 1517 MARTIN LUTHER

IN 1517, THE GERMAN monk and professor of theology, Martin Luther (1483–1546), nailed to the door of his local church a long condemnation of the church's practice of selling "indulgences"—documents that promised the buyer a reduction of time in purgatory. He declared that salvation came through a person's strength in faith and not through making such purchases. This practice was just one of many examples of the corruption of the Church at that time. Erasmus (*circa* 1466–1536) responded to this situation by promoting humanism, but Luther instead called for a strict adherence to the basic teachings of the Bible, which he translated into German, and a rejection of everything else—monks, ritual, and the decoration of churches and the veneration of saints. He taught that salvation is not from good deed, but a gift from god. Luther's refusal to retract his writings, a demand made by Pope Leo X and Holy Roman emperor Charles V, resulted in his excommunication and his condemnation as an outlaw.

## 1518 THOMAS MORE'S *UTOPIA*

SIR THOMAS MORE (1478–1535), Lord Chancellor of England, was the principal figure in the English Renaissance. He was a humanist Christian and, like his contemporary, Erasmus, regarded the happiness and well-being of humanity as the highest Christian ideal. His beliefs and his critique of the political and religious situation of his time are to be found in his *Utopia*, published in 1516. This depicts an imaginary society, inspired partly by Plato's *Republic*, that lives in accord with basic Christian teachings, such as the absence of private property, nonviolence, the abolition of hunting, religious tolerance, humane penalties for crime, and the rejection of wealth. More was executed for treason against Henry VIII in 1535.

*Portrait of Martin Luther (1483–1546).*

*French theologian and reformer, John Calvin (1509–64).*

### 1533 JOHN CALVIN

JOHN CALVIN, born in France, was inspired by the Protestant teachings of Luther. Expelled from France in 1533, he moved to Geneva, where he turned the city into a repressive theocratic dictatorship. Worship, beliefs, and morals were imposed by force and opponents were treated ruthlessly, excommunicated or, as often the case, executed. His follower, John Knox introduced a similar regime into Scotland. Fanaticism during this time took many forms— approximately 100,000 women were tried as witches and many were found guilty and executed. Music and festivals were banned and the persecution of Jews became widespread. Calvin's teachings, while they shared the simplicity of Lutheranism, differed in that he believed in predestination and opposed the ordination of bishops. These differences later became the basis for several wars between the Protestant states of Germany.

### 1540s HENRY VIII AND THE ANGLICAN CHURCH

THE ORIGIN OF the Anglican Church was not primarily theological or religious, but resulted from Henry VIII's (1491–1547) anger at the pope's refusal to allow him to divorce his first wife, Catherine of Aragon, for her failure to produce a male heir to the throne. Secession from the Catholic Church, which at the time controlled the whole of western Europe, was only possible because of the very low esteem in which it was generally held. While its clergy were Catholic by education and theology, it was supported by the new Protestant movement in northern Europe and this wide range of theological views remains in the Anglican Church to this day. Protestant influence was a significant factor (or excuse) behind Henry's decision to dissolve the monasteries and seize Church treasures.

## 1570s GIORDANO BRUNO DISCOVERS PROTESTANTISM

FILIPPO BRUNO (1548–1600) was born in northern Italy and took the name Giordano when he became a Dominican monk. As a monk, he studied the works of Aristotle and Thomas Aquinas but, in the 1570s, fearing prosecution for heresy, he fled and spent a number of years wandering throughout Italy and Switzerland, where he encountered Protestantism. His writings, such as *On the Infinite Universes and World* (1584), attracted the attention of the Inquisition, and he was imprisoned for eight years. After this time, he still refused to recant, and was burned at the stake by the Church in 1600. Although many of his ideas seem strange today, his freedom of thought and his views on the unity of the world had much influence on the philosophy that developed over the following century.

## 1572 ST. BARTHOLOMEW'S DAY MASSACRE

REFORMATION IN NORTHERN Europe and Counter-Reformation in southern Europe split France down the middle. As the Church was seen as part of the state, this led to civil war. A massacre of Huguenots (French Protestants) at Vassy in 1562 led to seven civil wars over the next 18 years. These were fueled by German and British support for the Huguenots and Spanish and Italian support for the Catholics. On August 23, 1572, over 8,000 Huguenots were killed in the St. Bartholomew's Day Massacre in Paris. The shocked response from other European nations forced a truce, but conflict continued to flare up. In 1627, Cardinal Richelieu, on behalf of the French government, led the siege of the Protestant stronghold of La Rochelle, and from 1618 to 1648 Austria and Germany were engulfed in the devastating Thirty Years' War.

*The assassination of Brion, tutor to the Prince of Conti (1558–1614) at the St. Bartholomew's Day Massacre in 1572.*

# Chapter 5

## The Seventeenth Century

MANY HISTORIANS CONSIDER the seventeenth century as the age of General Crises. In Europe, the Thirty Years' War raged along with the Great Turkish War. At the same time, there was revolt in Holland, the Polish-Lithuanian Commonwealth disintegrated, and England was in the raptures of its own civil war. As European colonization of the Americas continued in earnest, the exploitation of its incredible natural wealth resulted in great bouts of inflation, as riches were drawn into Europe from there and the rest of the world.

However, this was also a time of invention and the birth of modern science. The steam engine was invented toward the end of the century, a development that would soon change the world forever.

# Power and Politics

### 1600s THE DIVINE RIGHT OF KINGS

THE DIVINE RIGHT of kings was a concept that developed in the late sixteenth century and into the early seventeenth century. It simply stated that kings were appointed by God and could only be punished by God. Opposition to the monarchy was, therefore, impossible. In France, Spain, and the Holy Roman Empire, all Catholic countries, it was accepted almost as a matter of course. It became a further source of royal authority and power. It also gave the Church a privileged position. In Protestant countries, divine right was not popular. Charles I's belief in it in England was one factor in the outbreak of the Civil War in 1642 and also in Charles's execution in 1649. Overall, divine right stabilized but also ossified politics. Opposition became more difficult and the development of democracy was virtually impossible.

*The execution of Charles I (1600–49) of England.*

### 1649 THE DEATH OF A KING

THE STUART KINGS, James I (reigned 1603–25) and his son Charles I (reigned 1625–49), both tried to avoid dealing with Parliament as much as possible. By being frugal, James was able to avoid summoning Parliament for many years. Charles I also did not summon Parliament from 1629 until 1640, but he did not realize that if he was to do without Parliament he also needed to reduce his expenditure. When he summoned Parliament in 1640 to pay for a war with the Scots, he was faced with a barrage of complaints. For two years Charles and Parliament argued, fueled by tensions as to who should command an army to suppress an uprising

*Charles I (1600–49) demanding the Five Members in the House of Commons in 1642.*

in Ireland. Then, in August 1642, Charles lost his patience and decided to declare a war on Parliament—a war he was to lose. In 1646, Charles surrendered to Parliament and after three more years of arguing, in January 1649, the Parliamentary leaders reluctantly put Charles to death.

### 1658 AURANGZEB

AURANGZEB WAS THE last of the Mogul emperors. He seized power in 1658 when he rebelled against Emperor Shah Jahan, famous as the builder of the Taj Mahal. Under Aurangzeb (1618–1707),

the Mogul Empire began to break up. This was partly the result of his attacks on Hinduism, which led to rebellions by Hindus and Sikhs. It was also brought on by Aurangzeb's failure to control his own regional governors, who increasingly began to ignore his authority and raise taxes for themselves. Aurangzeb faced opposition from the Hindu Maratha princes from southern India and from the British, who had arrived in India in the early seventeenth century. When he died in 1707, the Mogul Empire had already begun to disintegrate.

## 1660 RESTORATION OF CHARLES II

CHARLES II (1630–85) WAS RESTORED to the English throne in 1660, after 11 years of the Republic. He was a very popular king, but as he grew older it became clear that he would produce no legitimate heirs to the English throne. Charles's successor would be his brother James, Duke of York. But James was a Catholic and many people were afraid that this would lead to a Catholic revival in England. Some Members of Parliament tried to prevent James from becoming king, while others supported him. His supporters became known as Tories, his opponents as Whigs. Both names were terms of abuse. These were the first political groups in Parliament. They were not really political parties, but they became the basis of the Liberal and Conservative parties of the nineteenth century.

## 1661 THE SUN KING

THE SUN KING was Louis XIV, King of France (1643–1715). He made France the most powerful country in Europe after fighting four wars and brought absolute monarchy to its height. Louis was only

*Perspective view of the palace, gardens, and park of Versailles, seen from the Avenue de Paris in 1668.*

five when he became king and did not rule in person until 1661. He followed the practice of centralizing power into his own hands. Louis also established a dazzling court at his new glittering Palace of Versailles, just outside Paris. The bishops and nobles of France flocked there to pay court to the king. Their days were often spent watching the king get up, the *lever*, or go to bed, the *coucher*. They were also expected to watch

*William (reigned 1689–1702) and Mary, joint rulers of the English throne after James II fled the country.*

him have breakfast, lunch, and dinner. Extra privileges were carrying the king's bedrobe or walking before him with a candle as he went to his bedroom. This ensured that the French nobility were kept where Louis could keep an eye on them. However, the last years of his life were to be beset by problems.

### 1688 THE GLORIOUS REVOLUTION

JAMES II WAS FORCED to flee from England in 1688, and was replaced by his daughter Mary, who became queen. Her husband, William of Orange, became king. In the years after 1689, a series of Acts of Parliament were passed to limit the power of the Crown. Parliament had to meet every year. Taxes could only be collected for one year at a time. The monarch had to be a Protestant and could not leave the country without Parliament's knowledge. These were attempts to place some limits on the power of the king, but the king could still appoint and dismiss ministers and decide all policy. William III, and his successors Queen Anne and George I, became less involved in the government of Britain and the post of prime inister developed, as well as the beginnings of the Cabinet. Britain was becoming a constitutional monarchy.

# War and Peace

### 1600s STATES IN CONFLICT

THE STRIKING DEVELOPMENT in seventeenth-century warfare was the sheer scale of armies. Gustavus Adolphus allocated half of Sweden's budget to military expenditure. Smaller states, such as Scotland and Switzerland, sold their manpower to the greater nations. The Thirty Years' War (1618–48) marked the beginning of modern warfare. During that conflict, King Gustavus Adolphus (1594–1632) of Sweden greatly improved army organization and discipline, introducing more powerful artillery and a lighter infantry musket that permitted soldiers to load and fire faster. During the wars of the English Civil War (1642–49), Oliver Cromwell (1599–1658) raised an extremely effective fighting force by conscription. Law fixed pay, supplies, and discipline, and for the first time, the scarlet coat became the badge of English troops.

### 1618 THE THIRTY YEARS' WAR

THE THIRTY YEARS' WAR was the last major European war of religion and the first all European struggle for power. Hostilities broke out on May 23, 1618, when a number of Protestant Bohemian noblemen threw two royal governors

*Oliver Cromwell (1599–1658), leader of the English Civil War.*

of their country out of the windows of the Hradcany Palace in Prague. The Bohemians appealed to the Protestant prince of Transylvania who, with the encouragement of his overlord, the Ottoman sultan of Turkey, was hoping to win the crown of Hungary from the Hapsburgs. They also elected Frederick V of the Palatinate as their new king. They hoped that Frederick's father-in-law, James I of England, and his uncle, Maurice of Nassau, virtual ruler of the United Provinces of the Netherlands, would lend him support.

## 1630s THE LION OF THE NORTH

IN JULY 1630, the Swedish king Gustavus Adolphus (1594–1632) landed in Pomerania to begin a series of victorious campaigns against the imperial armies. At Breitenfeld (September 17, 1631) and at the Lech River (April 15, 1632) he defeated Tilly, and at Lutzen (November 16, 1632) the Swedes defeated Wallenstein, although Gustavus Adolfus was killed. The intervention of France (1635) on the "Protestant" side cut across the religious alignments of the combatants. In 1640, both Catalonia and Portugal rebelled against Spain, although all three were Catholic. In 1643, the Protestant Christian of Denmark, fearing the increasing power of Protestant Sweden, restarted the old Danish-Swedish rivalry for the control of the northwestern entrance to the Baltic. Once again the Danes were heavily defeated and lost their monopoly control over the Sound.

## 1633 THE FIRST ENGINEER

THE EFFECTIVENESS of citadels for defense was greatly enhanced in the seventeenth century by the work of a French military engineering genius named Sébastien de Vauban (1633–1707). Retaining the basic features of the citadel structure, he devised a means of extending the outer works so far that no enemy could begin siege operations at close range. De Vauban was also a master of offensive siege craft; he developed the concept of using parallel trenches to connect the zigzag trenches used by besieging troops and the use of the ricochet shot from cannons plunging over the walls to drop on the defenders beyond the walls. The best examples of de Vauban's work can be seen at Neuf Brisach and Lille, typical of his "star fort" designs.

*The Vauban citadel on the island of Belle-Ile-en-Mer off Morbihan, France.*

*The Battle of Edgehill during the English Civil War.*

### 1640s THE ENGLISH CIVIL WAR

AFTER A DRAWN battle at Edgehill in Warwickshire (1642), the Royalists threatened to attack London. In 1643, the Royalists were victorious in most parts of England except London and the east. Charles and his army was defeated at Newbury (September 20, 1643) and the tide turned for the Parliamentarians for good in 1644, when the Royalists were beaten at Marston Moor in Yorkshire (July 2). In 1645, the Royalists were defeated by Thomas Fairfax's New Model Army at Naseby, and in 1646 Charles,

who had surrendered himself to the Scots, was turned over to Parliament and became a prisoner. After Charles I's execution (January 30, 1649), his son Charles II renewed the war, sustained by Royalists in Ireland and Scotland; but Cromwell defeated the Irish and then turned his sights on the Scots and then invaded Scotland, where he crushed the Scots at Dunbar (1650).

### 1650 MARITIME SUPREMACY

THE LEADING MARITIME nation of the first half of the seventeenth century was the Netherlands. From 1650, at the height of their prosperity, Spain ceased

*The Battle of Texel, August 21, 1673.*

to be a menace to the French and the British. Consequently, the Dutch were thrown into direct competition with the British fleets. Between 1650 and 1652, the British passed three Navigation Acts in an attempt to exclude the Dutch from their trade. By 1652, the British fleet consisted of over 60 large warships with over 100 guns on each ship. Three Anglo-Dutch Wars were fought (1652–54, 1665–67, and 1672–74). After these battles, the British overtook the Dutch as the world's major maritime power. As a result of the wars, the British gained New Amsterdam in North America, which became New York (1667).

*John Churchill (1650–1722), 1st Duke of Marlborough.*

### 1667 MARLBOROUGH

JOHN CHURCHILL (1650–1722), 1st Duke of Marlborough, entered the army in 1667. His career was to span the reigns of five monarchs. He first distinguished himself by helping defeat the rebellion of the Duke of Monmouth (1685). James I then raised him to the peerage and promoted him to lieutenant general. Only three years later, Churchill shifted his allegiance from the Catholic king to a Protestant Dutchman, William of Orange, who deposed James and ruled as William III. Churchill campaigned for William during the war against France in Flanders and a war against Ireland. When Anne became Queen in 1702, she appointed Marlborough Commander in Chief and First Minister. His marriage to Anne's intimate friend, Sarah Jennings, ensured his rise, first to Captain General of British Forces and then to Duke. During the long war against France, he won victories at Blenheim (1704), Ramillies (1706), Oodenarde (1708), and at Malplaquet (1709). Eventual conflicts with court led to his self exile. Marlborough is acknowledged as a master military strategist and as one of the great generals in British history.

# Society and Culture

## 1600s LIFE EXPECTANCY

DESPITE IMPROVEMENTS in medicine and a new understanding of the human body, life expectancy in Europe was a great deal shorter than it is today. Although the stirrings of improvement were already there in the seventeenth and eighteenth centuries, it was to be a very long time before the risks to life lessened. Many infants died either at birth or soon after, and many women died in childbirth. Infectious diseases created epidemics in which thousands died, especially in the unhealthy and overcrowded districts of large cities. Since Roman times, life expectancy had barely moved above 40 years old, less than that for women and even lower for others—for example, French peasants, who rarely lived for more than 22 years.

## 1601 A LAW FOR THE POOR

IN BRITAIN, VAGRANTS and beggars wandered the roads seeking shelter and sustenance, and had long been both a scandal and a security problem for the more settled population. These miserable outcasts from society created fear and trepidation, because what they were not given, they stole. In 1601, the government of Queen Elizabeth I took official action, and created a Poor Law, signaling for the first time that the state had assumed responsibility for the less fortunate populations. The law imposed a poor rate to fund poor relief, and appointed Overseers of the Poor in every parish to buy materials to provide work for the unemployed. The price of grain was controlled, and if famine struck, imported grain from abroad was distributed in the affected areas.

*In 1601, the Poor Law was introduced in England, creating a better environment for the lower classes.*

*Settlers in Jamestown, the first permanent English settlement in North America, trade with Native Americans in the fort, 1609.*

## 1607 ENGLISH SETTLERS IN NORTH AMERICA

THE JAMESTOWN SETTLEMENT was the first successful English settlement on the mainland of North America. The settlement, named after James I, who was the reigning monarch at the time, was founded in the colony of Virginia in 1607. A repeat of history was inevitable after Europeans settled in North America. Just as the Spaniards destroyed the Aztecs, Incas, and others nations farther south, there could be only one ending to the clash between the cultures of the ambitious, enterprising, but intolerant and ruthless newcomers and the seminomadic first Americans living their simple, traditional lives in the north. When the first English settlers established themselves in Virginia, the Native American helped them survive their first winter, teaching them how to hunt and trap animals and raise crops of corn and tobacco. In time, as the United States—which evolved from the early settlements—set out to claim the country from coast to coast, this was something the Native Americans would soon come to regret.

*The Taj Mahal, built by Shah Jahan (1592–1666) for Mumtaz, his beloved wife.*

## 1631 THE TAJ MAHAL

"A DREAM IN MARBLE" and "a poem in stone" are two of the many attempts to express the phenomenal beauty of the Taj Mahal, which the Mogul emperor Shah Jahan (1592–1666) built for his favorite wife Mumtaz, who died in 1631. The Taj, a marvel of intricate sculpture and mosaics, with walls, floors, and screens studded with precious stones, stands on the bank of the Jumna River near Agra and took 22 years (1631–53) to construct. More than 20,000 workmen were employed to build it, together with the surrounding gardens and fountains. Nearby stands a mosque, where Shah Jahan was able to see the Taj reflected in a stone set in the wall before him as he prayed.

## 1636 SAMURAI JAPAN

THE JAPANESE WORLD, frozen into stasis by the Decree of 1636, was based on duties and obligations from which there was no escape. Often brutally controlled by Shogun warlords and the samurai since the tenth century, the strictly disciplined Japanese lived in a hierarchical society in which failure, or perceived failure, to honor the warrior overlords could mean instant execution. The emperor, though a figurehead, was regarded as divine. The strict samurai Code of Bushido, in which loss of honor could be assuaged only by *seppuku* (ritual suicide), imbued the civilian mindset, producing a culture of great formality in which observing proper rituals and expected behavior and above all, automatic obedience to authority, was paramount.

## 1670 THE TRIAL OF WILLIAM PENN

THE JURY SYSTEM, brought to England by the Normans after 1066, was often abused by judges bullying juries for the verdict they wanted. This threatening behavior finally met its match in 1670, when the Quakers William Penn and William Mead were charged with riot for preaching their faith in public. The judge was intent on a "guilty" verdict, but the jury disagreed. What was more, they refused to give in, despite imprisonment, fines, and threats. Ultimately, the Lord Chief Justice, Sir John Vaughan, ruled that judges could not "lead (juries) ... by the nose." The "not guilty" verdict stood and the case, known as "Bushell's Case" from the name of the foreman, Edward Bushell, established the right of British juries to independent verdicts.

*A view of Lincoln's Inn, where William Penn (1644–1718) studied law.*

139

# Exploration and Empires

## 1602 BEGINNINGS OF CONFLICT

THE ENGLISH East India Company sought profits in Southeast Asia, and in 1602 the company established a base at Bantam. The Dutch were already located there, but they were unwilling to share in the wealth of the spice trade. Conflict sprang up between the traders, and the English traders left in Bantam were prevented—sometimes by violence—by the Dutch, Portuguese, and even the Javanese from engaging in commerce. The Portuguese had a fort at Amboina, one of the main ports in the Spice Islands, but the Dutch seized it immediately after the English had reached a treaty with its governor in 1606, rendering the deal void.

*The mosque of Muhammad Ali in Egypt.*

## 1610 THE MUSLIM WORLD AND ITS NEIGHBORS

TO ISLAM, THE WORLD had always been divided into two camps: the House of Islam, representing the lands ruled by the faithful, and the House of War, which includes everybody else. While Muslim states tended to ignore going out to the rest of the world, they did welcome visitors who brought useful technology, especially if they chose to accept Islam. A combination of events in about 1610 led to a substantial number of English and Dutch pirates settling in the lands of the Barbary corsairs of North Africa. These immigrants provided navigational and shipbuilding information that helped transform the corsairs into the terror of the seas. Jewish physicians who had studied in the West were also much sought after at this time.

## 1619 COEN IN THE EAST INDIES

THE DUTCH East India Company had started its life committed to trading alone, avoiding the commitments a proper empire would require. However, it would not be long before it became apparent to the board of directors of the company that a monopoly of trade would ensure much higher profits than free competition. In 1619, the Dutch sent Jan Pieterszoon Coen to the East Indies. Coen had very clear ideas of what he wanted to do. First, he founded the Dutch post at Batavia (modern Djakarta, Indonesia) to serve as a center for all inter-Asian trade. Then, he forced all rival traders out of the islands of Southeast Asia. The attacks on the English culminated in 1623, with a massacre at their main post at Amboina.

## 1632 THE WAY TO THE PACIFIC

RUSSIAN EXPLORERS learned of a Siberian tribe, the Yakuts, in about 1620. The high-quality furs the Yakuts traded stimulated the greed of traders. In 1632, Pyotr Beketov took an armed force and conquered the Yakuts. He then carried on southward to the country of another Siberian tribe, the Tungus, and conquered them, too. A post in the land of the Tungus was the base for a journey eastwards in 1639 by a party of 20 men led by Ivan Moskvitin. This little band followed the Ulya River to its mouth, at the Sea of Okhotsk. These were the first Russians to reach the Pacific coast.

*Barbary pirates attacking a Spanish ship.*

## 1643 TO THE CHINESE BORDER

THE EXPEDITION to the Ulya River uncovered news of large silver deposits along another river to the south. In 1643, Vasily Poyarkov traveled to the Amur to find out the truth of this, but behaved so badly toward the local tribe that another expedition led by Yerofey Khabarov in 1649 had a hostile reception. In 1651, Khabarov returned, ready for war. The Amur tribes paid tribute to the Chinese emperor, but that did not deter the Russians. A fort was built at the confluence of the Amur and Sungari rivers. Khabarov and his Cossacks defeated a Chinese assault in April 1652. An uneasy peace between China and Russia in the Amur country continued, until the Russians agreed to withdraw in a treaty between the two empires in 1689.

## 1654 EXPANSION OF THE DUTCH EMPIRE

COLLECTION AND DISPERSAL points of slaves became important targets in wars. Dutch forces seized posts or constructed new ones in Brazil, and the need to supply slaves to these territories caused the seizure, in 1654, of one of the oldest Portuguese bases in Africa at Elmina, near the mouth of the Volta River. Other European states built their own posts on the coast nearby, including the Swedes, the Danes, and the Prussians, countries almost entirely without American possessions. The islands of the Caribbean were handed around European states like real estate in a modern city. The Dutch had captured Curaçao in 1634 from the Spanish. The French settled Guadeloupe and Martinique, and in 1697 the French forced Spain to grant them half of the island of Hispaniola, which eventually became Haiti.

## 1682 PETER THE GREAT'S WARS OF EXPANSION

THE TEN-YEAR-OLD Romanov heir to the throne, Peter became czar in 1682. In 1695, he embarked on a campaign of

*Peter I the Great (1672–1725).*

*The saving of Vienna from the Turks led by Kara Mustapha Pasha, 1683.*

expansion that resulted in wars with the Turks and Sweden. Although initially Peter experienced more defeats than victories, by the end of his reign, in 1725, the Russian Empire had regained the lands around Narva that they had previously held during the reign of Ivan the Terrible, and also Estonia and Livonia. This had enabled the construction of a new city, christened St. Petersburg. Peter's campaigns had also led to the acquisition of land around the Caspian Sea, including the strategic city of Baku. However, his two wars against the Turks produced no lasting gains.

## 1699 THE TURKISH RETREAT

IN 1683, THE TURKS made a second attempt to capture Vienna. This, too, failed, but this time the Hapsburg Empire was able to recover substantial areas conquered by the Turks 150 years before. Even at the time, the peace treaty signed in 1699 was recognized as a turning point in relations between the Turks and Europe. The eighteenth century was an era of continuing retreat by the Turks under Russian and Hapsburg pressure until, in 1798, the fringes of their empire became, like India, the battleground for outside powers, such as the French and British.

# Trade and Industry

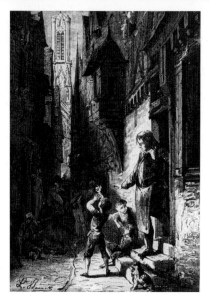

*Hans Lippershey, inventor of the first telescope.*

### 1600s THE INVENTION REVOLUTION

A SCIENTIFIC REVOLUTION took place over much of Europe in the 1600s, with the invention of many items that had industrial, agricultural, or commercial uses and a huge impact an life. Among these were: the telescope (1608, Hans Lippershey, Dutch); the steam turbine (1629, Giovanni Branca, Italian); the adding machine (1642, Blaise Pascal, French); the barometer (1643, Evangelista Torricelli, Italian); the air pump (1650, Otto von Guericke, German); the reflecting telescope (1668, Isaac Newton, English); the calculating machine (1671, Gottfried Wilhelm Leibniz, German); and the steam-powered pump (1698, Thomas Savery, English).

### 1600s THE DUTCH AND ENGLISH EAST INDIA COMPANIES

THE ESTABLISHMENT of the Dutch East India Company (1600) and English East India Company (1602) gave great power and organizational strength to their respective nations..The Dutch dominated in East Asia. By the 1640s, they had driven the Portuguese from Malacca and Ceylon and established themselves in Java, becoming masters of the spice trade. In the Americas, the English colonies in Virginia (1607) and Massachusetts (1620) soon overtook the Dutch colony in New York (1626). The French began to colonies Canada, starting at Quebec (1608). The most lucrative European ventures were in the smaller islands of the Caribbean, where plantations—worked by imported African slaves—yielded sugar, a commodity much in demand at home. English, French, and Dutch entrepreneurs had, by the 1640s, taken the bulk of this trade away from the Portuguese and the Spanish.

### 1609 BANKS

THE FIRST BANK opened in Amsterdam, the Netherlands, in 1609. By the mid-seventeenth century, banks were commonplace in Europe. In Japan, feudal clans ran banks, which issued their own paper money. As paper money became more widely used, the gold it represented generally stayed in storage. Goldsmiths saw an opportunity. They could lend a little of the actual gold out and make money by charging the borrower for it. Many of the early banks failed because they lent too much gold. If many savers came to collect at the same time, there was not enough to go around. To prevent this, most governments now regulate the amount a bank can lend. The world's first central bank, the Bank of England, was established in 1694.

*The Bank of England in Threadneedle Street, London.*

## 1630 THE BEGINNINGS OF THE SLAVE TRADE

AN ENGLISHMAN, John Hawkins, piloted the first slave ship to Spanish waters in 1562. African slavery and agricultural plantations began to become important only after about 1630, when sugar plantations became firmly established. The entrepreneurs of the slave economy in the Americas were, in the end, mainly Portuguese, English, French, and Dutch. Their impact on the native inhabitants was huge. The colonists brought disease, their own religions, culture, and styles of life that penetrated from the initially mainly coastal settlements right across the continent. The horse, for example, a Spanish import into the Americas, became the basis of a nomadic lifestyle in which buffalo were hunted. This so-called Plains Indian culture spread across the North American prairies in the seventeenth century.

## 1649 RUSSIAN RUNAWAYS

IN RUSSIA in the mid-seventeenth century, the idea of being tied to the land took on an almost literal meaning. The czar had insufficient money to pay salaries to his officials and to army personnel. Instead, he rewarded them with grants of land. Of course, land without peasants to work it was valueless. To prevent peasants from running away, the czar had laws passed authorizing landholders to chase and capture runaways. A law of 1649 required each man to remain at his post, in the place and walk of life in which he had been born. The practice never quite matched the theory. Runaways often escaped from Russian society altogether and settled elsewhere in Asia. Exceptionally, a person could rise to a top official post.

*Sir John Hawkins, who traded with the Spaniards in kidnapped Africans.*

*The rise of the slave trade was caused by increasing demand for workers on sugar plantations.*

### 1650s SUGAR PLANTATIONS

THE IMPETUS for the slave trade came from the trend in the 1650s of drinking tea, coffee (first introduced to Europe in 1516), and chocolate. People liked to stir in some sugar to disguise the natural bitterness. The demand led to a sudden growth in sugar plantations in the West Indies, the ideal place to grow sugar cane, and slaves seemed the ideal means of providing labor. During the sixteenth century, about 1,000 slaves were imported from the west coast of Africa to the West Indies. Within the next hundred years, another 800,000 were imported. British slave merchants accounted for 40 percent of Europe's trade in slaves and made an estimated overall profit of £12 million out of trading more than 2.5 million Africans.

### 1694 THE NATIONAL DEBT

THE RAPID RISE of England's power was facilitated by the invention of a new instrument of credit, the national debt. This allowed public borrowing for emergencies on very advantageous terms. The central idea was that Parliament should be responsible for repayment. Previously, governmental borrowing had been in the king's name and debts were regarded as his personal obligation. In 1694, Parliament established the Bank of England, one of whose principal functions was to lend money to the government on the understanding that Parliament would guarantee repayment and raise the necessary funds by levying taxes. This meant that costs could be spread over several years.

# Science and Technology

### 1600s GALILEO

INFLUENCED BY COPERNICUS, an Italian scientist called Galileo Galilei (1564–1642) founded new scientific methods of deducing laws to explain the results of observations and experiments. He showed that different-size objects with the same density would display the same constant acceleration when dropped simultaneously, and that, allowing for friction, a body moving on a horizontal smooth surface will neither accelerate nor decelerate. These demonstrations angered orthodox scientists, because they seemed to contradict instinctive preconceptions about physics. He also used the newly invented telescope to observe that the planets did indeed revolve around the sun, which he was forced to recant by the Catholic Inquisition.

*Italian Galileo Galilei (1564–1642), whose experiments founded a new era in scientific understanding.*

### 1600s GLASS SHEET

A PROCESS was developed in the 1600s that enabled the production of sheet glass for the first time. This meant that large single-pane windows and mirrors could be made, giving birth to a whole new industry. It involved pouring the required quantity of molten glass onto a casting table, where it was carefully spread and rolled out to an even thickness and cooled slowly to prevent it from cracking. The development of larger, coal-fueled furnaces had proved essential for supplying molten glass in sufficient quantities for sheets of a reasonable size. Techniques for making high-quality optical glass were improved in the 1700s, allowing for considerable improvement in optical instruments, such as the telescope and microscope, which required precise and accurate lenses.

### 1600 MAGNETISM

JUST AS SOME SCIENTISTS were experimenting with electricity, others were playing around with magnetism, although no one had yet linked the two. William Gilbert (*circa* 1545–96) was fascinated by the natural magnetism of loadstone. In 1600, he published a book called *On Magnets*, following 18 years of experimentation. He believed that magnetism was the force attracting everything to the earth and, therefore, that space must be a vacuum. Otto von Guericke (1602–86) extended Gilbert's ideas. He demonstrated how to create a vacuum with his famous horse experiment in 1652, showing that 16 animals could not pull two evacuated brass hemispheres apart. He then made a sulfur ball, which when rubbed would attain magnetic qualities, mysteriously glow in the dark, and make crackling noises.

*Christiaan Huygens in Salomon Costers clockmaker shop.*

## 1608 THE FIRST TELESCOPE

THE ADVANCES IN SCIENCE were aided by the invention and development of instruments. The telescope was invented in 1608 by Dutchman Hans Lippershey (*circa* 1570–1619), as a military reconnaissance device. Galileo had adapted it within a year and began to change the human view of the universe radically. The fundamental effect that the telescope had was to call orthodox scientific beliefs into doubt, where every aspect of science and technology was required to be fully investigated. It is held that Galileo noticed the phenomenon by which a pendulum takes the same time to complete a swing, whatever the length of the arc. This led another Dutchman, Christiaan Huygens (1629–95), to develop the pendulum-regulated clock, which, in turn, enabled scientists to measure time accurately enough to verify Galileo's astronomical theories.

## 1609 THE FIRST MICROSCOPE

JUST AS SOME SCIENTISTS were interested in the study of the universe, so others were interested in studying the minutiae of things. The telescope, which might have been called the "macroscope," spawned an alter ego in the form of the first optical microscope in 1609. The invention of a Dutchman, Zacharias Janssen (1580–*circa* 1638), the microscope transformed scientific knowledge of the way things are designed and function at a cellular level. Study by magnification initiated various new approaches to biology, chemistry, geology, and so on. William Harvey (1578–1657), an English physician, discovered the circulation of blood thanks to the microscope. This, in turn, led to more dynamic and progressive approaches to medicine, now that blood was understood to be the medium for transporting vital chemicals to parts of the body.

### 1643 TORRICELLI'S GENIUS

THE INTRODUCTION OF PUMPS for removing flood water from mines revealed a strange phenomenon. It was found that water could only be sucked up a tube for some 33 feet (10 m) or so, after which it would go no higher. An assistant of Galileo, called Evangelista Torricelli (1608–47), set to work on this problem in 1643. He had a moment of genius, reasoning that the air was in fact like a lake, which asserted a pressure as it increased with depth. Cleverly, he opted to experiment with mercury instead of

water, because it was 14 times more dense, which meant being able to scale down his apparatus. He filled a glass test tube with mercury and inverted it with the open end held submerged in a dish of mercury to keep an air seal. He found that the mercury column dropped to a length of about 2½ feet (76 cm) and stopped, with a small space above it. This was evidence that the weight of air, or air pressure, was supporting the column of mercury, and that the space must be a vacuum.

### 1670 NEWTON'S TELESCOPE

BY THE TIME Isaac Newton (1642–1727) started his astronomical observations, it was very difficult to make telescopes any larger. The design developed by Galileo was a refracting telescope, which required lenses to become bigger and bigger if a greater magnification of the stars was desired. An alternative design needed to be invented. It was Isaac Newton himself who first built the new type of telescope, called the reflector telescope. A concave mirror was used to focus the light collected, instead of a lens. Large mirrors were cheaper and easier to make, and they had the added advantage of being far less heavy and so easier to mount than lenses. Newton's first reflector telescope was made in 1670; it

*Evangelista Torricelli's (1608–47) barometer experiment.*

*Isaac Newton (1642–1727), philosopher, mathematician, scientist, and astronomer.*

James Watt (1736–1819) was repairing a Newcomen engine when he realized that the design could be improved by incorporating a separate condenser. This allowed for the working cylinder to remain hot and increased the efficiency of the engine considerably. The Watt steam engine was such an improvement that it went on to power the Industrial Revolution. The late eighteenth century saw it adopted in all kinds of ways for driving machinery in factories.

led to the construction of some very large instruments, which effectively opened up the skies for closer scrutiny.

### 1682 STEAM ENTERS THE PICTURE

THE FIRST PRACTICAL application of steam was in Papin's pressure cooker of 1682. He noticed and recorded the physical forces created by steam as it expanded and contracted, which inspired Thomas Savery to build a steam-operated mine pump between 1698 and 1702. By 1712, Thomas Newcomen (1663–1729) had invented the first "proper" steam engine, featuring a piston and cylinder, and this design was widely used for pumping the water from mines for several decades. A mathematical instrument maker named

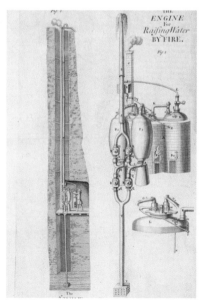

*Thomas Savery's steam pump, known as the "miner's friend."*

# Religions, Belief, and Thought

### 1600s MODERN SCIENCE

BACON (1561–1626) AND DESCARTES (1596–1650) are generally seen as the founders of modern science. Bacon stated that science should be about the collection and organization of observed facts, so that general principles could be derived from them. Before him, the tendency was either to indulge in theoretical speculation or simply to describe the world without explaining it. Descartes argued that all matter ultimately consisted of measurable particles and that all we need to do is to measure how these particles behave. All other properties, such as color and texture, are unreal or can be reduced to the basic quantities of size and shape.

### 1602 CAMPANELLA'S *CITY OF THE SUN*

TOMMASO CAMPANELLA (1568–1639) was born in southern Italy and became a Dominican monk when he was 14 years old. He rejected the scholastic and Aristotleian philosophy that he was taught and claimed that all knowledge of the world was obtained directly through the senses. This strictly empirical position contrasts with his later interest in astrology and white magic. Although

*Tommaso Campanella (1568–1639) was imprisoned for nearly 30 years for his "heretical" ideas.*

denounced as a heretic and imprisoned for almost 30 years for holding these views, he spent several of his final years acting as astrological adviser to the pope. His *The City of the Sun* (1602) depicts an imaginary society governed by philosophers, in which the state provides education for all; there is no private property and all things, including wives, are held in common.

## 1646 GEORGE FOX AND THE QUAKERS

THE SOCIETY OF FRIENDS, or "Quakers," was originally founded in England by George Fox (1624–91) the son of a rural weaver. He lived during a time of considerable social unrest and war. He rejected the religious and political consensus by proposing an unusual approach to Christianity. Following his own inner experiences in 1646 and 1647, he rejected the formal institutions of the Church and emphasized direct awareness of the divine. Quaker meetings involve no liturgy or ritual and are characterized by long periods of silence and contemplation—during which they were once said to "quake" in awe of God, hence their name. Quakers are renowned for their active concern with peace issues and social justice and for the democratic way in which they run their affairs. An American offshoot, the Shakers, was founded by Mother Ann Lee in 1774.

*A meeting of Quakers, a group of independent religious organizations established in the mid–17th century.*

# Chapter 6

## The Eighteenth Century

WHILE THE PREVIOUS century is noted as the age of General
Crises, the eighteenth century did not see particular calm either.
A North American war raged between England and France,
Russian-Turkish wars teetered back and forth, Opium Wars in
China erupted due to trade differences between the Chinese
and the West, while the French Revolution kept the nerves of
monarchs of the rest of Europe strained.

Meanwhile, isolated Australia was discovered and became
a British penal colony, while India saw the end of the Mogul
Empire and the rise of the East India Company.

With the dawn of machinery, such as steam power and the
cotton gin, technology was about to transform the world.

# Power and Politics

*Various Indian nobles and a British soldier pay tribute at the palace of an Indian ruler.*

## 1700s THE BRITISH IN INDIA

THE BRITISH LANDED in India for the first time in 1603. They were representatives of the East India Company, for which a charter had been granted by Elizabeth I in 1600. For more than a century, they occupied coastal trading posts, such as Madras, but in the mid-eighteenth century they were able to defeat both the Dutch and the French and take control of the trade of the subcontinent. In 1784, Pitt's India Subcontinent Act prevented the East India Company from interfering in the affairs of Indian states, but in the early nineteenth century, after the Maratha Wars, the company acquired more influence across India. By the 1820s, almost all of India was governed, directly or indirectly, by the East India Company.

## 1763 THE TREATY OF PARIS

THE TREATY OF PARIS in 1763 brought to an end the French and Indian War, which was an extension of the Seven Years' War in Europe (see page 161). The war had resulted in a comprehensive victory for Britain over France. The French forces had been driven out of North America and India, and the French navy had been crushed at Quiberon Bay in 1759. The British army had even won a victory on the continent at Minden in the same year. The end of the war had two principal effects. First, it built up resentment in France against Britain, which led to the search for an opportunity to gain revenge, and second, and much more importantly, it led to increasing opposition from the colonists to British rule, especially when this involved increased taxes to help pay for the cost of the war.

## 1773 THE BOSTON TEA PARTY

THE CENTER OF RESISTANCE to British rule in the 1760s and 1770s was the port of Boston in Massachusetts. Because they relied on trade, Bostonians were far more affected by restrictions imposed by the British government than other agricultural colonies to the south. In 1770, this led to an attack on a group of British soldiers that resulted in the deaths of five Bostonians. In December 1773, when tea from India arrived in Boston, it was dumped into the sea by Bostonians disguised as Indians. This protest became known afterward as the "Boston Tea Party." In June 1774, the port of Boston was closed and the colony of Massachusetts lost many of its rights of self-government and justice. Representatives of all the colonies, except Georgia, met at Philadelphia in September 1774 in the First Continental Congress. They agreed to refuse to import British goods from December 1774.

## 1775 THE MARATHA WARS

THE MARATHAS were Hindu princes from southern India who attacked the remnants of the Mogul Empire in the mid-eighteenth century. They were organized into a loose confederacy and competed among themselves for leadership. Their success against the Mogul Empire brought them into conflict with the British, leading to the first Maratha War from 1775–82. A second war broke out in 1802, which resulted in the Marathas being defeated at the battles of Assaye and Argaum by Sir Arthur Wellesley (who later became the Duke of Wellington). This led to the collapse of Maratha power. They retained control of their lands, but were under the indirect control of the British.

*Tea being thrown into the sea by disguised Bostonians in retaliation against British trade restrictions.*

## 1776 THE DECLARATION OF INDEPENDENCE

WAR BROKE OUT in North America between the colonists and the British in April 1775. Much of the early fighting centered on Boston, which the British were forced to evacuate in March 1776. Congress then announced that the authority of the British crown was at an end. The Declaration of Independence was drawn up by Thomas Jefferson on July 4. The actions of the colonists set a new precedent in power and politics. They asserted the right of a people to throw off their allegiance to their king and establish for themselves a new and different form of government. The next step was the Articles of Confederation and Perpetual Union, which were signed in November 1777. This set out the basis for a United States of America, which came into being in 1781, when the British forces in North America surrendered.

## 1787 CONSTITUTION

SIGNED ON September 17, 1787, the Constitution created the United States of America. Until then the states had only been united by the Articles of Confederation. The Constitution came into effect in June 1788, when the ninth state, New Hampshire, ratified it. The drafting of the Constitution had proved difficult. Until the 1770s, the states had all had their own governments and it had been opposition to British rule that had united them. Once the British left, some of the old rivalries reappeared. States were reluctant to raise taxes for the Federal government, and there were disagreements over trade and between the agricultural states of the South and the industrialized states in the North. In addition, the smaller states, such as Connecticut and Rhode Island, feared that they would be swamped by the larger states, such as Massachusetts and New York. What resulted was a compromise.

*Drafting the Declaration of Independence.*

## 1789 THE BASTILLE

IN MAY AND JUNE of 1789, while the Estates General was arguing at Versailles, bread prices in Paris reached record levels. On July 14, 1789, a crowd of Parisians attacked the Bastille, a royal fortress in Paris that was used as a prison and an arsenal. They were looking for weapons to defend Paris against a possible attack by Louis XVI's forces. The attack was a complete success and the governor of the prison surrendered, but the mob killed him immediately. The fall of the Bastille was a symbol that the power of the king could be challenged, and it had been the working people of Paris who had played the most important role in the events. It was an ominous step for the aristocracy.

*The siege of the Bastille, July 14, 1789, one of the first steps toward revolution in France.*

## 1792 THE JACOBINS

IN SEPTEMBER 1792, the National Assembly was set up in France. This soon fell under the control of the Jacobins, who were members of a club that met in a monastery in the rue St. Jacques. Their leader was Maximilien Robespierre. The monarchy was abolished and Louis XVI was put on trial and executed in January 1793. Robespierre then initiated the Reign of Terror, in which all of his political opponents, including members of his own party, were brought before revolutionary tribunals and then executed, particularly by the guillotine. The guillotine was a new device and became the preferred method for beheading people. Robespierre became virtual dictator of France, even introducing a Law of Suspects, which allowed for people suspected of planning crimes to be tried.

# War and Peace

### 1700 THE GREAT NORTHERN WAR

SWEDEN, THE DOMINANT power in northern Europe when the war began, fought against an alliance intent on seizing its empire. After Charles XII inherited the Swedish throne (1697), Denmark, Saxony, and Russia attacked Sweden (1700). Charles defeated the Danes, then turned his attention to Russia, destroying the Russian army that was besieging Narva (1700). Charles toppled Augustus from the throne of Poland (1704) and broke his power in Saxony (1706). In 1707, Charles was decisively defeated at Poltava (1709) by Peter the Great and fled to the Ottoman Empire. Russia seized Livonia, Estonia, and the Gulf of Finland. Charles returned to the north in 1714, but was killed during a campaign against Danish-ruled Norway (1718). This signaled the emergence of Russia as the strongest power in the Baltic.

### 1713 UTRECHT AND BEYOND

THE TREATY OF UTRECHT (1713) ended France's attempts to dominate Europe. However, there was still the question of colonies and trade. The Dutch were no longer a problem, and the Spanish were content to ally themselves with France when it suited

*Bringing home the dead king, Charles XII.*

them. The Anglo-Spanish War of Jenkins' Ear (1739–48) proved to be the first flashpoint, followed by the Austrian War of Succession (1740–48), in which Britain and France fought from 1743. After a brief pause, France and Britain clashed in the Seven Years' War (1756–63), which carried on as the War of Independence (1775–83), although this was effectively over after Cornwallis surrendered at Yorktown in 1781.

## 1740 THE WAR OF THE AUSTRIAN SUCCESSION

EMPEROR CHARLES VI died without a male heir, in 1740, and his lands passed to a daughter, Maria Theresa. Two months later, Frederick II of Prussia, anticipating a partition of Hapsburg domains, invaded Silesia. A Prussian victory at Mollwitz, in 1741, hastened the formation of an anti-Hapsburg coalition that included Bavaria, Spain, and France, as well as Prussia. Illustrious victories by Frederick II in 1745 compelled Maria Theresa to sign the Treaty of Dresden on December 25, 1745, reaffirming Prussian control over a combined Austrian, English, and Dutch force at Fontenoy, but had lost Canada. A general peace was finally concluded at Aix-la-Chapelle on October 18, 1748.

## 1756 THE SEVEN YEARS' WAR

THE SEVEN YEARS' WAR pitted Britain and Prussia against Austria, France Russia, Saxony, Sweden, and (after 1762) Spain. On the European continent, hostilities began in 1756, when Frederick II (the Great) of Prussia, anticipating an assault from Maria Theresa of Austria and Elizabeth of Russia, launched a surprise offensive through the electorate of Saxony, a minor Austrian ally. Sweden had aligned itself against Prussia, and Frederick's military advance into Bohemia led to a Prussian defeat at Kolin in June 1756. A Russian army then marched into East Prussia in August, and

*Frederick II (1712–86), King of Prussia.*

Austrian troops occupied Berlin for several days in October. Only Frederick's outstanding victories at Rossbach in November, and at Leuthen a month later, prevented the allies from overwhelming his kingdom.

## 1763 PRUSSIAN SOVEREIGNTY

COSTLY PRUSSIAN SUCCESSES at Zorndorf in 1758, and again at Leignitz and Torgau in 1760, only drained Frederick's limited resources. He suffered another defeat, against the Russians, at Kunersdorf in 1759. By the end of 1761 the Austrians had moved into Saxony and Silesia, and Russian troops held Prussian Pomerania. With enemy armies closing in around him, Frederick seemed incapable of further resistance. At this critical moment the Russian empress died (January 1762) and was succeeded by Peter Ill, one of Frederick's devoted admirers. Peter immediately withdrew from the war, and Austria, unable to defeat Prussia alone, was compelled to end the fighting in Germany. A treaty confirming Prussian sovereignty over Silesia was signed at Hubertusberg in 1763.

## 1775 AMERICAN REVOLUTION (AMERICAN REVOLUTIONARY WAR)

THE AMERICAN REVOLUTION was caused by colonial opposition to British exploitation and antimonarchist sentiment. The spark that ignited wholesale revolution, came at Lexington, Massachusetts, on April 19, 1775. General Gage despatched a small force to seize illegal military stores at Lexington. The local colonists' militia, known as minutemen, exchanged fire with the

*The Battle of Bunker Hill, near Boston, during the American Revolutionary War, also known as the American War of Independence.*

British troops and the Battle of Lexington and Concord began the Revolution. The second Continental Congress met in May 1775 and adopted the rebel militias as the Continental Army; George Washington was appointed commander in chief. The British were reinforced by the arrival in Boston of William Howe, Sir Henry Clinton, and John Burgoyne with additional troops raising their force to 10,000.

## 1790s VALMY AND JEMAPPES

THE NATIONS OF EUROPE began moving against revolutionary France even before the execution of Louis. In August 1792, a joint Prussian-Austrian army invaded northeastern France. They were met at Valmy, the day being won by the French. Other French forces pushed back the Austrian army at the Battle of Jemappes. In January 1793, the infamous orders to execute King Louis XVI and Marie-Antoinette were issued. Britain was transformed from a concerned observer to an implacable foe. The Austrians were driven from the Netherlands, and The United Provinces (northern Holland) were annexed. By 1795, Prussia, Spain, Hanover, and Saxony had opted out of the coalition, leaving Britain and Austria to continue the fight against France's revolutionary government.

## 1799 RISE OF BONAPARTE

AUSTRIA WAS NOW FIGHTING a lone war on the continent of Europe. In Italy, Napoleon Bonaparte expelled the Austrians from northern Italy. They joined up with Joubert's troops, marching out of southern Germany, and advanced on Vienna. A joint Austrian-Russian army

*Napoleon Bonaparte (1769–1821).*

managed to wrest most of northern Italy away from the French. Napoleon seized power in 1799 and a fresh French army defeated the Austrians in Italy. By the end of 1800, the French were driving into southern Germany and the Austrian government sued for peace, bringing the French Revolutionary Wars to a close in early 1801.

# Society and Culture

*The Bridgewater Canal, the first of many canals built to open up trading routes between the major cities in Britain.*

## 1759 THE CANALS

INCREASE IN INDUSTRIAL production created problems. It meant that increased transport was required to carry goods to markets, and in the mid-eighteenth century, Britain's roads were dusty, pitted, muddy, icy, and dangerous, depending on the time of year. Factory owners had no faith in their carrying a regular supply of goods safely. The solution was water transport and after 1759, an artificial waterway, the Bridgewater Canal, was built to connect Manchester to the coal mines at Worsley, a 5¾ miles (9 km)

west of Manchester. A network of canals followed, built by gangs of strong, but rough-living navvies (navigators) who moved from location to location.

## 1770s DANGER IN THE MINES

MINES WERE EVEN MORE unhealthier than the mills and factories, if that were possible. Damp, cold, dark, dangerous, they were nevertheless the workplace for men, women, and children, who spent long hours underground. Children of four or five sat all day opening and shutting doors. Pregnant women hauling trucks loaded with coal risked miscarriages or worse. The railroads inside the mines could be death traps, if, for instance, workers lost their hold on a truck and were knocked down and run over. Gas escaping from the coalface could choke them to death. Ceilings could cave in and bury or trap them. Yet, there was no protection, and if mineworkers could not work, they faced dismissal.

## 1770S THE AGE OF ENLIGHTENMENT

THE HUMANISM of the Renaissance had its effects on philosophy and politics, and gained its most powerful impetus in the eighteenth century. This was the Age of Enlightenment, which sought to remake society in the light of pure reason. The ancient Greek concept of democracy came to the fore with revived ideas about representative government. The French political philosopher Jean-Jacques Rousseau (1712–78) set out his own theories of democracy, of the right to elementary education. The Scots economist Adam Smith (1723–90), author of *The Wealth of Nations* (1776), advocated the untrammeled workings of free enterprise and the importance of free trade. These ideas were revolutionary, given the values they sought to replace.

## 1787 THE ABOLITION SOCIETY

BRITAIN HAD BECOME the greatest slave-trading nation in Europe, yet it was here that the first positive moves were being made to get the inhumane trade banned. In 1787, philanthropists, driven by religious belief, formed the Abolitionist Society. Abolitionists interviewed slave-ship captains and crews to build up a picture of the horrors being perpetrated onboard slave ships during transportation. They faced objections from the large plantation owners, from those who believed Africans to be "natural" slaves, and from others who maintained that the slave trade was an excellent training ground for British sailors. Parliament finally banned the trade in 1807, 20 years later. Another 26 years went by before slavery itself was abolished in all British possessions.

*Granville Sharp (1735–1813), one of the earliest philanthropists to fight for the abolition of slavery.*

*French philosopher, author and liberal thinker, Jean-Jacques Rousseau (1712–78).*

### 1789 IDEAS OF REVOLUTION

THE FRENCH REVOLUTION was well primed with liberal ideas through the writings of Voltaire (François-Marie Arouet, 1694–1778) and Jean-Jacques Rousseau (1712–78). Its rallying cry of *Liberté, égalité, fraternité* (Liberty, equality, brotherhood) largely encapsulated their principles. The people became paramount in French revolutionary thinking, which also required a complete break with the repressive past. Now France was not the king's property as before, but belonged to all who lived there. A new calendar was introduced, with the year 1789 as Year One, as well as a new religion, and the Cult of the Supreme Being, to replace the old Catholicism. These innovations did not last, but the primacy of the people, which the Revolution promoted, had come to stay.

### 1790S THE DECLARATION OF EUROPEAN FEUDALISM

ALTHOUGH FEUDALISM had ceased in Britain after 1350, it still persisted in France and Russia. In France, the liberalizing revolution of 1789 brought it to an abrupt and bloody end. Russia was much more isolated from European trends and it was not until 1861 that Czar Alexander II (1818–81) freed the serfs and abolished feudalism. Russian feudalism had taken a particularly harsh form, and the serfs had been "property," sold along with the feudal estates they worked on. The czar was assassinated by anarchists in 1881, but even 20 years of freedom had not released their servile mindset. When anarchists called for rebellion against the czar, they refused, clinging pathetically to their traditional belief that the czar was the "Little Father," their protector and friend.

## 1790s BRITAIN STANDS BACK

IN BRITAIN, the notion of the French revolutionary concepts made little or no headway. The British, in fact, gave sanctuary to the many French aristocrats, or "aristos," who fled to their neighbor across the English Channel to escape the revolutionaries' vengeful slaughter of their class. British kings were not absolute monarchs, but constitutional sovereigns, subject to the will of Parliament.

Although most ordinary people had no voting rights, they had not been brutally suppressed like the French feudal peasants had been. There was also a fairly high degree of religious toleration in Britain, although anti-Catholic and anti-Nonconformist laws persisted. There was no deep-seated popular resentment against monarchy, nobility, or the aristocratic classes on which revolution could flourish in Britain.

*Westminster Palace, home to the British Parliament.*

# Exploration and Empires

### 1730s THE TURKS AND POLAND CRUSHED

SUCCESSIVE RUSSIAN rulers from the Empress Anna to Catherine the Great initiated wars against the Turks and took part in wider European conflicts throughout the eighteenth century. The first war against the Turks, launched in 1735, ended in a humiliating political settlement in 1739, in which the tremendous gains the Russians had made were given up when their Hapsburg allies signed a peace treaty. During the reign of Catherine the Great (1762–96), however, further gains were made at the Turks' expense. Russia also participated with the Hapsburgs and Prussia in three partitions of Poland, which extinguished that once-powerful eastern European state.

### 1741 THE WAR FOR NORTH AMERICA

THE GROWING WEALTH of the British colonies along the Atlantic coast of North America, in part based on the profits from slavery, attracted more and more settlers. These newcomers were desperate for land, and this resulted in a series of wars with French colonies in the St. Lawrence River Valley and around the Great Lakes. Although these coincided with the wars in Europe, they were fought independently. Fighting broke out in 1741, halted briefly in 1754, and resumed in 1754. At the end of the conflict in North America, in 1760, the British had pushed the French out of their main colony on the mainland—Quebec.

*Equestrian portrait of Catherine II the Great, of Russia.*

## 1757 THE END OF ISLAMIC INDIA

A NEW HINDU power that could withstand the advance of the Mogul armies arose in southern India during the end of the seventeenth century: these were the Marathas. The strength of numbers of the Marathas, combined with continued internal unrest in the Mogul Empire, helped to overthrow the effective power of the sultan in Delhi. He became effectively a figurehead ruler, and India was once more divided into warring states. Included among these parties at war were the European traders, who brought the conflicts from home to India. In 1757, the army of the East India Company, led by Robert Clive, defeated the army of the Naxab of Bengal at Plassey. The effect of this victory was to make England the strongest power in India and put an end to Mogul power.

## 1769 JAMES COOK

THE WORLD had not been completely explored or mapped, and there still remained many unresolved questions about the Pacific. The English sea captain James Cook (1728–79) helped answer many of these through his adventurous forages into the unknown seas in those parts. He plotted many unexplored areas in this part of the world from 1769 on.

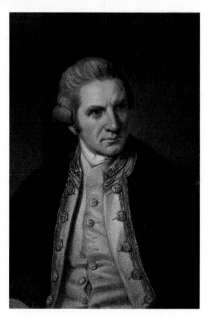

*Captain James Cook (1728–79), whose expeditions into the Pacific opened up the world to further settlement.*

Cook produced a chart of New Zealand and, after landing in Botany Bay, he claimed the Australian southeast coast for Britain, calling it New South Wales (1769). Cook also made an exploration of the Great Barrier Reef, and proved that New Guinea was not connected to Australia. He made another voyage to New Zealand between 1772 and 1775, before being killed in the islands of Hawaii by natives in 1779.

## 1780s DEFINING THE BOUNDARIES

FRENCH AID TO the American colonists, starting from 1778, tipped the balance of the war in favor of the Americans. In 1781, a large British army trapped at Yorktown, Virginia, surrendered. Fighting an alliance of France, Spain, and the American colonists was beyond British resources. In 1783, a treaty ended the war, but enforcing this independence was not easy. Britain saw no reason to give up valuable fur trading posts around the Great Lakes, while Spain hoped to gain territorial advantages in the lands north of Florida and east of Louisiana. It took a major war with the Native Americans of the Midwest and the aggressive deployment of soldiers in the South to secure the 1783 borders. By 1796, the borders of the United States had finally been firmly established along the Great Lakes and the Mississippi River.

## 1788 THE PENAL COLONY

ALTHOUGH SPANISH and French missionaries, traders, and whalers increasingly colonized the Pacific, Australasia was left to Britain, who decided to use New South Wales as a penal colony. Eleven ships carrying 700 convicts, 36 women, and guards, plus provisions for two years, arrived in Botany Bay in 1788 and settled around Sydney Cove. Few people traveled beyond the Great Dividing Range that stretches for 7,000 miles (4,800 km) up the east coast. The British had no powerful neighbors to threaten the colony, but faced the problem of economic viability and a population composed largely of criminals. In 1801, however, Napoleon Bonaparte (1769–1821) sent Thomas-Nicolas Baudin to the Australian coast. In response, Britain sent Matthew Flinders to survey the entire coastline of the country, which he called Australia.

*The governor of the newly established penal colony in New South Wales, inspecting convict settlers.*

*Pyramids Battle, or Cairo Battle, on July 21, 1798, between the French army led by Napoleon Bonaparte and the Mameluk army led by Mourad Bey.*

## 1793 CHINA IN CHAOS

CHINA'S RULERS REJECTED an attempt by Britain to widen the scope for traders in 1793. Trade took place, only on a controlled basis, in a few ports. However, the most popular import was an addictive drug, opium. The social havoc caused by opium led the Chinese to attempt blocking the supply, and started the First Opium War (1839–42). At the end of this conflict, Britain had acquired Hong Kong, and freer trade had been agreed. China now entered into chaos. In 1850, a dangerous revolt that threatened the ruling Manchu dynasty broke out in the south of the country. The Tai-ping rebellion eventually took control of central China for many years, until it was suppressed in 1864.

## 1798 FRANCE AND EGYPT

DURING THE WARS between France and the rest of Europe, the French government decided to threaten Britain's link with India by invading Egypt. In July 1798, they arrived off the Egyptian coast. The French conquered Egypt, but abandoned it following the defeat of their fleet and army by the British. In 1802, the French army left, and after several years of instability, Mohammed Ali came to power in 1809. Wanting to be an independent ruler, he pursued this aim single-mindedly, frequently with the support of the French. At the time of his death in 1849, Egypt controlled the Nile Valley as far as Khartoum, and both sides of the Red Sea coast.

# Trade and Industry

### 1700s TARIFFS

A TARIFF IS a schedule of customs duties generally imposed by a government on imports, and sometimes also on exports. Tariffs were originally levied to raise revenue. They were imposed mainly as instruments of government economic policy, possibly to protect domestic industries against foreign competition. It was common for a government to levy high, discriminatory tariffs to display hostility toward another. Equally, friendly nations might be accorded preferential treatment. Almost every peace treaty between warring powers in Europe after 1700 contained a most-favored nation clause, compelling the two sides to extend tariff treatment as favorable as that accorded to any other nation.

### 1709 COAL AND IRON

ABRAHAM DARBY (*circa* 1678–1717) independently developed the use of coal (in the form of coke) for blast furnaces to increase their output. This turned Europe and then North America into the

*The world's first iron bridge, built over the Severn in England in 1779.*

workhouses of the world for the next two centuries. Darby, who had used coke in smelting copper, founded the Bristol Iron Company in England in 1708. He acquired premises at Coalbrookdale, along the Severn River, near supplies of low-sulfur coal. In 1709, he made marketable iron in a coke-fired furnace. Soon, he was able to demonstrate superior cheapness and efficiency of coke by building much larger furnaces than were possible with charcoal as a fuel. The quality of the iron permitted the manufacture of thin castings, which were as good as brass for making such items as pots and other hollow wares. It was at Coalbrookdale that the world's first cast-iron bridge was built (1779).

## 1750s CHANGE IN EUROPE

IN WESTERN EUROPE, the most important change in agriculture in the mid-eighteenth century was the spread of potato cultivation. In the environment of, for example, Germany, the calorie content of a potato crop was about four times that of a grain crop. In the Balkans and Hungary, corn played a similar role in enlarging food-production capacity. In communications, France led the way in developing all-weather roads and a system of canals that connected with natural waterways. In manufacturing, England took the lead, offering plenty of scope for private enterprise and hands-on inventiveness. New crafts were also created by imitation of the products of other countries. By trial and error, Europeans learned how to replicate Chinese porcelain and many other valuable Chinese products, the manufacturing process of which was kept secret often for hundreds for years.

## 1760s THE COTTON INDUSTRY

RICHARD ARKWRIGHT (1732–92), an inventor and businessman, invented the first spinning frame, which could produce strong cotton thread. Arkwright was also the first person to use one of James Watt's steam engines to drive machines for spinning and weaving in a cotton mill. These machines could spin not just one thread at a time, as on a hand-powered spinning wheel, but hundreds of threads. Manchester became the center of the lucrative cotton industry in Britain and was sometimes known as "Cottonopolis." The city grew rapidly during the Industrial Revolution, but the people who worked in Manchester's cotton factories lived in poverty, in unhealthy, filthy, overcrowded slums, without running water, on unpaved streets lacking drains or sewers.

*Richard Arkwright's (1732–92) prototype spinning machine.*

## 1776 FREE-TRADE THEORY

THE FIRST FREE-TRADE theorists were a group of eighteenth-century followers of the economist François Quesnay. They maintained that the free movement of goods accords with the principles of natural liberty. Government intervention is justified only to the extent necessary to ensure free markets. This is because a nation's well-being is best secured if individuals are allowed freedom to pursue their economic interests. The free-trade system, which prevailed during the nineteenth century, received its most eloquent expression in *The Wealth of Nations* (1776), by the Scottish economist Adam Smith (1723–90). The policy stands in opposition to mercantilism, which put a high value on national self-sufficiency, guaranteed, if necessary, by high protective tariffs.

## 1782 WATT'S STEAM ENGINE

JAMES WATT (1736–1819) was the most important engineer of the Industrial Revolution. While working at the University of Glasgow, he was asked to repair a working model of a steam engine used for pumping water that had been invented by Thomas Newcomen in 1705. Realizing he could build much better engines, from the 1760s onward he applied himself to this. Using only one-quarter of the coal needed by earlier engines, these were cheaper and more powerful. In partnership with Matthew Boulton in Birmingham, Watt built steam engines that could drive all kinds of machinery, for example, to lift coal to the surface in mines. In Watt's first steam engine, a coal fire heated water to make steam. In 1782, he built the first rotary steam engine, with cogs and wheels, so that the engine could turn wheels and drive machinery. The watt, the unit of electrical power, is named after him.

*James Watt's (1736–1819) steam engine.*

## 1789 END TO SERFDOM

SERFDOM IN RUSSIA was a system in which the peasants were theoretically free tenants but were, in fact, in servitude to the landowners, who exploited them mercilessly, demanding ever-larger shares of the crops. By the late seventeenth century, serfs were usually heavily in debt to their masters and were virtually chattel slaves. The system persisted until the mid-nineteenth century in Russia and other parts of eastern Europe. Czar Alexander II (reigned 1855–81) abolished serfdom throughout Russia in 1861. In western Europe, feudalism and serfdom had almost disappeared by the eighteenth century, and the French Revolution of 1789 put the final nail in their coffin. Former serfs had by then attained a degree of economic independence and even became small landowners in their own right.

*Eli Whitney's (1765–1825) cotton gin.*

## 1793 THE COTTON GIN

TWO NOTABLE agricultural inventions of the eighteenth century were the seed drill, developed by the English agriculturalist Jethro Tull (1674–1741), and the cotton gin, invented in 1793 by the American inventor Eli Whitney (1765-1825). The seed drill cuts a furrow in the soil and then drops the seed through a tube. It sows the seed in rows, permitting cultivation between the rows and, thus, reducing the need for weeding. The seed drill featured a rotary mechanism on which all subsequent sowing implements were based. The cotton gin cleaned the cotton by separating the seeds from the fibers of the short-staple cotton plant (work hitherto done by hand). The efficient design remains in use today, almost unchanged.

# Science and Technology

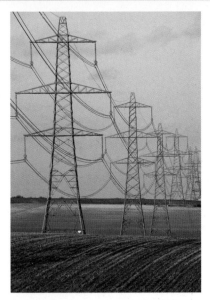

*The 18th century saw the discovery and first uses of electricity; today, it is an integral part of our landscape.*

## 1700s ELECTRICITY ENTERS THE PICTURE

VARIOUS EXPERIMENTS were conducted over the early half of the eighteenth century in an effort to understand the nature of electricity, more out of curiosity than through any recognition of its potential. One of Newton's pupils, Francis Hauksbee, invented a device called an Influence Machine in 1706. It was a glass globe that demonstrated the glow of air molecules by friction and the way electricity would attract various items of metal and threads. Stephen Gray discovered in 1729 that a thread would carry the attractive force down its length from the machine. In 1745, the Leyden jar was developed by Kleist and Musschenbroek as a means for storing electricity, and by 1749, electricity saw its first practical application, firing mines and other explosives. In 1786, Luigi Galvani showed that electricity stimulated movement in frogs' legs by inventing the cathode and anode cycle, which led in 1796 to fellow Italian, Alessandro Volta, building his Voltaic Pile battery, comprising of alternating layers of copper and zinc.

## 1700s NEWTON'S MATHEMATICS

ISAAC NEWTON (1642–1727) was an English physicist, astronomer, natural philosopher, alchemist, theologian, and mathematician, who laid the foundation for the discipline of modern physics by demonstrating that scientific principles are of universal application. He investigated various phenomena during his lifetime, making some notable discoveries and developing explanatory laws. His publication, *Philosophiae*

*Naturalis Principia Mathematica* (1687), is considered one of the most influential books in the history of science. In the 1700s, he developed theories on calculus, based on the work of fellow mathematician John Wallis. He also described three laws of motion and defined the nature of weight, mass, force, acceleration, and inertia. His most famous work concerned gravity, on which he expounded in 1685, saying, "Every particle of matter in the universe attracts every other particle with a force whose direction is that of the line joining the two, and whose magnitude is directly as the product of the masses, and inversely as the square of their distances from each other."

## 1720s CALCULATING MACHINES AND COMPUTERS

SEVERAL CALCULATING MACHINES were conceived before the Industrial Revolution. John Napier (1550–1617), Blaise Pascal (1623–62), and Gottfried Leibniz (1646–1716) all came up with devices. In the 1720s, Basile Bouchon devised a machine that worked on the punched-card principle of the Jacquard loom. In 1835, Charles Babbage (1792–1871) a British inventor and mathematician, conceived and drew up plans for his programmable computer named the "analytical engine." Due to its complexity, the machine was never made, but it embodied the principles on which modern digital computers are based. The American Herman Hollerith, made a tabulating machine that was used to take a census in 1890. It introduced individual punched cards as a means for sending or blocking signals, which could then be counted to calculate the census results.

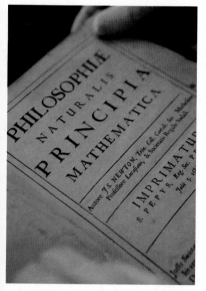

Philosophiae Naturalis Principia Mathematica *(1687) by Sir Isaac Newton (1642–1727).*

## 1733 TEXTILE AUTOMATION

AS THE INDUSTRIAL REVOLUTION gathered pace, one of the first large-scale industries to be affected by technological developments was the textiles industry. Many thousands toiled in textile mills, where processes had traditionally been very labor intensive. Then suddenly, engineers started introducing machines for automating processes that obviated the need for large workforces. The machines introduced included John Kay's (1704–64) flying shuttle in 1733, James Hargreaves' (*circa* 1720–78) spinning Jenny in 1767, Richard Arkwright's (1732–92) spinning frame in 1769, Samuel Crompton's (1753–1827) spinning mule in 1779, and Edmund Cartwright's (1743–1823) power loom in 1785. Added to these, James Watt's (1736–1819) steam engine was introduced in 1769 as a power supply, instead of water.

*Sir Richard Arkwright (1732–92), inventor of the first automated spinning machine.*

*James Hargreaves' (circa 1720–78) spinning Jenny, a machine that could spin eight bobbins at one time.*

## 1757 PRECISION ENGINEERING

ONE OF THE KEY FACTORS in the success of new industrial processes leading into the Industrial Revolution, was the ability of engineers to make very precise components for their new machines and apparatus. One area that demanded extreme accuracy, and, therefore, spearheaded such techniques, was instrumentation for navigation. The sextant was an instrument for calculating position by aligning the horizon with a specific star or the sun. When it had a telescope added to it in 1757, its potential for accuracy was improved considerably, but the divisions scribed on the scale (six for each degree) now needed to be marked far more accurately. The solution eventually came in 1774 with the Ramsden dividing engine. It introduced the concept of using a tangent screw or worm gear for making minute adjustments. The worm gear was then incorporated into lathes and other machinery and hailed the beginning of mass production of precision-made components in almost all areas of industry. The concept of interchangeable parts was also born, because the new machinery would now make things to exactly the same specifications every time.

it in 1770 in Paris. It was a cumbersome machine: difficult to steer and constantly running short of steam. Richard Trevithick (1771–1833) was the first to build a steam-powered locomotive, which he ran on the Penydarren Railway in Wales in 1804. By the 1820s, locomotives

*The first steam car tested by the inventor Nicolas Cugnot (1725–1804).*

## 1770 STEAM VEHICLES

AS WELL AS DRIVING the wheels of industry, the steam engine was recognized before long as a means for propelling vehicles. The first recorded example was a carriage designed for pulling field guns. Nicolas Cugnot (1725–1804) designed and constructed

were becoming a familiar sight and the brittle cast-iron tracks had to be replaced with wrought iron as the locomotives became heavier and more powerful. The first steam-powered boat was made by Claude d'Abbans and took to the water in 1783. The engine, made by Frèrejean et Cie, rotated a large paddle wheel.

*English chemist Henry Cavendish, who discovered hydrogen.*

### 1781 DISCOVERY OF HYDROGEN

WORK ON GASES eventually led to the realization that materials are either made up of pure elements or they are made from molecules, which comprise combination of elements. Henry Cavendish (1731–1810) discovered hydrogen by experimenting with acids on metals. In 1781, he ignited a mixture of hydrogen and air and was amazed to find that he had created water, which was thought to be an element. By 1814, a Swedish chemist called Jöns Berzelius (1779–1848) had devised various symbols to represent elements and compounds, and he went on to publish tables indicating atomic and molecular weights of over 2,000 chemicals. The Periodic Table, based on atomic mass, was devised in 1869 by Russian chemist, Dmitri Mendeleyev (1834–1907). The table grouped similarly massed elements together vertically and ranked them horizontally according to characteristics. It had to include blank spaces as well, indicating that there must be elements as yet undiscovered, which have since been found or artificially created by scientists.

### 1792 COAL REFINING AND APPLICATIONS

WILLIAM MURDOCH (1754–1839) invented an apparatus for processing coal by "destructive distillation," in 1792. By heating coal to very high temperatures without the presence of air, it would break down into component fractions, including gases, liquids, and solids, all of which proved to have useful applications during the Industrial Revolution. Coal gas was used for lighting and as a fuel for the internal-combustion engine. Coal tar was used for waterproofing canvas to make tarpaulin. Naptha was used as a solvent for rubber in the Macintosh process. Pitch, bitumen, and asphalt were used for building road surfaces and other sealing applications, such as in roofing.

Coke was the carbon content of the coal, bereft of all the other hydrocarbons listed above, and was used as fuel industrially and domestically. Its most important role by far was as the fuel in blast furnaces for producing the vast quantities of iron and steel consumed in the Industrial Revolution.

### 1796 INOCULATION/VACCINATION

INOCULATION FROM SMALLPOX had been practiced for many years before the Industrial Revolution by using infected tissue from a sufferer to induce a mild form of the disease in a healthy person, who would then develop resistance to the full-blown disease. There were inherent risks, however, which actually resulted in a higher overall mortality rate. In 1796, a British scientist called Edward Jenner (1749–1823) managed to inoculate a boy against smallpox by using cowpox vesicles. Cowpox was a related disease, which caused the boy to develop the antibodies in his system necessary to fight off smallpox. This became known as a nonvariolous vaccination, and established the practice of using either dead or related pathogenic organisms for inoculating against serious diseases.

*Dr. Edward Jenner (1749–1823), giving the first vaccination against smallpox.*

# Religions, Belief, and Thought

### 1700 THE BA'AL SHEM TOV AND HASIDISM

RABBI ISRAEL BEN ELIEZER, the "Ba'al Shem Tov," or "Master of the good name," was born in the Ukraine in 1700. After living in Spain, he worked as a lime digger in Romania. He became a herbalist and earned the title of "ba'al shem," and while practicing herbalism, he promoted his religious teachings through simple stories and parables. His teachings of joy in response to the immanence of God in the world and of the superiority of spiritual emotion over intellectual religious understanding proved highly popular among the uneducated Jews of eastern Europe. He meditated in the forests, taught that God was present in nature, and was prone to spontaneous singing, dancing, and storytelling. The emphasis upon sincere prayer and continual awareness of God's presence differed markedly from the legalistic and oppressive Judaism of his time.

### 1749 JOHN WESLEY AND THE METHODISTS

JOHN WESLEY (1703–91) was the founder of the Methodist movement, an offshoot of the Church of England.

*Founder of the Methodist movement, John Wesley (1703–91).*

The name derives from the methodical approach he applied to studying the Bible for developing personal devotion. He promoted his approach at outdoor sermons throughout Britain, to which he dedicated 12 years of his life. His decision to employ lay preachers in support of his mission, then ordain them, led to a split with the Church of England and in 1748 he created the Methodist Church. Reinforced by the profuse production of hymns by his brother, Charles, the movement spread rapidly in North America and Wales.

## 1762 ROUSSEAU'S *EMILE*

JEAN-JACQUES ROUSSEAU (1712–78) was renowned as the greatest liberal thinker and advocate of democracy and freedom in the eighteenth century. His writings covered every discipline from education to politics and from theology to science. All his doctrines were held together by his two underlying beliefs: the innate goodness of human nature and the natural world; and the corrupting influence of artificial culture. In his *Émile* (1762), he presented healthy education as a result of innate human curiosity about the world and not as a result of coercive lessons. The only healthy governments were those that emerged from a social contract between free and equal citizens. His thoughts on true Christian living involved allowing God to act in our lives and in nature and in minimizing our ignorant interference with this process.

## 1770s JEREMY BENTHAM AND UTILITARIANISM

JEREMY BENTHAM (1748–1832) was an English jurist, philosopher, and legal and social reformer. His utilitarian theory of ethics is that an act is good to the degree that it contributes to the greatest happiness of the greatest number of people. If an act gives one unit of pleasure to three people and causes two units of pain to another person, then it is better to do this act than not to do it. This "scientific" approach to ethics distinguishes it from approaches such as the Christian one, which are based on justice or on the intentions of the person acting. This position was developed by his student, John Stuart Mill (1806–73), in his book, *Utilitarianism* (1861).

*English Utilitarian philosopher Jeremy Bentham (1748–1832).*

*Johann Wolfgang von Goethe (1749–1832).*

## 1770s GOETHE'S CRITIQUE OF REDUCTIONISM

JOHANN WOLFGANG VON GOETHE (1749–1832), Germany's greatest literary figure, was one of the foremost critics of reductionist science in the eighteenth century. He argued that as the natural world can only be known through subjective and qualitative experience, the process of reducing these experiences to mathematical quantities was not empirical. He felt that scientists were deliberately blinding themselves to the reality of the natural world and replacing it with an abstraction. This allowed them to treat nature as an inanimate object and to exploit it for their own ends. To counter this problem, he attempted to develop a theory of color that incorporated the direct sensory experience of different colors. It is generally felt that his critique is of more value than the alternatives he developed.

## 1776 ADAM SMITH: *THE WEALTH OF NATIONS*

ADAM SMITH (1723–90) was a Scottish economist and philosopher and the founder of modern economics. His most important publication, *An Inquiry into the Nature and Causes of the Wealth of Nations* (1776), where he explores the functions of the market and explains how free trade, free enterprise, and the free division of labor can work together for

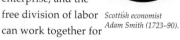

*Scottish economist Adam Smith (1723–90).*

the benefit of all. He describes this as the action of a "hidden hand." In common with the French *laissez–faire* economists, he advocated free international trade.

He is seen today as a politically "right-wing" thinker who advocated the selfish pursuit of profit. However, it is often forgotten that he also wrote and lectured extensively on social ethics, justice, and meaningful work. He was the author of the *Theory of Moral Sentiments* (1752) and donated the majority of his own wealth to charity.

## 1789 THE FRENCH REVOLUTION

"LIBERTÉ, ÉGALITÉ, FRATERNITÉ" was the rallying cry of the revolutionaries who stormed the Bastille in 1789 and overthrew the monarchy. The French Revolution was a series of political events that abolished the absolute power of the king and the rich landowners and replaced it with a Republic elected by all the people. The new government adopted the "Declaration of the Rights of Man and of the Citizen," declaring everyone equal and free and subject to fair taxes. Perversely, this was imposed through a reign of terror. The Revolution, despite its violence and tyranny, inspired political radicalism across Europe.

## 1792 ROBERT OWEN AND NEW LANARK

ROBERT OWEN (1771–1858), a manager of a spinning factory and disillusioned with poor working conditions, became a practical utopian. He sought in 1792 to create a new type of community in the village of New Lanark, Scotland, where originally children as young as five worked 13 hours a day. He created schools, increased the minimum working age to ten, decreased the working day, and supported trade unions, factory reform, and votes for all. He started another community, New Harmony, in the United States, which his son managed. His ideas were published in *A New View of Society* (1814).

*The town of New Lanark, Scotland.*

# Chapter 7

## The Nineteenth Century

THIS WAS A PERIOD in history marked by the collapse of many great empires, including those of the Spanish, Portuguese, Chinese, and Mogul empires. Their fall paved the way for the British Empire, the German Empire, and the United States to develop their interests and their power bases, prompting military conflicts but also advances in science and exploration.

The British Empire became the world's leading power, controlling one-quarter of the world's population and one-third of the land area. This was an era of invention and discovery that lay the foundation for the technological advances of the twentieth century. The Industrial Revolution began in Europe.

# Power and Politics

*The Buffalo Hunt.*

## 1800s NATIVE AMERICANS VS. SETTLERS

THE STATES OF THE Union in North America began to expand after the Constitution was ratified. This began the long period of conflict between the colonists and the Native Indians. In Georgia, the Cherokees, who had developed an advanced culture with newspapers, schools, and libraries, were evicted from their homelands. President Jackson forced them to west of the Mississippi, which was to become their final home. The journey west became known as the Trail of Tears. This was to be only the first of a series of evictions, culminating in the obliteration of the Sioux at the Battle of Wounded Knee in 1890.

## 1815 THE HAPSBURGS

THE HAPSBURGS, the Austrian royal family, ruled a large empire that covered much of central Europe. At the end of the Napoleonic War, they had been given most of northern and central Italy. Their empire was governed from Vienna by the emperor, but was very multinational and multilingual in character. To the east, there were Hungarians, Czechs, Slovaks, and Ruthenians; to the south, there were Italians, Croats, and Slovenes; and to the north, there were Poles. The Hapsburgs knew that of all the empires of Europe, theirs was the most vulnerable to nationalism. For 33 years, from 1815 to 1848, any sign of nationalism was eradicated without mercy.

## 1820s NATIONALISM

NATIONALISM, THE CONCEPT of the nation state was uncommon in the eighteenth century. Then autocratic power was exercised by hereditary royal families, not by the people whom they ruled. The French Revolution and Napoleon's empire created a new sense of national identity in France and abroad; as early as the 1790s, there were demands for reform in both Britain and Austria. The demands in Britain succeeded in the 1830s, but elsewhere autocracy struck back using repression. In the 1820s, radical movements in Europe were crushed by the armies of Russia, Austria, and Prussia.

### 1844 THE *ZOLLVEREIN*

THE *ZOLLVEREIN* was an economic union set up by Prussia in 1819. The Rhineland had been given to Prussia at the Treaty of Vienna in 1815 and the Prussians set common tariffs for all their territories, creating a "customs union," or Zollverein. Other German states joined, and by 1844, almost all of Germany was included. Although the Zollverein was not a political force, it led to Prussia being seen as the leader of Germany, with the result that many German states were drawn into a Prussian sphere of influence and away from Austria. It laid the basis for the nation-state of Germany, and challenged the German Confederation, set up in 1815, and dominated by Austria.

### 1857 THE INDIAN MUTINY

IN 1857, THERE WAS REVOLT against the East India Company by members of its own army. To the British, it was seen as mutiny; to Indians, it marked the beginning of Indian nationalism. The revolt began when a new cartridge was introduced. Muslims came to believe that it was smeared with pig fat. Hindus came to believe that it was smeared with cow fat. East India Company control broke down in many parts of northern India, and in 1858 the British government took over the government of India. In the

*The Indian Mutiny in 1857.*

1860s and 1870s, a number of nationalist movements were set up, culminating in the Indian National Congress, which led the fight for independence in the twentieth century.

### 1862 BISMARCK

OTTO VON BISMARCK (1815–98) became Chancellor of Germany in 1862. He was a conservative Prussian politician who wanted to extend Prussia's dominance in Germany by uniting the country under the King of Prussia. He followed the policy of *realpolitik,* which meant that he was ready to use any means to achieve his ends. In 1864, Bismarck, in alliance with Austria, declared war on Denmark and took Schleswig. In 1866, he signed a treaty with France and then picked a quarrel with Austria. The French remained neutral, but the Austrian army was crushed in seven weeks. When the peace terms were discussed, Bismarck insisted on being lenient to Austria; he knew that he would want its support in the future.

### 1871 ALSACE-LORRAINE

THE PROVINCES OF Alsace and Lorraine were taken by Germany at the end of the Franco-Prussian War. They became part of the new German Empire. This was bitterly resented in France. For more than 40 years, the statue in Paris, which represented the city of Strasbourg, the capital of Alsace, was draped in black cloth. *Revanchisme* (revenge) became

*Meeting between Otto von Bismarck (1815–98) and Napoleon III (1808–73) at Donchery.*

important in French politics. The French actress, Sarah Bernhardt, refused to appear on stage in Germany. When she was asked to name her fee by a theater manager, she sent a telegram back with the words "Alsace-Lorraine." It was obvious that sooner or later France would attempt to regain the two lost provinces, and the main battle plan of the French army, "Plan 17," involved a direct assault of the French army from Champagne into neighboring Germany.

### 1878 AUSTRIA VS. RUSSIA: SEEDS OF WAR

TURKISH POWER in the Balkans began to collapse in the middle of the nineteenth century. Greece became independent in the 1820s, and Romania, Bulgaria, and Serbia emerged at the end of the nineteenth century. This created an area in southeast Europe in which there were many small states, but no dominant great power. Both Russia and the Austrian Empire tried to advance into the Balkans. Austria was given control of Bosnia and Herzegovina in 1878 and annexed the territories in 1908. Russia formed an alliance with Serbia; they had a common script and the same religion. It was to be the clash between these two powers that was to lead to the outbreak of World War I in 1914.

## 1882 THE DUAL AND TRIPLE ALLIANCES

THE DUAL ALLIANCE, signed between Germany and Austria in 1879, became an important part of Bismarck's plan to give Germany security. If either power was attacked by Russia, the other would declare war. In 1882, the Dual Alliance was extended to become the Triple Alliance with the inclusion of Italy. While these agreements gave Bismarck some security, they isolated Russia, so in 1881 he had arranged the Alliance of Three Emperors, between Germany, Austria, and Russia. This agreement was renewed in 1884, but in 1887 Russia refused to sign. Bismarck quickly concluded a secret treaty with Russia, designed to prevent Russia from forming an alliance with France.

## 1894 THE DUAL ENTENTE

IN I887, WILHELM II became emperor of Germany. He soon disagreed with Bismarck and demanded his resignation. As a result, Russia refused to renew the Reinsurance Treaty in 1890, and relations between Russia and France grew closer. In January 1894, they signed the Dual Entente, which was intended to counter the Triple Alliance. Both powers agreed to defend the other if attacked by Germany and to mobilize their forces immediately if the powers of the Triple Alliance mobilized. The Dual Entente created the situation that Bismarck had tried for so long to avoid, the possibility of a war on two fronts, with Germany caught between the armies of France and Russia.

*Emperor Wilhelm II (1859–1941) of Germany.*

# War and Peace

*The death of Nelson at the Battle of Trafalgar, 1805.*

### 1805 TRAFALGAR AND AUSTERLITZ

IN ONE OF HISTORY'S most famous military maneuvers, Napoleon marched his main Grande Armée into Germany and surrounded the Austrian army. With their strategic center breached, the Austrians were unable to prevent the French occupation of Vienna, and in December 1805 the remaining allied army catastrophically lost the Battle of Austerlitz to Napoleon, knocking Austria out of the wars for several years. In the Atlantic, the French and Spanish navies were caught by the British fleet after their attempt to secure the English Channel for Napoleon. The resulting naval battle off Cape Trafalgar was one of the greatest in history, for its time, and resulted in the destruction of both the French and Spanish fleets, but at the cost of Nelson's life.

### 1813 THE BATTLE OF LEIPZIG

THE NEW ALLIED coalition of Great Britain, Russia, Prussia, Spain, Portugal, Austria, and Sweden slowly ground down the remaining French armies. Austria especially had not suffered a significant military defeat in eight years, and her relatively intact armies were to form the backbone of the 1813 and 1814 campaigns. Despite victories at the battles of Lutzen, Bautzen, and Dresden, the French Army suffered a crushing defeat at the huge three-day Battle of Leipzig in October 1813. By 1814, allied armies were advancing into France from every direction and despite continuing French resistance, Paris surrendered on March 31, 1814. A few days later, Napoleon surrendered to the coalition unconditionally, and was exiled to the island of Elba in the Mediterranean.

## 1835 THE TEXAN WAR OF INDEPENDENCE

IN NOVEMBER 1835, a convention of Anglo-American settlers set up a provisional state government and declared that Texans were fighting for the rights due them under the Mexican Constitution. A Texan army was quickly gathered and marched to attack the Mexican garrison at San Antonio. For 13 days, the small force defended the Alamo against more than 5,000 Mexican troops. On March 6, the Alamo fell. The Texans had almost 800 men when they faced Santa Anna's force of about 1,600 soldiers at San Jacinto. Taking the Mexican army by surprise, most of Santa Anna's troops were killed or wounded. Santa Anna was captured the next day, and in Velasco, on May 14, he was forced to recognize Texas's independence and to withdraw south of the Rio Grande.

*The Mexican army taking the Alamo, 1835.*

## 1845 MAORI WARS

IN 1841, NEW ZEALAND became a separate colony of Great Britain, and British government and settlements were established. The resultant loss of Maori tribal lands triggered the Maori revolts against British rule from 1845 to 1848 and again from 1860 to 1870. At Gate Pah, in 1864, the British attacked the Maori stockade with an overwhelming force. After a bombardment and several assaults the stockade fell with the loss of over 100 men. The Maoris had lost just 30, having abandoned their defenses just before the final assault. Peace was permanently established in 1871, however, after which the Maoris gained representation in the New Zealand Parliament that had been established in 1852.

*Hospital at Scutari, detail of Florence Nightingale on the ward.*

## 1854 CRIMEAN WAR

IN 1853, CZAR NICHOLAS I of Russia demanded the right to protect Christian shrines in Jerusalem, then part of the Turkish Empire. As a first step, his troops moved into the Turkish Balkans. By August 1854, Turkey, with the help of Britain, France, and Sardinia, had driven the Russian forces out of the Balkans. The allied troops landed in the Crimean peninsula on September 16, 1854, and laid siege to the Russian fortress of Sevastopol. Ferocious battles were fought at the Alma River, at Balaclava, and Inkerman. During the siege of Sevastopol, disease took a dreadful toll of French and British troops. Florence Nightingale's heroic work as head of the hospital service did much to improve conditions. By September 1855, Sevastopol was in allied hands.

## 1865 UNION

THROUGHOUT THE AMERICAN Civil War, the South were disadvantaged in terms of manpower and materials. The more populous and industrialized North could always deploy larger and better equipped armies in the field. The South, however, boasted some of the most talented commanders of the century: Stonewall Jackson, J.E.B Stuart, Jubal Early, and their senior commander, Robert E. Lee. Lee sustained the South far beyond their true capacity, defeating numerous Union generals in well-managed battles. He failed to defeat the Union army at Gettysburg, and in 1864 faced Grant, the new northern commander. Forced on to the defensive, he nevertheless inflicted heavy losses on Grant at the battles of the Wilderness, Spotsylvania, and Cold Harbor. Early in April 1865, he met Grant at Appomattox and surrendered the army of Northern Virginia.

## 1874 INCREASES IN MILITARY EXPENDITURE

BETWEEN 1874 AND 1896, European military expenditure increased by 50 percent. The czar, fearful of the horrors of modern warfare and concerned by the rise in spending, called a disarmament conference at The Hague in 1899. Even the Americans, who had only just recovered from a devastating civil war, took the position that any reduction in arms should be considered potentially dangerous to peace. In the event, the conference was doomed to failure and no meaningful agreements were reached.

## 1879 THE ZULU WAR

CONVINCED THAT THE independent Zulu kingdom adjoining the new British possessions in South Africa was a serious threat, an ultimatum was delivered ordering the Zulus to disband their army. Knowing that the Zulus would refuse, a British and colonial army under Chelmsford crossed the Buffalo River in January 1879. Hopelessly underestimating the tactical ability of

*The Battle of Isandhlwana during the Zulu War, 1879.*

the Zulus, Chelmsford split his forces and left the way clear for the enemy to attack the British camp. A full six British companies were slaughtered, in addition to several hundred colonial troops. A wing of the huge Zulu army crossed the Buffalo, but was driven off at high cost by a small force at the hospital station at Rorke's Drift.

## 1881 THE MAHDI

IN 1881, MUHAMMAD AHMED declared himself the Mahdi, the prophesied Muslim messiah who would rid the world of evil, and launched a holy war on infidel occupiers of Sudan. The Mahdi led a victorious attack on Al Ubayyid in 1883, and went on to capture the Darfur region of western Sudan, defeating an Egyptian army led by British Colonel William Hicks. In 1884, General Gordon was dispatched to Khartoum to evacuate Egyptian troops. The Mahdi's forces besieged Khartoum for ten months. On January 26, 1885, two days before British reinforcements arrived, Khartoum fell and the entire garrison were massacred. The British reconquered Sudan in 1898.

# Society and Culture

## 1800s LIFE AS A CONVICT EXILE

IN 1788, A BRITISH CONVICT FLEET
of 11 ships sailed for Botany Bay in
Australia. The worst punishment for
convicts except for the death penalty was
transportation to an unknown land as
far from Britain as possible. Fortunately,
when they reached Australia, the convicts
were able to use their work skills to
build houses and streets. They even built
prisons. Others were put to work laboring
on the land to produce food. Some,
however, resorted to crime and were sent
as prisoners to nearby Norfolk Island.
The conditions there were so frightful
that prisoners about to be hanged told
a visiting priest that they welcomed the
punishment since it would "take them
out of this terrible place."

## 1825 THE END OF SPANISH AMERICA

BY 1810, SPANIARDS, Natives Americans,
and the mixed-blood "mestizos," the
products of intermarriage, were united
in one stern and uncompromising
purpose: to end the tyrannical Spanish
rule in South and Central America.
Led by "El Libertador," the Venezuelan
Simón Bolívar (1783–1830), Colombia

*Simón Bolívar (1783-1830), South American revolutionary leader.*

(1819), Venezuela (1821), Ecuador (1822),
Peru (1824), and Bolivia (1825) fought
savagely against the Spaniards, neither
side giving respite. Bolívar and his fellow
liberators, José San Martin of Argentina
and Bernardo O'Higgins of Chile, were
defeated by Spanish troops several
times before the rulers, at last, suffered
a disastrous defeat at Boyacá, Colombia,
on August 7, 1819. Virtually the whole
Spanish army surrendered. Meanwhile,
Mexico and other Central American states
also wrenched their freedom from the
Spaniards and by 1825, Spanish rule in the
Americas had been brought to an end.

## 1840s CHINA HUMBLED AND REVIVED

IN 1839–42, THE BRITISH went to war with China over the Chinese reluctance to open its ports to the trade in Indian opium, which the British sought to use as currency for valuable imports, such as Chinese porcelain, silk, and tea. China, outclassed by the modern weapons used by the European power, had to yield Hong Kong and open five "treaty" ports. Another Opium War, in 1860, wrested more concessions from the Chinese emperor, who had to allow the British, French, and other foreigners to create enclaves on Chinese territory, where these trading nations would be immune from Chinese law. Later, these events became a strong motive for the Communist Mao Zedong (1903–76), who became ruler of China in 1949 and made it a recognized power in the world once again.

## 1864 THE RED CROSS

IN 1859, HENRY DUNANT (1828–1910), the Swiss philanthropist, was forced to draw the same conclusions about the state of medicine and medical care in war as Florence Nightingale when he witnessed the Battle of Solferino, at which there were 40,000 casualties. Dunant saw injured soldiers lying in agony and ignored on the battlefield, many bleeding to death from dreadful wounds as the fighting raged in the battle around them. Dunant, like Nightingale, was shocked and appalled by the situation, but he also refused to shrug off a condition that had been accepted as a consequence of war for centuries. In 1864, he founded the International Red Cross Organization to help in the care of battle casualties on both sides in a conflict. This humanitarian work extended before long to protection

*The Battle of Solferino, which shocked Henry Dunant into founding the Red Cross.*

for prisoners of war and ultimately extending to the relief of suffering throughout the world.

## 1865 FREEING THE SLAVES OF THE SOUTH

IN THE UNITED STATES, the southern states had relied heavily on slaves to work on the cotton and other plantations and by 1860, the South quarreled with the nonslave North, especially over what Southerners felt was undue federal interference from Washington. The matter was settled by the victory of the North in the American Civil War (1861–65), after which the slaves were freed. Some Southerners refused to accept that slaves were no longer slaves and in 1866, the Ku Klux Klan secret society was founded to reassert white supremacy. The Klan's aim was to terrorize the former slaves and anyone who supported them. The Klan disbanded in 1869, but was revived and still persists, although in a weaker form, to this day.

## 1872 NEW ARMED FORCES

THE JAPANESE had long been a warlike nation and had even turned war into sport, with martial arts kung fu, ju-jitsu, and kendo. Modern technological warfare, however, was entirely new in their experience when, after 1872, their army was trained by the Germans and their navy by the British. All this meant that modern battleships and weapons were acquired by a people who, barely 20 years earlier, had been so terrified by Perry's steam-assisted sailing ships that they called them *kurofune*, "smoking dragons." What was more, before modernization, so that no one could escape the bonds of isolation, the Japanese had been forbidden to build vessels that could sail more than a certain distance out to sea before they sank.

## 1880s MORE WESTERNIZATION

ANY OTHER NATION but the obedient Japanese might have suffered cultural collapse at the pace and extent of changes that, ultimately, enabled them to leap from a medieval society to a modern one within 40 years, one-tenth of the time it had taken in Europe. By 1882, the Bank of Japan had been established. The

*Brothers Auguste and Louis Lumière, French photographic manufacturers who invented the cinematograph.*

Cabinet was reorganized along German lines. Government papermaking and cotton-spinning plants were established, with steam power introduced into some 200 factories by 1890. Railroads, steamships, and electric power plants were constructed. The Japanese were soon catching up so fast that they were absorbing innovations not long after they first appeared in the West—for example, telephones, invented in the United States in 1869, and the movie theater, first introduced in France in 1895.

*A petrol-powered Panhard Levassor Phaeton with starting handle, 1896.*

### 1885 THE MOTOR CAR

MACHINES CAN LIBERATE. This was certainly true of the bicycle, which, after about 1890, enabled women, who took up cycling with especial enthusiasm, to travel farther than had ever been possible before. The same could be said of the motor car pioneered in Germany after 1885 by Gottlieb Daimler (1834–1900) At first a plaything for the rich, the car enabled many townspeople to venture out into the countryside for the first time. Country people were not always pleased at the invasion, but when the car gave thousands the kind of mobility that the horse could never offer, it increased knowledge and understanding of rural life and brought people, however reluctantly, closer together.

### 1895 POPULAR ENTERTAINMENT

THE BROTHERS Auguste (1862–1954) and Louis (1864–1948) Lumière gave the first movie performance in Paris in 1895. The images were so realistic that the audience, seeing a train coming toward them on screen, panicked. However, the movie theater quckly went on to become a rival to the music hall, and vaudeville theater. The music hall, sentimental, tuneful, and rowdy, expressed working-class aspirations. The better life for which they now felt able to hope was tempered by sadness at their distance from it. The first movies had no sound unless the pit orchestra chose to play an accompaniment. The United States was in the forefront of sound movie's development in the following decades.

# Exploration and Empires

*Sydney from St. Leonard's Road, North Shore, Australia.*

## 1800s SHEEP AND SETTLEMENT

BY 1800, THERE WERE 5,000 convicts around Sydney, Australia, and the introduction of Merino sheep from South Africa (1794) gave the colony an export product to attract free settlers. Coastal settlements sprang up, including Perth (1829), Melbourne (1835), and Adelaide (1836). By the 1830s, there were 100,000 settlers. A regular steamship service between Sydney and Britain from 1856 increased the population to one million by the 1860s, by which time convict transportation had ceased. The discovery of gold in Victoria (1851) led to an influx of settlers, but wool remained the main export commodity. Australia's colonies became self-governing in 1850 and British troops left in 1870.

## 1801 AFRICA VS. THE UNITED STATES AND EUROPE

THE MUSLIM countries of western North Africa had always derived their income from what to European eyes was piracy, but to Islamic ones was the duty of fighting the infidel. In 1801, the ruler of Tripoli declared war on the United States. This opened a series of minor military engagements between the North African states and European and American powers, which culminated in 1830 with a full-scale French invasion of Algiers. The French combined military might with a policy of settling French colonists in pacified regions. By 1847, the whole of the coastal strip and the fertile land between the Mediterranean Sea and the Sahara had fallen under French control.

## 1815 THE AGE OF IMPERIALISM

IMPERIAL EXPANSION was a continuous condition after 1815, as nations sought the prestige and profit of overseas conquest. In Africa, this became a "scramble" as new colonial powers (such as Germany and

Italy) increased the momentum to secure territories before their rivals. Peace was maintained between the colonists through the Berlin Conference (1884–85), which helped divide Africa into "spheres of influence." Great Britain made the greatest gains, including the territories of Egypt (1882), Nigeria (1884), British Somaliland (1884), Southern Rhodesia (1890), Northern Rhodesia (1891), and Sudan (1898). France also made significant gains, mainly in North and West Africa, including the French Congo (1875–92), French West Africa (1886), and Madagascar (1895–96). During the "scramble," Germany quickly built up its own African and Pacific empire, covering 1 million square miles (2.6 million sq km) and Italy seized Tripoli (1861), Eritrea (1889), Somaliland (1893), and Libya (1912).

## 1830s DARWIN'S VOYAGES OF DISCOVERY

THE GROWING VALUE of overseas trade caused governments to demand ever more accurate information about destinations in the far, and still largely unexplored, corners of the world. One British voyage to survey the South Atlantic and Pacific coasts of South America carried the naturalist Charles Darwin (1809–82). His studies of South American plant and animal life during the 1831–35 voyage of HMS *Beagle* contributed greatly to his theory of evolution. Darwin's researches encouraged the exploration of the Amazon Basin between 1848 and 1861 by the naturalists Alfred Wallace (1823–1913), Henry Bates (1825–92), and Richard Spruce (1817–93). The information acquired by scientific expeditions such as these was of great use to investors seeking new natural resources to exploit, and contributed to the development of a colonial economic relationship between South America and Europe.

*The Madagascar Expedition, with French soldiers in a street in Tananarive.*

## 1846 THE SUEZ CANAL

IN 1846, A GROUP OF Austrian, French, and British investors agreed that the time had come to cut a canal between the Mediterranean and the Red Sea, thereby providing a shorter sea route between Europe and the Far East. In 1858, a stock issue raised the money, work began in 1859, and the canal opened ten years later. The canal was vital to Britain, who now chose to interfere in Egypt's internal politics. In 1881, a group of Egyptian army officers seized control and the threat to the canal caused the British to occupy Egypt in 1882.

*The Suez Canal is an artificial sea-level waterway in Egypt, connecting the Mediterranean Sea and the Red Sea.*

## 1853 JAPAN AND CHINA RESIST

IN 1853, AMERICAN WARSHIPS arrived in Tokyo Harbor. They forced the Japanese government to sign a treaty opening Japanese ports to trade. The leaders of Japan made a determined effort to catch up with the European powers. The discipline of Japanese society enabled the process of modernization to proceed rapidly. In 1894, Japan fomented a war with China, and emerged victorious in 1895. As part of the settlement, Japan acquired Korea. In 1899, a resistance movement popularly known as the "Boxers" began a rebellion in China, which resulted in a siege of the foreign diplomat's compound at Peking. An international army crushed the rising, ending China's hopes of regaining control.

## 1860s CROSSING AUSTRALIA

THE FIRST CROSSING of Australia (1860–61) was completed by Irishman Robert Burke and William Wills riding on camels, the first use of the animals in the country. Both perished on the return journey.

British surveyor John MacDonnell Stuart completed the first south-north crossing (1860–62) on his third attempt after overcoming water shortages, Aborigine hostility, and heat. During the 1860 trek, Stuart found and named the MacDonnell Ranges and came within 150 miles (240 km) of the center of Australia. Such crossings enabled the government to begin linking Australia by telegraph and railroad. By 1900, explorers had reached most of the "outback," but the demanding terrain and temperatures they experienced had confirmed the belief that the interior was unsuitable for settlement.

## 1885 THE FIRST STIRRINGS OF NATIONALISM

VIOLENT RESISTANCE to colonial rule had been common for centuries, but the first systematic political challenge arose with the Indian National Congress (established 1885). This aimed to further the powers of Indians who were already entering the civil service. Similar movements later emerged elsewhere, such as the National Congress of British West Africa (est. 1918) and the South African Native National Congress (est. 1912). Despite these movements, only Britain offered any measure of self-government to its colonies by making Canada, New Zealand, Australia, and South Africa into independent "dominions." Such freedoms were, however, restricted to colonies where white settlers were a large or dominant section of the population.

*British troop commander in Boer War campaign being cheered by his troops.*

## 1099 THE BOER CHALLENGE TO THE BRITISH EMPIRE

THE GREATEST CHALLENGE to British power in this century arose in South Africa in the form of the Boers (Dutch settlers). Two Boer republics had become enclosed by British territories, and conflict between the settlers began to arise. Increasing friction between the Boers and the British escalated into war after Cecil Rhodes (1853–1902), Prime Minister of Cape Colony 1890–96, attempted to seize the diamond and gold areas of the Boer republics. Throughout the Boer War (1899–1902) the British suffered serious defeats at the hands of the Boers, until many of the Boer communities were placed in concentration camps. Their property was destroyed, denying the soldiers supplies and, thus, turning the fortunes of the war.

# Trade and Industry

### 1802 TELFORD'S ROADS

THOMAS TELFORD (1757–1834), nicknamed "the Colossus of roads," was one of the most important civil engineers of the Industrial Revolution. From 1793, he built canals, including the Ellesmere Canal, to carry raw materials and finished goods from Wales to the Mersey River. In 1802, he was made responsible for building and repairing a network of roads in the Scottish Highlands. He invented a new solid-gravel road surface that could take wheeled vehicles and withstand harsh weather. The 875 miles (1,400 km) of new roads and 11 bridges he built changed the whole way of life in the Highlands. Telford's supreme achievement was the building of a 288 miles (460 km) road from London to Holyhead, North Wales, which took 15 years. He used explosives to blast away rock to make new passes. Of the several bridges along the route, the Menai Straits suspension bridge is the most famous.

### 1803 THE OPENING UP OF AMERICA

IN 1803, THE UNITED STATES bought the lands west of the Mississippi from France for $11,250,000. The Louisiana Purchase doubled the country's size. Thousands of people now began to move westward to settle in and cultivate the new territories. The new settlers drove out the Native Americans who lived on the Plains. The move west picked up speed after the American Civil War in the 1860s. The first American railroad was opened in South Carolina in 1830. By 1880, the U.S. rail network was bigger than that of Europe. Rail transport made the development of the country possible in spite of the great distances between places. Goods could be sent cheaply and easily to market in exchange for factory-made equipment for farm use.

*Thomas Telford (1757–1834), Scottish civil engineer.*

*The U.S. railroad network joins East and West, May 10, 1869.*

## 1824 TRADE UNIONS BECOME LEGAL IN BRITAIN

TRADE UNIONS are organizations of employed workers, formed mainly for the purpose of collective bargaining. Journeymen's guilds existed in the Middle Ages (journeymen being workers hired on a daily basis), but modern trade unionism was a product of the Industrial Revolution. In Britain in 1799, the Combination Law made all unions illegal and they had to function largely as secret societies until 1824, when the law was repealed and unions became legal organizations for negotiating terms of wages and hours of labor. In the U.S. they were known as labor unions. In 1825, it was the carpenters of Boston that were the first to stage a strike to demand a 10-hour working day. The labor union movement then grew steadily in numbers and influence.

## 1830 THE SCRAMBLE FOR AFRICA

FRANCE, WHOSE first major African territory was acquired with the conquest of Algeria in 1830, dreamed of "civilizing" Africa, while building a vast empire across the top of the continent. Britain championed a scheme for a "Cape to Cairo" railroad. British motivation was mixed: trade, territorial power, missionary zeal to Christianize the continent, and the wish to populate much of the world with British settlers to guarantee the future of the Anglo-Saxon race. The Germans arrived late on the scene (1884), but thereafter expanded rapidly. The Italians tried but failed to take Ethiopia in 1896. The Belgians and Portuguese also staked claims, essentially to African resources. Clashes inevitably occurred between the European imperialists and, indeed, contributed to the international tensions that precipitated World War I.

## 1839 OPIUM WARS

IN THE 1830s, many Chinese had begun to smoke opium, and the British and other Europeans were happy to supply the drug, which was produced mainly in India. When Chinese officials forbade its import, European traders got around this by smuggling and bribery. In 1839, the Chinese sent a commissioner to Canton to clamp down on the illegal importing of Opium. When the Chinese destroyed a large cargo of the drug, war broke out. The British landed troops and took the city of Shanghai. In the Treaty of Nanking (1842), four ports in addition to Canton were opened to European trade and Hong Kong was ceded to the British. Fighting resumed in 1856, and in 1860 an Anglo-French force seized Peking. Other Western nations received privileges and even went one better, gaining exemption from Chinese law for their nationals living on Chinese territory.

## 1848 GOLD RUSHES

JAMES MARSHALL was building a mill on the banks of the Sacramento River, California, in 1848, when a sudden gleam in the water caught his eye. It was gold. Within a year, thousands of people gripped by gold fever were rushing to California. Prospectors came even from as far away as Europe in the hope of making their fortunes. The Californian Gold Rush had started. The same thing happened after gold was found in the Australian outback in 1851. As is often the case, most of the prospectors were not lucky, but wherever there was gold, mining towns would spring up and populations exploded. Eventually, the demand for coins outstripped the amount of gold being produced in the world. Minted coins were then given a symbolic value unrelated to the amount of precious metals they contained. Nowadays, most gold is stored, nearly half of it at Fort Knox Gold Depository. Only exceptionally is the precious metal used for coins.

*Riverboats moored in the port of Sacramento, originally a mining town founded during the Gold Rush of 1848.*

## 1850s MASS PRODUCTION

THE AMERICAN CIVIL WAR created a demand from the government for cheaper guns with interchangeable parts, which could be repaired quickly on the battlefield. Beforehand, all parts had been made in workshops, but now they were made in engineering factories. All the parts were standardized. Finishing was no longer done by hand but by machine tools. Once these systems were in place, mass production became possible. The skilled craftsman was replaced by the unskilled or semiskilled worker, whose job was to be responsible for one small, specialized operation. This was the basis for the production line, which Henry Ford developed in the 1920s for automobile manufacture.

## 1850s THE INDUSTRIAL REVOLUTION IN EUROPE

IN EUROPE, MACHINE SHOPS first developed in Liège, Belgium, after 1807, and soon afterward in France. Germany took the lead in the 1850s in the new technologies of chemicals and steel. The firm of Krupp, founded in 1811 in the Ruhr region, produced armaments as well as steel wheels for trains on the expanding German railroad system. Before World War I, Krupp pursued a benevolent social policy toward its machine-shop workers. A major contribution to the steel industry was the invention of the blast furnace for refining ore. The blast furnace operated on the principle that a blast of air forced through a mixture of solid fuel and ore burns away

*Silesian furnaces at Borbeck, Germany, 1855.*

impurities and converts them to slag, which is insoluble and can be skimmed off, leaving a more pure form of steel.

## 1895 RUBBER

SEEDS FROM THE rubber tree were brought from Brazil in 1876. The first commercial planting of rubber in Malaya occurred in 1895 and development was rapid in the European-controlled countries of Southeast Asia. Here, the temperature and humidity are high all year round and there was a large, cheap, and skilled labor force. The rapid growth of the motor-vehicle industry after 1905 greatly stimulated natural rubber production. The Japanese occupation of Southeast Asia in World War II, however, blocked much of the world's natural rubber supply and boosted the development of a massive synthetic rubber industry, particularly in the United States.

# Science and Technology

*Power loom weaving, 1834.*

## 1800s MASS-PRODUCTION TECHNIQUES

THE MOST CRUCIAL development in the latter half of the eighteenth century was mass production. Textiles and ceramics saw huge expansion of their industries, bringing a shift of labor force from working the fields to working in town factories. Henry Maudslay of Britain introduced a new lathe in 1800, dubbed the "go-cart," which revolutionized the production of precision parts. Championed by Marc Isambard Brunel (1769–1849), Maudslay went on to develop a production line for the mass production of ships' blocks. By 1808, he had perfected five machines, which only needed ten unskilled men to operate them. In the United States, Elisha King Root began developing mass-production techniques associated with farming. In 1832, he established a factory for producing steel ax heads, and in 1837 John Deere began mass producing steel plowshares. Both tools were essential for clearing and dressing vast tracts of land for agricultural use in the United States and Russia during the second quarter of the nineteenth century.

## 1820s ASPHALT AND CONCRETE

IN THE LATE 1820s, John McAdam (1756–1836) of Scotland devised a new process for making hard-wearing road surfaces. He used a mixture of heated bitumen or asphalt and stones, which would set by cooling to provide a smooth, durable top layer. His invention was dubbed "Macadamizing." It became such a success, the process has remained a ubiquitous form of road surfacing throughout the world ever since. Portland cement was invented by Joseph Aspdin of Yorkshire, England in 1824. It proved to be a versatile building material indeed. By 1867, steel-reinforced concrete had been patented by Joseph Monier of France. The first reinforced concrete building was erected in the United States in 1872 and the first concrete road was laid in 1892, also in the United States.

## 1826 PHOTOGRAPHY AND CINEMATOGRAPHY

THE FIRST PHOTOGRAPHIC image was taken in 1826 by Joseph-Nicéphore Niepce (1765–1833) in France. His long-time assistant, Louis Daguerre (1789–1851) made an improvement to the process, which came to be known as the daguerreotype in 1839. The first photographic printmaking process, using the negative-positive method on paper, was invented in 1835 by William Henry Fox-Talbot, which meant duplicate copies could, for the first time, now be made. The first color photograph, taken by James Clerk-Maxwell (1831–79), and the invention of the single-lens reflex (SLR) camera by Thomas Sutton both occurred in 1861. The first successful attempt at producing a moving photographic image was made by Louis Aimé Augustin Le Prince in New York in 1885. Cinematography had been invented.

*French photography pioneer Louis Daguerre (1789–1851).*

*Alexander Graham Bell (1847–1922), inaugurating the New York-Chicago telephone system.*

## 1835 TELEGRAPH TO TELEPHONE

IT WAS THE INVENTOR of the Morse code, Samuel Morse (1791–1872), who built the first electric telegraph in 1835. Electrical pulses were sent along the telegraph wire using his code; at the receiving end, a series of clicks were heard, which had to be deciphered by the operator. This was the first modern form of telecommunication. In 1876, Alexander Graham Bell (1847–1922) made an assemblage of components devised in part by other electrical scientists, which he had improved upon for practical application. He had invented the telephone by doing so, and was able to transmit the first spoken message via an electrical wire. Important in their own right were the microphone and loudspeaker he had developed, which found plenty of other applications.

## 1859 EVOLUTION

TWO ENGLISHMEN were responsible for the discovery of the theory of evolution. Both of them were aware that the variety in species, including humans, seemed to suggest an ability for living things to change over time. Charles Darwin (1809–82) spent five years as a naturalist onboard the HMS *Beagle*,

*Alfred Russel Wallace, Welsh naturalist and explorer.*

1831–36. He visited the countries of South America and the Galápagos Islands. What he saw led to the development of his theory, but he spent many more years looking for tangible evidence before publishing his theories. Alfred Russel Wallace (1823–1913) was 14 years younger than Darwin. He became a professional naturalist, making a living by collecting specimens of plants and animals to send back to Europe from South America and Southeast Asia. By 1858, he had arrived at the same idea of "evolution by natural selection" as Darwin, and sent an outlining essay to him. When Darwin received this he was shocked to realize that he had spent too long expounding his own theory and quickly published *On the Origin of Species by Natural Selection or the Preservation of Favored Races in the Struggle for Life* in 1859.

## 1867 ANESTHETIC AND ANTISEPTIC

ONCE SCIENTISTS BEGAN to understand that microorganisms were responsible for infection and disease, a whole new approach to medicine and surgery was initiated, thanks to the microscope and the accidental discovery that it was possible to sterilize food by heating it. Joseph Lister (1827–1912) was the first surgeon to introduce an antiseptic into his routine, in 1867. He used a spray or carbolic acid (phenol), an extract from coal tar, to kill and inhibit pathogens. By 1874, Abraham Groves (1847–1935), had introduced the practice of sterilizing surgical instruments and wearing rubber gloves. Anesthesia,

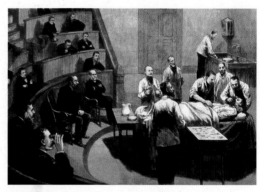

*Dentist William T.G. Morton, giving the first public demonstration of ether anesthesia in the Boston hospital.*

although practiced for centuries in the form of alcohol as an analgesic, became more of a science at this period. William Morton, an American dentist, coined the word "anesthesia" in 1846, when he adopted the use of rectified sulfuric ether.

## 1877 THE PHONOGRAPH

HAVING INVENTED a way of transmitting human voice, the telephone, a way for recording audible messages was sought. In 1877, the famous inventor Thomas Edison (1847–1931) invented and made the first public demonstration of such a machine, which he called the phonograph. It comprised a cylinder held on a rotating drum, which was covered in tin foil. Sound waves were converted, via a vibrating needle touching the foil, into a spiraling sound track or line onto the surface of the tin foil. When the machine was operated in reverse, the same needle would pick up the characteristics of the scribed line and an amplifier transmitted an audible form of the recorded sound. The gramophone record, a horizontal disk, as opposed to Edison's drum, was invented by Emile Berliner (1851–1920) in 1887. The first gramophone records were made from shellac, a hard and brittle resinous substance derived from the lac insect.

*Gramophone player.*

## 1888 RADIO WAVES

BOTH THE TELEGRAPH and telephone communication systems relied on a physical wire link to be able to convey a transmitted message. This type of technology had obvious limitations. Wire could be cut and frequently had to be laid over long distances at great expense, although the first submarine telephone cable was successfully laid across the Atlantic Ocean in 1857, linking

*Guglielmo Marconi (1874–1937) testing the wireless telegraphy across the English Channel.*

the voices of the United States and Europe for the first time. Twelve years after the invention of the telephone, in 1888, a German scientist named Heinrich Hertz (1854–94) discovered the existence of radio waves. This led the brilliant Italian, Guglielmo Marconi (1874–1937) to make the first successful transmission using the newly discovered radio waves. Marconi quickly demonstrated that radio waves could be sent without the receiver even being visible. In 1901, the first radio transmission all the way across the Atlantic was made, and the domestic "wireless" was only a few years away. Marconi's invention had an immediate impact on world communications, particularly early on with shipping, because the telegraph and telephone could not be used.

## 1895 RADIOACTIVITY AND X-RAYS

WHILE EXPERIMENTING with a cathode ray tube in 1895, which would later be developed into the television, Wilhelm Röntgen (1845–1923) noticed a new phenomenon. Invisible rays being emitted by the device, which he dubbed X-rays, were causing various chemicals to glow. He then discovered that the rays, although invisible to the eye, would affect a holographic plate. What was more, the

*Wilhelm Röntgen (1845–1923) won the Nobel Prize for his discovery of X-rays.*

X-rays had the ability to travel through some solid materials and not others, which meant that they could be used to see inside the body and look for breaks in bones, or pieces of metal, such as bullets or segments of shrapnel. X-rays are high-frequency, electromagnetic radiation waves. Röntgen's discovery made an enormous contribution to medical diagnosis, which had previously relied on a great deal of guesswork and painful manipulation of the patient.

# Religions, Belief, and Thought

## 1800s AMERICAN TRANSCENDENTALISM

RALPH WALDO EMERSON (1803–82) and Henry David Thoreau (1817–62) initiated a philosophical and literary movement known as American Transcendentalism, which drew upon the teachings of the *Bhagavad Gita* and other Eastern texts to provide a basis for experiencing the divine in the natural world. Despite its somewhat exotic origins, the movement's values, such as self-reliance and simple living, fitted well with American society and have inspired many significant events from the first World Parliament of Religions in Chicago to the conservation movement and the creation of national parks.

Moroni appeared to him and told him about the *Book of Mormon*, a record of the early inhabitants of the Americas and their prophets. In 1827, Joseph Smith received the *Book of Mormon*, which was written on plates of gold, and he translated it into English in 1829. This book supports and verifies the Bible and contains witnesses of Jesus Christ

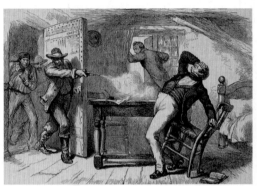

*Illustration of the murder of Joseph Smith, founder of the Mormon Church, along with his brother Hyrum.*

## 1830 JOSEPH SMITH AND THE MORMON CHURCH

THE CHURCH OF Jesus Christ of Latter Day Saints was founded by Joseph Smith (1805–44), following a vision in 1820 in which he was visited by Jesus Christ and God the Father. In 1823, the angel

from ancient America. For this reason, it is called the *Book of Mormon*: Another Testament of Jesus Christ. Joseph Smith organized the Church with himself as the prophet in 1830. Opponents drove him and his supporters out of several states, and in 1844, Joseph Smith was killed in

Carthage, Illinois. Most of the remaining members of the Church moved to Utah and founded Salt Lake City under the leadership of Brigham Young.

### 1836 COMMUNISM

KARL MARX (1818–83), a middle-class German Jew, studied philosophy at the University of Berlin from 1836 before editing a radical newspaper. After the failed 1848 revolt in Germany, he fled to England, where he attempted to provide a scientific foundation for socialism through his books, *The Communist Manifesto* and *Das Kapital*. In both these books, he countered the utopian socialism of Proudhon and Bakunin. Like the English economists, he saw production based on land, labor and capital, but he pointed out that whoever controls the mode of production controls the economics and politics of the country. When production is controlled by landowners, it causes feudalism; when controlled by investors, it causes capitalism; when controlled by laborers, it causes socialism. Public ownership of the means of production was seen as the basis for fair and meaningful work.

*Karl Marx (1818–83), the first exponent of Communist ideals.*

### 1836 THE BIRTH OF RAMAKRISHNA

RAMAKRISHNA WAS a Hindu mystic from Bengal, India. Earlier in life, as a priest he practiced *bhakti*, devotional prayer to the god Kali. He experimented with prayer, meditation, and worship in several of the other major religions, including Islam and Christianity, and had ecstatic visions as a result of each of these. He is chiefly remembered for teaching that there is one God common to all religions. His life is commemorated in the work of the Ramakrishna Mission, created by his disciple Swami Vivekananda (1863–1902).

## 1840s REFORM AND CONSERVATIVE JUDAISM

THE 1840S MARKED the emergence of several distinct movements in Judaism that split from traditional Orthodoxy. These were rooted in recognition by Jews that they were citizens of their host nations and not a nation within a nation. Reform Judaism, which developed among immigrants to the United States, was an attempt to adapt Judaism to Western society by distinguishing between the unchangeable and universal teachings of Judaism and those that were merely cultural traditions. Conservative Judaism made a similar distinction but treated far more of the teachings as unchangeable. This approach was opposed by the Zionists, who saw themselves primarily as citizens of the future nation of Israel—a stance that brought them into conflict with the societies they lived in.

## 1859 EVOLUTION AND SOCIAL DARWINISM

*ON THE ORIGIN OF SPECIES*, by English biologist Charles Darwin (1809–82), was published in 1859. Alfred Russel Wallace independently reached similar conclusions about the nature and process of evolution. The

On the Origin of Species *by Charles Darwin (1809–82).*

idea that species developed over time, and that humans had developed from apes, shook the intellectual world and, especially, Christianity. Other scientists, using his idea of the "survival of the fittest," concluded that Europeans had conquered the world because they were more evolved (although Darwin did not say this). Social Darwinists believe that life is an endless struggle and that only the most assertive and aggressive people, businesses, and nations survive. Peter Kropotkin, in his *Mutual Aid*, countered this argument by pointing out that the ability to cooperate was a form of fitness that encouraged survival.

## 1893 SWAMI VIVEKANANDA AND THE REDISCOVERY OF HINDUISM

SWAMI VIVEKANANDA (1863–1902) was a disciple of Ramakrishna and the most important recent systematizer of Hindu thought. In developing a philosophy that brought together all the main strands of the Hindu tradition, from *advaita* (meditation) to *bhakti* (devotion), he virtually created modern Hinduism. The central teaching is that God is beyond all concepts and images and can be known directly through meditation, but that God also takes forms and so devotional worship is also a true form of religion. As well as providing a means to unite Hinduism, it provided a means to bring harmony between all faiths; and this resulted in worldwide attention when he spoke at the 1893 World Parliament of Religions.

## 1893 GANDHI'S CAMPAIGN BEGINS

MOHANDAS GANDHI (1869–1948), known as Mahatma (meaning "Great Soul") is revered today as the father of the Indian nation. Born near Bombay in 1869, he studied law in England, then as a barrister moved to South Africa. He first experienced the apartheid policy when he was thrown out of a first-class railroad coach at Pietermaritzburg in 1893.

From then on he campaigned for justice using *ahhimsa* (nonviolence) or what he called *satyagraha* (truth force). In 1909, he established Tolstoy Farm, a self-sufficient vegetarian community for his satyagrahis. On returning to India in 1914, he dedicated himself to obtaining Indian independence from the British Empire through nonviolent action. With independence, the country underwent partition into Muslim Pakistan and largely Hindu India. Over one million died in the resulting religious conflict. However, Gandhi promoted religious harmony. Hindu extremists, angered at this policy, assassinated him in 1948.

*Mohandas Gandhi (1869–1948).*

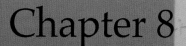

# Chapter 8

## The Twentieth Century and Beyond

WITH TWO WORLD WARS devastating many nations, the United Nations was formed to help prevent future wars. However, antagonism between the new superpowers, the Soviet Union and the United States, resulted in the Cold War. Near the end of the century, the Soviet Union collapsed, and the United States became the sole superpower.

As a result of changes in politics, economics, society, culture, science, and medicine, the century saw a major shift in the way people lived. It was a century that started with horses as the main mode of transport, but ended with our exploration of space. Now, early in the twenty-first century, the offer of more efficient communications, advancements in technology, and faster transportation promises a world that will change more rapidly and widely than ever before.

# Power and Politics

### 1904 THE ENTENTE CORDIALE

THROUGHOUT THE SECOND half of the nineteenth century, Britain had avoided any long-term European commitments. British politicians took part in conferences and agreements, but undertook no treaty obligations. In 1902, however, Britain signed a treaty with Japan, and in 1904 it signed the much more important Entente Cordiale with France. These treaties brought to an end the period of "Splendid Isolation" in British foreign policy. Three years later, in 1904, Britain signed an entente with Russia, so creating the Triple Entente. This effectively meant that Europe was now divided into two armed camps, each made up of three powers and each with a series of built-in clauses, which involved automatic and immediate military action. The stage was now set for a showdown.

### 1914 SARAJEVO

THE ARCHDUKE Franz Ferdinand, heir to the Austrian throne, and his wife were assassinated, shot dead by a Serbian terrorist Gavrilo Princip on June 28, 1914. Under normal circumstances this incident would have passed without major repercussions, but the buildup of alliances

ASSASSINAT DE L'ARCHIDUC HÉRITIER D'AUTRICHE ET DE LA DUCHESSE SA FEMME A SARAJEVO

*The assassination of Archduke Franz Ferdinand and his wife Sophie at Sarajevo on June 28, 1914.*

and the consequent heightening of tensions in the Balkans turned what would have been a political matter into an international tragedy. The Austrian government had been looking for an excuse to crush Serbia, which stood in their way in the Balkans. When Russia mobilized in support of the Serbs, Germany automatically became involved, and this brought in France. By August 12, all the major European powers were involved in a catastrophic fighting match in the form of World War I, which would last for more than four years.

## 1917 THE OCTOBER REVOLUTION

FROM MARCH TO OCTOBER 1917 Russia was ruled by the Provisional Government. This had no legal standing, but it was intended to govern until a general election could be held, planned for November. The Provisional Government gradually became more and more unpopular, partly because it decided to continue the war against Germany, but also because food shortages

*Portrait of Russian revolutionary and Communist theorist Leon Trotsky (1879–1940).*

and inflation grew even worse. On October 24–25, the Bolsheviks overthrew the Provisional Government in a coup planned and led by Leon Trotsky, Lenin's second in command. A month later the general election was held. This was won by the Socialist-Revolutionary Party, but when the Assembly met in January, Lenin dissolved it by force and began to rule as a dictator.

## 1919 THE RISE OF FASCISM

FASCISM DEVELOPED in Italy after the end of World War I. The term came from the Roman word *fasces*, a bundle of rods and an ax, that was carried before a Roman magistrate. They represented the power of a magistrate to order corporal punishment and capital punishment. The fasces became the symbol of the Italian Fascist Party. Fascists believed in a strong central government headed by a dictator. They thought that ordinary people should be prepared to sacrifice their own personal liberty for the good of the state. For example, they believed that men and women had different roles in society. The Fascist Party opposed foreign influences and instead wanted Italy to be self-sufficient. They described this economic system as "Autarky."

## 1920s THE WARLORDS

IN THE 1920S, THE central government in China broke down and power fell into the hands of local rulers who became known as the "Warlords." Although some, such as Yen Hsi-shan of Shensi, ruled efficiently, most were simply local rulers taking advantage of the situation. The Warlords were eventually crushed in military campaigns led by Jiang-Jieshi, which gave him even more power within the Kuomintang and led to a split in 1927 between the Nationalist members on one side and the Radicals and Communists on the other. The Communists, led by Mao Zedong, set up a commune in Kiangsi, where they lived until 1934. They were then forced to leave and set out on the Long March to the province of Shensi. The Long March became part of Chinese Communist history.

## 1922 MUSSOLINI

BENITO MUSSOLINI was the leader of the Fascist Party in Italy. He had fought in World War I and had been angry at the treatment Italy had received at the Treaty of Versailles. From 1919 to 1922, he organized a propaganda campaign through his newspaper *Il Popolo d'Italia*. He portrayed himself to be a strong man who, given the chance, could solve Italy's many problems. His supporters, known as the Blackshirts, were organized into Fascizi di Combattimento. In some parts of Italy—Bologna, for example—they were the main source of law and order. They investigated crimes, punished criminals, broke up strikes, and attacked any opponents. In October 1922, Mussolini organized a "March on Rome" by his Blackshirts. This was intended to put pressure on the government; in fact, it led to Mussolini

*Prince Yuan Shi-k'ai of China.*

*Italian dictator Benito Mussolini (center), leading the Blackshirts in the Fascist "March on Rome."*

being appointed prime minister of Italy. He went on to become the first dictator in western Europe.

## 1928 THE FIVE-YEAR PLANS

IN 1928, STALIN announced the First Five-Year Plan. This was an attempt to develop the Soviet nation through revitalizing and modernizing industry, which Stalin believed was 100 years behind the West. Every factory, coal mine, and industrial plant in the Soviet Union was set a series of targets for the next five years, which they had to meet. The targets were worked out in Moscow by the state-planning agency, Gosplan. The First Five-Year Plan also included the collectivization of all the farms in the Soviet Union. Farmers and peasants were forced to amalgamate their farms into state farms. Second and Third Five-Year Plans followed in the 1930s. Overall, industrial production increased by about 400 percent, but the plans encouraged quantity, not quality. Fifty percent of Soviet Union manufactured tractors broke down and could not be repaired.

## 1933 HITLER IN POWER

HITLER WAS BORN in Austria, but became Chancellor of Germany in January 1933. He was given total power when the Enabling Act was passed in March the same year. This allowed him to govern without the Reichstag, the German Parliament, for the next four years. By then, Germany had been changed completely. All political parties and trade unions had been banned. Children were indoctrinated in Nazi ideas by schools and youth organizations, such as the Hitler Youth. Almost all married women had been forced to give up work and were encouraged to have at least four babies. Newspapers, movie theaters, books, the arts, music, and radio were all controlled by the Nazis, and their laws were enforced by the secret state police, the Gestapo. A total dictatorship had been set up in Germany.

## 1936 THE SPANISH CIVIL WAR

THE SPANISH CIVIL WAR broke out in the summer of 1936. It was fought between the forces of the Popular Front, the elected government of Spain, and the rebel Falangists, led by General Francisco Franco. The Falangists wanted to overthrow the Popular Front Republicans, who had begun to undermine the power of the Church and the position of the landowners. Because Franco was a Fascist, he received aid from Mussolini, who sent 70,000 men, and Hitler, who sent the Condor Legion of 10,000 men.

*Spanish Civil War Poster.*

Hitler used the war as an opportunity to try out the strength of his new armed forces and to practice "Blitzkrieg," the strategy of mobile warfare that he was to use at the beginning of World War I.

## 1945 THE IMPACT OF WORLD WAR II

DURING WORLD WAR II, Gandhi organized the "Quit India" campaign. This was a response to the British Government's decision to announce that India had declared war on Germany without consulting Indians. Gandhi's campaign increased the influence of the Muslim League, led by M.A. Jinnah. When the war ended in 1945, Jinnah demanded a separate Muslim state, Pakistan. For the first time, there was widespread violence between Hindus and Muslims, especially in Calcutta in August 1946, when Jinnah attempted to put pressure on the British to allow "partition." It became increasingly obvious that the two religions could not coexist.

## 1945 HIROSHIMA

ON APRIL 12, 1945, Harry S. Truman became President of the United States upon the death of Franklin Roosevelt. On his desk he put the notice, "The Buck Stops Here." Just over three months

*The leaders of the Big Three meeting at Potsdam (from left): British Prime Minister Winston Churchill, President Harry S. Truman, and Soviet leader Joseph Stalin.*

later, he had to take one of the most momentous decisions ever taken. While at the Potsdam Conference, he was told that the "atomic bomb" was ready to be used on Japan. After a very lengthy discussion, Truman decided to use the bomb. He was told by his chiefs of staff that one million casualties would be caused if Japan were to be invaded. The first atomic bomb was dropped on August 6, 1945, on the city of Hiroshima; some 70,000 people were killed. The bomb not only marked the beginning of a new period in the history of humankind, but also increased the hostility between Truman and the Soviet leader Stalin, who had not been told about the bomb in advance. It became a factor in the development of the Cold War.

### 1945 THE HOLOCAUST

THE HOLOCAUST is the name given to the mass slaughter of Jews and other groups by the Nazis. Hitler believed that he could purify the German race by ridding it of all foreign groups. This also included Gypsies, Slavs, cripples, and the mentally ill. At first, the Nazis tried to force Jews to leave Germany by making it more difficult for them to earn a living. Jews were attacked on the street and their property smashed. After the outbreak of war, Hitler forced Jews to live in ghettos and then, from January 1942, began mass murder in extermination camps using poison gas. By the end of the war in 1945, about six million people had been killed.

*Deportation of Polish Jews in open cattle coaches at the "reloading point" in Warsaw, guarded by German soldiers.*

## 1946 THE IRON CURTAIN

IN 1945 AND 1946, Stalin built the "Iron Curtain" across Europe. It was a barrier that ran for 1,000 miles (1,600km) from the Baltic to the Adriatic, cutting Europe in two. Its purpose was simple: to prevent any Western influence from reaching the eastern European countries controlled by Stalin. In particular, it cut Germany into two sections: the Soviet zone and the three Western zones. The Iron Curtain received a very hostile reception in the

*A woman passing through the Russian border after the construction of the Iron Curtain.*

West, which surprised Stalin. At Yalta and Potsdam, he had agreed that the West could do as it liked in western Europe

and he assumed that, therefore, he could do as he liked in the East. As always, Stalin's main preoccupation was security, and the Iron Curtain seemed to him a natural step. To the West, it correctly suggested the beginning of another form of dictatorship.

## 1949 THE COMMUNIST REVOLUTION

IN 1949, AFTER YEARS of fighting, the Chinese Communist Party seized power. Mao Zedong set up a program of industrial development based on the Soviet Union's Five-Year Plans. However, the distrust of intellectuals and technical experts held back progress. Much of the work in building dams and other large-scale enterprises was done by manual labor. In the late 1950s, the "Great Leap Forward"—an experiment in rapid farming and manufacturing processes— was not progressing as quickly as expected originally. However, the "Cultural Revolution" of the late 1960s was successful and led to a period of reconstruction from 1970.

## 1950s EUROPEAN UNION

THE FIRST MOVES toward European union took place in the years after World War II. In March 1948, the Brussels Treaty was signed by Britain, France, Belgium, the Netherlands, and Luxembourg. This included plans for economic, social, and military cooperation. In May 1948, a Congress of Europe to discuss plans for European union was held, and in May 1949 the Council of Europe was set up, with headquarters at Strasbourg in France. In May 1952, a European Defense Community was set up by Italy, France, the Netherlands, West Germany, Belgium, and Luxembourg. This could have led to an integrated European army, but it collapsed when the French Parliament rejected the treaty in 1954. This was the first sign that national politics could make integration increasingly difficult.

*The first road convoy to arrive in Berlin after the lifting of the Berlin Blockade and the end of the Berlin Airlift.*

## 1955 NATO AND WARSAW PACT

THE NORTH ATLANTIC Treaty Organization (NATO) was set up in 1949 after the Berlin Blockade. It was a military alliance involving countries on either side of the North Atlantic. It changed relations between East and West by uniting the countries of the West, which led to the stationing of forces from the United States in western Europe for the first time. The most important clause in the NATO treaty was that an attack on one country was considered to be an attack on all of them. In other words, the East could not pick off democratic countries without the risk of a war with NATO countries. The Soviet Union did not react to NATO until West Germany was admitted as a member in 1955. After this it set up the Warsaw Pact, a military alliance between the Communist countries of eastern Europe.

*Joseph Bech signing a treaty at a Brussels conference on western European union.*

## 1960s THE EEC

THE EUROPEAN Economic Community (EEC) developed three main organizations. The Commission, in Brussels, was made up of representatives from all of the member countries, who were appointed by their governments. Each "commissioner" was responsible for an area of policy. The role of the Commission was to carry out EEC policies. These policies were decided by the Council of Ministers, which was made up of politicians from each of the member states. It could meet anywhere. At important meetings, the prime ministers would attend; on other occasions, it would be the minister responsible for the area of policy to be discussed, for example, farming. Finally, there was a European Parliament in Strasbourg, which contained elected representatives from each member country. The Parliament could discuss, argue, and even question commissioners, but it had no legislative power.

## 1961 THE BERLIN WALL

THE BERLIN WALL was built in August 1961. It separated families from one another and trapped people who had crossed into the other side of Berlin. For 12 years, people had been escaping from East Berlin to West Berlin, and in 1961 the number reached thousands every week. Most of the people who escaped were skilled workers, doctors, or engineers. The Wall was an attempt to stop the drain

*Between the walls that divided East and West Germany in Berlin, from 1961.*

of people from East to West. It was very effective, but it did not stop people trying to escape. The Wall also increased tension between the superpowers. President Kennedy visited West Berlin in 1963 to show his support for its citizens.

## 1961 BAY OF PIGS INVASION

UNTIL 1959, CUBA was governed by the pro-American dictator Batista. In 1959, however, he was overthrown by a group of rebels led by Fidel Castro. The United States cut off all aid to Cuba, and, in turn,

*Prisoners from the Bay of Pigs invasion being returned to the United States.*

Castro nationalized all American assets and property in Cuba. Khrushchev took advantage of the situation by agreeing to buy 1 million tons of Cuban sugar every year at inflated prices. This brought Cuba Soviet influence and Castro set up a Communist regime. Many American citizens were horrified. Communism now

existed only 70 miles (115 km) off the coast of Florida. Eisenhower authorized an attempt to overthrow Castro by landing a force of Cuban exiles at the Bay of Pigs. The landing actually took place in April 1961, after John F. Kennedy had became president, and turned out to be a disaster. The 1,500-strong force of Cubans were all killed or captured.

## 1972 SALT

IN 1969, THE SUPERPOWERS began Strategic Arms Limitation Talks. These were aimed at limiting the number of the very biggest nuclear weapons. The first treaty, known as SALT 1, was signed in 1972. Its most important clause was a five-year moratorium on the building of strategic weapons. This agreement did not lessen the risk of nuclear war—the superpowers had more than enough weapons already—and it did not effect intermediate or tactical weapons, but it was the first agreement of its kind. SALT 2 was agreed in 1979; this was a much more important treaty because it limited the number of strategic weapons that the two superpowers could build. Each would have no more than 2,500. However, the treaty was never ratified by the U.S. Congress, because of the Soviet invasion of Afghanistan in December 1979.

## 1980s SUPERPOWERS COLLIDE

IN 1981, RONALD REAGAN became President of the United States. He was a fierce opponent of Communism and relations between the superpowers deteriorated. In 1980, the United States had boycotted the Olympic Games in Moscow and in 1984 the USSR boycotted the Games in Los Angeles. Disarmament talks made no progress for years. The situation was made worse by internal politics in the USSR. Leonid Brezhnev, who had been president since 1964, was very ill and corruption was widespread. When he died in 1982, Yuri Andropov replaced him, but he also soon fell ill and died in 1984. His successor, Konstantin Chernenko died in 1985. For five years, there had been little prospect of real change, either internally or externally.

*Leonid Brezhnev, General Secretary of the Soviet Union Communist Party Central Committee and the USSR head of state.*

## 1985 GORBACHEV

IN 1985, MIKHAIL GORBACHEV became the President of the Soviet Union and announced his policies of *Perestroika* and *Glasnost*. *Perestroika* meant the restructuring of the Soviet economy and *Glasnost* meant openness. Gorbachev was aware that the Soviet Union was bankrupt and he had to find ways of saving money. He restarted disarmament talks with the United States. He was able to develop a close friendship with Western leaders, which enabled a number of treaties to be signed. In 1989, Gorbachev and President George H. W. Bush announced the end of the Cold War.

## 1989 THE WALL COMES DOWN

SINCE 1945, THE SOVIET UNION had kept military forces in eastern Europe. Those countries had been cut off from the West by the Iron Curtain that Stalin had built in 1945–46. The most famous example of the Iron Curtain was the Berlin Wall, which had been built on Khrushchev's orders in 1961. These actions had been very expensive. In 1989, Mikhail Gorbachev began to withdraw forces from eastern Europe in an effort to save money. The West German government paid the expenses of the forces that left East Germany. As Soviet troops left, country after country

*Crowds in the Potsdamer Platz in Berlin begin to break down the Wall, November 1989.*

withdrew from the Warsaw Pact, throwing off Communism, finally, in November 1989; crowds in Berlin began to knock chunks out of the Berlin Wall. By the end of the year, pieces were being sold as souvenirs.

## 1990s–2000s UNITY AND EXPANSION

THE EEC became the European Community in the 1970s and the European Union in the 1990s. The name change indicated a higher level of integration, with taxes and laws being brought more closely into line. In 1992, the Single Market meant that goods and people could move freely between EU countries. Monetary union, agreed by a majority of member states in 1997, became a reality with the introduction of the Euro currency in 2002. The Union began to be seen as a political

force in world affairs and there was talk of an EU military force. Euro-skeptics saw this as a move toward a federal state. Expansion to 25 members in 2004 was likely to test the practicality of such a goal.

## 2001 THE UNITED STATES REELS IN SHOCK ON 9/11

ON SEPTEMBER 11, 2001, Americans were traumatized by a string of coordinated suicide attacks carried out by members of terrorist organization al-Qaeda against the United States. In the morning of that day, 19 terrorists hijacked four commercial passenger airliners. The hijackers deliberately crashed two of the airliners into New York's Twin Towers at the World Trade Center; both towers collapsed within hours, destroying and damaging many nearby buildings. The hijackers crashed a third airliner into the Pentagon in Washington, DC. The fourth plane crashed into a field near Shanksville in Pennsylvania after some of its passengers and flight crew endeavored to fight off the hijackers. There were no survivors. The total death toll of the attacks was around 2,750, although the precise figure may never be known. The overwhelming majority of casualties were civilians, including nationals of over 70 countries.

## 2001 WAR IN AFGHANISTAN

Less than a month passed after the attacks on the United States on September 11, 2001, when President George W. Bush ordered air strikes against Kabul, Jalalabad, and the Taliban stronghold in Kandahar. The war in Afghanistan began on October 7, 2001, as

*Cypriot president Tassos Papadopoulos (left) and foreign minister George Iacovou sign the Accession Treaty to join the European Union April 16, 2003, in Athens, Greece.*

the U.S. military's Operation Enduring Freedom was launched, along with British involvement. The invasion of Afghanistan was aimed at deposing the Taliban regime who were harboring Osama Bin Laden and other high-ranking al-Qaeda members. It also intended to put these people on trial and destroy the organization of al-Qaeda. It has been an ongoing international military campaign led by the United States and the United Kingdom with the support of other NATO and non-NATO countries.

## 2004 THE EUROPEAN UNION EXPANDS

THE 2004 EXPANSION of the European Union (EU) was the largest ever single expansion of the EU, in terms of both territory and population, but not in terms of its GDP. The concurrent accessions included the following countries: Cyprus, Czech Republic, Estonia, Hungary, Latvia, Lithuania, Malta, Poland, Slovakia, and Slovenia. Seven of these countries were members of the former Eastern Bloc, with one from the former Yugoslavia and the remaining two being Mediterranean islands. Part of the same wave of expansion was the inclusion of Bulgaria and Romania in 2007, which were unable to join in 2004, but constitute as part of the fifth enlargement. The Treaty of Accession 2003 was signed on April 16, 2003, in Athens, between the EU members of the time and the ten acceding countries. The treaty was ratified and entered into force on May 1, 2004, amid ceremonies around Europe.

## 2007 BENAZIR BHUTTO IS ASSASSINATED

BENAZIR BHUTTO (1953–2007) was a Pakistani politician who led the Pakistan Peoples Party (PPP). Bhutto was the first woman elected to lead a Muslim state, twice being the Prime Minister of Pakistan (1988–1990; 1993–1996)—Pakistan's first and only female Prime Minister. Bhutto was sworn in as Prime Minister for the first time in 1988, but was removed from office 20 months later under the order of then-president Ghulam Ishaq Khan for alleged corruption. In 1993, she was reelected but was removed yet again in 1996 on similar charges, this time by President Farooq Leghari. She went into self-imposed exile in Dubai in 1998. Bhutto returned to Pakistan on October 18, 2007, after reaching an agreement with President Pervez Musharraf, whereby she was granted an amnesty. She was assassinated on December 27, 2007, by a suicide bomber after departing for a PPP rally in the Pakistani city of Rawalpindi, two weeks before the scheduled general election, in which she was a leading opposition candidate.

*Former Pakistan prime minister, Benazir Bhutto (center) was killed in 2007, in a suicide attack at a campaign rally.*

## 2009 FIRST AFRICAN AMERICAN PRESIDENT

AFTER A LONG CAMPAIGN that promised the American public "Change" and in a landmark presidential ballot, the United States elected its first African American president in 2008. Barack Obama, formerly a senator from Illinois, announced his candidacy for the presidency in Springfield, Illinois, on February 10, 2007. By August 2008, he was declared nominee of the Democratic Party for the 2008 presidential election. On November 4, 2008, projections indicated that Obama won the election, making him the President-elect and the first African American President of the United States.

# War and Peace

### 1900 DREADNOUGHT

THE DEVELOPMENT of steel manufacturing allowed enormous steps to be made in the production of ships from 1870 onward. By 1900, the thin steel battleships, with a displacement of 16,500 tons and a speed of 18 knots, were fast becoming the norm. Britain had intensified the fleet buildup in 1899, concerned that the joint fleets of France and Russia rivaled her own. The first *Dreadnought* was laid down in 1904; it was a significant improvement on anything produced elsewhere in the world. This British vessel, with a speed of between 18–25 knots boasted ten 1-foot (30-cm) guns and would become the model for capital ships until World War II. Britain and Germany now dominated the seas around Europe.

### 1901 AFTER PRETORIA

NO SOONER HAD the British begun to reduce the number of troops in South Africa than Boer leaders, among them such soldiers and future statesmen as Louis Botha and Jan Christiaan Smuts, launched extensive and well-planned guerrilla warfare against the occupying British troops. The fighting continued for the next year and was finally only quelled through the severe tactics of the new British commander in chief, Kitchener. He exhausted the Boers by devastating the Afrikaner farms that sustained and sheltered the guerrillas, placing both African and Afrikaner women and children in concentration camps, and building a strategic chain of formidable iron blockhouses for his troops. British losses totaled about 28,000 men. Afrikaner losses were about 4,000 men, plus more than 20,000 civilians, who died from disease in the concentration camps.

*The warship HMS* Dreadnought.

## 1914 THE WAR IN THE EAST

THE EASTERN WAR began on August 17, 1914, when Russia invaded eastern Prussia in a full-scale offensive. Two days later, General Alexander Samsonov's Second Army attacked around the right flank of the German Eighth Army, commanded by General Friedrich von Prittwitz. He proposed abandoning most of East Prussia, including Königsberg. He was immediately replaced by Field Marshall Paul von Hindenburg and his new chief of staff, Erich von Ludendorff. By August 27, they had fallen on Samsonov's army, taking it in both flanks. The Battle of Tannenberg was over by August 30, when Samsonov's command disintegrated at a cost of 92,000 captured. By September 5, German forces under General August Mackensen defeated Rennenkampf at the Battle of Masurian Lakes, where the Russians suffered over 100,000 casualties.

## 1916 THE SOMME OFFENSIVE

ON JULY 1, 1916, the British and French launched the Somme offensive. The offensive was launched against some of the heaviest German fortifications on the entire Western Front. The British general Haig at first resisted the idea, but the French commander Joffre won the argument and the campaign began. The Somme offensive saw the first use of tanks, and was preceded by the war's

*Battle of the Somme, France, 1916, with over a million casualties.*

greatest artillery barrage. Despite these advantages, the general slaughter of Allied troops that occurred was infamous, with the British suffering 65,000 casualties on the first day alone. When the October rains finally put an end to the prolonged carnage, 400,000 British, 200,000 French, and 450,000 Germans had become casualties. The Allies only captured a few miles of ground, but the Germans responded by withdrawing to their new Hindenburg line in early 1917.

*The French defense at Verdun, France, 1916.*

## 1916 THE VERDUN BULGE

IN 1916, THE GERMAN commander in chief, Erich von Falkenhayn put into action his idea for "bleeding white" the French army. His plan was to attack a point that the French would not allow to fall, and assure that the point was well covered by artillery. His target was the "Verdun Bulge," which his troops first assaulted on February 21, after the most concentrated bombardment of the war. The campaign carried on for four terrible months, during which 300,000 Germans and 460,000 French became casualties. This series of battles, one of the greatest slaughters in history until this time, only marginally achieved the original German goals. The French were indeed "bled white," but not as severely as von Falkenhayn had hoped.

## 1918 THE YANKS ARE COMING

THE BRITISH ATTACKED at Arras, nothern France, on April 9, suffering 84,000 casualties, but achieved no breakthrough. Before this battle had ended, the new French commander Nivelle launched his own offensive from Soissons to Rheims. This offensive ground to a halt on its first day, and by the time the assault finished, the French had suffered 220,000 casualties; many French soldiers mutinied. In November, the British launched an attack toward Cambrai using hundreds of tanks. All three German lines were broken, but within days, German counterattacks drove the British back to their starting positions. The last great German offensive was launched on March 21, 1918, with a 6,000-gun barrage and a heavy gas attack. The Allies suffered 350,000 casualties, but more troops were rushed in from across the Channel, and American soldiers began arriving.

## 1936 THE SPANISH CIVIL WAR

DURING ITS FIRST MONTHS, the Spanish Civil War acquired international political and ideological significance. Within less than a year from the conflict's onset, Fascist Italy sent about 70,000 ground troops to aid the Nationalists, and Nazi

Germany provided planes, pilots, arms, and technicians. The USSR sent weapons and advisers to the Republicans; the Comintern organized thousands of liberals and leftists from 53 foreign countries into volunteer International Brigades, formed to fight fascism. Both sides engaged in mass arrests and executions in the name of anti-Communism or anti-Fascism. Serving as a battleground for conflicting nations and as a proving ground for new weapons, the Civil War later became known as a dress rehearsal for World War II.

### 1939 BLITZKRIEG

ON SEPTEMBER 1, 1939, waves of German bombers hit railroads and snarled the Polish mobilization. Four

*Diving German "Stuka" bombers, 1940.*

days later, two army groups broke through narrow fronts and were sending armored spearheads toward Warsaw and Brest. This was *blitzkrieg* (lightning war): the use of armor, air power, and mobile infantry in a pincers movement to encircle the enemy. On September 17, a second, deeper encirclement closed 100 miles (160 km) east, near Brest Litovsk. By September 20, practically the whole country was in German or Soviet hands.

### 1940 THE BATTLE OF BRITAIN

FOLLOWING THE FALL of France, Hitler hoped that Britain would accept German control of the European continent and seek peace. Instead, Britain shunned the chancellor's overtures of July 1940, and in August the German Luftwaffe of Hermann Göring began an all-out attack on British ports, airfields, and industrial centers and, finally, on London. The goal was to crush British morale and wipe out the RAF in preparation for Operation Sea Lion, an invasion of England. The first great air battle in history was the Battle of Britain. For 57 nights, an average force of 160 bombers attacked London. The outnumbered RAF, employing the effective Spitfire fighter and aided by radar, destroyed 1,733 German aircraft, while losing 915 fighters of their own.

## 1941 THE DESERT FOX

ITALY MANAGED to overrun British Somaliland in August 1940. However, Mussolini's triumph was short-lived, for by the next summer the British recaptured that territory and drove the Italians from their East African possessions. In September 1940, Mussolini moved a second army of Italians and North African troops across the Libyan border to establish themselves about 60 miles (100 km) inside Egypt. The British struck back in December in a surprise attack that carried them halfway across Libya by early February 1941. In March 1941, Germany's Afrika Korps, commanded by General Erwin Rommel, arrived at Tripoli. By mid-April, Rommel had reconquered all of Libya except Tobruk; his exploits earned him the nickname "the Desert Fox."

## 1941 PEARL HARBOR

IN LATE 1941, more than 75 U.S. warships were based at Pearl Harbor, Hawaii. All U.S. aircraft carriers were elsewhere. On December 7, at 7:50 a.m., the first wave of Japanese planes struck Pearl Harbor, bombarding airfields and battleships moored at the quays. A second wave followed. Eighteen ships were hit, and more than 200 aircraft destroyed or damaged. The attack was, however,

*Japanese air attacks on Pearl Harbor, December 1941.*

a colossal political and psychological blunder, for it served as the catalyst that brought the United States into the war.

## 1943 TANK WARFARE

ON THE EASTERN front, since Stalingrad, the Germans had shortened their lines, while the Soviet troops were stretched over a massive front with a bulge westward around Kursk. On July 5, 1943, the Germans, using their new Tiger and Panther tanks, struck at this Soviet salient. Hitler committed more than 1,000 planes against the Red Army's enormous concentration of troops, artillery pieces, and tanks. The encounter developed into one of the largest and most vicious armor battles ever fought.

More than 3,000 tanks were engaged on the grasslands. On July 12, 1943, the Soviets moved in fresh tank divisions, and the advantage finally swung to the Russians. Manstein, having lost 70,000 men, half his tanks, and over 1,000 planes, was forced to withdraw.

*At the Battle of Kursk, a German Panzer VI Tiger is positioned between Bielgorod and Orel on July 1943.*

## 1944 D-DAY

ON JUNE 6, 1944, waves of Allied troops moved ashore between Cherbourg and Le Havre in history's largest amphibious operation, involving about 5,000 ships of all kinds. About 11,000 Allied aircraft operated over the invasion area. More than 150,000 troops disembarked at Normandy on D-Day. For more than a month, the Germans resisted while Allied forces were being built up on the crowded beaches. On August 15, 1944, a fleet of Allied warships appeared off the French Mediterranean coast between Toulon and Cannes. They unloaded an army of U.S. and French troops. Speedily taking Marseilles and Nice, the Allies headed northward along the Rhone River. German troops in western France were now threatened with isolation.

## 1945 THE ORIGINS OF THE VIETNAM WAR

FRENCH INDOCHINA, which included Vietnam, Cambodia (Kampuchea), and Laos, was occupied by Japanese forces during World War II. Communist leader Ho Chi Minh and his Viet Minh declared Vietnam an independent republic in 1945. The United States supported French rule. When fighting erupted between France and the Viet Minh in 1947, the United States aided the French and backed Emperor Bao Dai. By 1953, they were providing 80 percent of the cost of France's war effort. In 1954, the French, hoping to win a decisive victory, lured the Viet Minh into a battle at Dien Bien Phu but were, in turn, besieged there. Defeat at Dien Bien Phu made France withdraw from Indochina.

## 1950 INVASION

THE KOREAN WAR began between North Korea (supported by China) and South Korea, aided by the United Nations (UN), although the bulk of the troops were provided by the United States. North Korean forces invaded the South on June 25. The Security Council, due to a walkout by the USSR, voted to oppose them. By September 1950, the North Koreans had overrun most of the South, with the UN forces holding a small area, the Pusan perimeter, in the southeast. The course of the war changed after the surprise landing of American troops later the same month at Inchon on South Korea's northwest coast. This dramatic counterattack caught the North Koreans off guard and it was their turn to retreat in confusion.

*Memorial to the Korean War in Washington, DC.*

## 1954 GENEVA AND BEYOND

FOLLOWING THE Geneva agreement of 1954, there were five years of relative calm until, in 1959, relations between North and South Vietnam again became critical. The regime in Saigon tried to eliminate the Communists in the south, and the Communist government of Ho Chi Minh in Hanoi decided to assist a new rebellion. By the end of 1960, the anti-Diem forces in the south formed a national-liberation front and in 1961 Diem, who had depended on aid from the United States since 1951, sought extra protection. By 1963, there were about 16,700 U.S. troops in South Vietnam.

## 1964 TONKIN GULF INCIDENT

AFTER THE TONKIN Gulf Incident in August 1964, in which the U.S. Navy claimed two of its ships were attacked by North Vietnamese boats, a resolution was passed by the U.S. Congress to take unlimited action to resolve the crisis. An attack on an American base at Pleiku in February 1965 was used as the justification for starting air attacks on the North. The United States began sending in combat troops to Vietnam (April 1965). The political crisis in Saigon was eased with the emergence of Nguyen Cao Ky as prime minister (1965–67), and the establishment of a new constitution in 1966 and the election of Nguyen Van Thieu as president in 1967.

*American advisers and South Vietnamese troops gathered in front of a tank during the Vietnam War.*

## 1969 CAMBODIA

THE WAR CONTINUED throughout 1969–71 and spread across the region. The United States brought Cambodia into the war, securing the removal of Sihanouk's neutral regime in Phnom Penh. Heavy bombing of Cambodia drew that country into the conflict and ultimately resulted in the Khmer Rouge government. Anxious to break the stalemate, North Vietnam launched a new and much heavier offensive against the South Vietnamese army in the Quang Tri province and in the region of An Loc (north of Saigon) in the spring of 1972. There were now fewer than 100,000 American troops in Vietnam and so they responded with an even more intense bombing routine of the north, the mining of Haiphong Harbor, and unlimited air support for South Vietnamese troops on the ground.

## 1972 THE PARIS TREATY AND AFTER

CONTACTS BETWEEN Hanoi and Washington during 1972 led to the signing of the Paris Treaty in 1973. American forces finally left South Vietnam in March 1973, and for two years the South Vietnamese government sought to continue the American policy of pacification. However, the Viet Cong revolutionary government of South Vietnam was making substantial political gains. In late 1974, North Vietnam breached the cease-fire. By April 1975, the Communist forces took Saigon. The war was over and Vietnam was reunited as the Socialist Republic of Vietnam in July 1976.

## 1973 YOM KIPPUR WAR

IN OCTOBER 1973, Egypt and Syria joined forces to launch an attack on Israeli forces. The Syrians, aided by troops from Jordan and Iraq, initially made some gains in the north, but by October 11, they had been turned back, and the Israelis advanced into Syria. In the south, the Egyptians crossed the Suez Canal and penetrated about 6 miles (10 km), into Sinai before they were stalled. On October 16, the Israelis counterattacked and invaded Egypt itself. A cease-fire took effect on the Syrian front on October 22, and in Egypt two days later.

### 1979 THE RUSSIAN INVASION OF AFGHANISTAN

ON DECEMBER 25, 1979, Soviet forces invaded Afghanistan and quickly won control of Kabul. However, the government, dependent on Soviet military forces, was unpopular, and a rebellion intensified. The anti-government guerrilla forces operated from bases around Peshawar, in Pakistan and Iran. Weapons and money from the United States, Saudi Arabia, Iran, and China sustained them. By 1986, about 118,000 Soviet troops and 50,000 Afghan government troops were facing perhaps 130,000 guerrillas. Estimates of combat fatalities range from between 700,000 and 1.3 million people. The Soviets completed a withdrawal in 1989.

### 1982 THE FALKLANDS WAR

NEGOTIATIONS TO settle a sovereignty dispute between Argentina and Britain over the Falkland Islands began in the mid-1960s at the UN. The talks were still in progress in April 1982, when Argentine forces invaded the islands. They were defeated by a British task force and formally surrendered on June 14. Although numerically superior, the Argentines were outfought by the British. Casualties were comparatively light, despite the use of modern weaponry. Argentina continued to

*The HMS* Invincible *returns to Portsmouth, carrying British troops home from the Falklands War.*

claim the islands. The British government refused to negotiate, but the two nations resumed diplomatic relations in 1990.

### 1991 YUGOSLAVIA'S BREAKUP

THE WARS IN YUGOSLAVIA began in 1991 after Slovenia and Croatia declared their independence. In July of that year, the Yugoslav People's Army, which consisted mainly of Serbs, intervened in Slovenia trying to remove the Slovenian government. Slovenian troops repelled the Yugoslav forces after ten days. The war in Bosnia began in the spring of 1992, when the new government declared independence from Yugoslavia. Serbian nationalists within Bosnia violently occupied more than 60 percent of Bosnian territory; thousands of Muslims and Croats were murdered. The International Criminal Tribunal for the former Yugoslavia in the

The Hague indicted over 50 Bosnians for massacring civilians during the war: the majority were Serbs, including Bosnian Serb leader Radovan Karadžić and military commander Ratko Mladić.

## 1990s–2000s WARS IN THE GULF

IRAN AND IRAQ fought a costly war between 1980 and 1988, in the course of which Iraq's leader Saddam Hussein authorized the use of poison gas on Kurdish Iraqi villages. In August 1990, Iraq invaded Kuwait. The UN demanded Iraq's withdrawal while an American-led coalition was assembled, chiefly of forces supplied by the United States, Saudi Arabia, Britain, France, Egypt, and Syria. By January 1991, some 500,000 allied personnel were pitched against a slightly larger Iraqi army. With air superiority, the allied land assault, Desert Storm, was successful within days. Kuwait was liberated and the Iraqi army scattered, captured, or killed. However, Saddam Hussein was left in power. Fears remained about the existence of so-called "weapons of mass destruction" (WMD). By 2002, Iraq was under pressure to cooperate with UN weapons inspectors. The American and British governments claimed Iraq was concealing stocks of WMD, and in March 2003, President George W. Bush demanded that Saddam Hussein step down as president. When this was rejected, American and British forces began an air and ground assault on Iraq. Within a month, Baghdad was occupied and combat was declared ended on May 1. However, insurgents continued to attack American and British occupation forces, and the Allied death toll soon exceeded the number of those killed in the war. Saddam Hussein was captured in December 2003. After the capture of President Hussein, he was tried and executed in December 2006 by the new Iraqi government. In February 2009, President Barack Obama announced an 18-month withdrawal window for combat forces, with about 50,000 troops remaining in the country. So far, the war has claimed at least 5,000 coalition military personnel lives. Civilian losses are estimated at 100,000 or more.

*President George W. Bush waves to U.S. troops.*

## 1999–2006 KOSOVO WAR CRIMES TRIALS

SINCE MAY 1999, the International Criminal Tribunal for the former Yugoslavia has prosecuted crimes committed during the Kosovo War. Many Serbian and Yugoslavian commanders have been indicted so far for crimes against humanity and violations of the laws of war in Kosovo in 1999, including Yugoslavian president Slobodan Milosevic and the Serbian president Milan Milutinovic. The indictment against nine prominent figures has alleged that they directed, encouraged, or supported a campaign of terror and violence directed at Kosovo Albanian civilians and aimed at the expulsion of a substantial portion of them from Kosovo. It has been alleged that about 800,000 Albanians were expelled as a result. In particular, in the last indictment as of June 2006, the accused were charged with murder of 919 Kosovo Albanian civilians from 1 to 93 years old. Milosevic died in custody during the trial in 2006. Many other cases are still ongoing.

## 2000s LONDON, MADRID, AND MUMBAI BOMBINGS

Following the 9/11 attacks on the Pentagon and World Trade Center in 2001, a War on Terror was launched along with the hunt for al-Qaeda member Osama Bin Laden, the prime suspect for masterminding the attacks. Osama Bin Laden's declaration of a *jihad*, or holy war, against the United States, and his calling for the killing of American civilians in 1998, are seen by investigators as evidence of his motivation to commit his acts of terrorism. The effect of the War on Terror was an increase in the threat of international terrorists plotting further attacks against the world's major cities. On the morning of March 11, 2004, a series of coordinated bombings against a commuter train

*Kosovo Liberation army soldiers positioned on a hill above the Yugoslav army head to the trenches after mortars were fired by the Yugoslavs in Bukos, Pristina.*

*The Madrid train bomb attacks in March 2004 killed 191 people and injured over 1,800 in the worst terror strike Spain has ever known.*

system in Madrid, Spain, killed 191 people and wounded over 1,800. An official investigation determined the attacks were directed by an al-Qaeda-inspired terrorist cell, although no direct al-Qaeda participation has ever been established. The bombings occurred three days before Spain's general elections, which resulted in the defeat of the incumbent José María Aznar's Partido Popular. On July 7, 2005, a series of four bomb explosions struck London's public transport system during the morning rush hour. All four incidents were suicide bombings that killed 52 commuters as well as the four bombers. More than ten coordinated shooting and bombing attacks took place across India's largest city of Mumbai by Islamic terrorists from Pakistan. The attacks began on November 26, 2008, and lasted until November 29, killing at least 173 people and wounding over 300. By the early morning of 28 November, all sites except for the Taj Hotel had been secured by security forces. Action by guards from India's National Security on November 29 ended with the death of the last remaining attackers at the Taj Hotel, ending the incident. The only attacker captured alive was Ajmal Kasab. He revealed that the attackers came from a Pakistan-based terrorist organization.

# Society and Culture

### 1900 REPRESSION RULES

REPRESSION REMAINED the reaction of authority under challenge, even while humanitarians gained ground elsewhere in the world. In 1900, the Boxer Rebellion, or the Righteous Harmony Society Movement, of China, opposed to the powerful influence of foreigners in China, was put down. Captured Boxers were beheaded. In Russia, protests against czarist rule in 1901, 1902, and 1905 were put down no less forcefully. However, Russia could

no longer afford this kind of response. Millions of peasants lived in appalling poverty and deprivation, and anarchists were willing to murder and terrorize to get what they wanted. Eventually, the Russian czar Nicholas II (1868–1918) and his entire family faced the ultimate terror—their capture and slaughter by the Bolsheviks in 1918.

### 1903 VOTES FOR WOMEN

WOMEN SOUGHT THE VOTE as early as 1880, but their polite requests got nowhere in the male-dominated political world. After 1903, when Emmeline Pankhurst (1858–1928) founded the Women's Social and Political Union in Britain, her suffragism was more militant. Suffragettes chained themselves to railings, smashed windows, set fire to mail boxes, and one, Emily Davison, committed suicide by throwing herself in front of King George V's horse during a race in 1913. Violence was matched by violence, notably the force-feeding of hunger-striking suffragettes, the practice of which so damaged Mrs. Pankhurst that it contributed to her death. Her efforts, however, made such a prominent issue of votes for women that after they

*Cover illustration of 100,000 workers marching to commemorate Bloody Sunday in Russia, 1905.*

*English suffragette Emmeline Pankhurst (1858–1928) making an open-air speech.*

had undertaken men's jobs during World War I, some were enfranchised in 1918. All adult women in Britain were allowed to vote after 1928.

### 1914 THE WAR TO END ALL WARS

THE DECLARATION of war on August 4, 1914, was greeted by the public in Britain, France, and Germany in the traditional European way: by cheering crowds, excitement, and patriotic flag-waving. Only three months later, this jubilant mood was replaced by disillusionment as lethal modern weapons forced the combatants in France to retire into trenches and largely remain there, among the mud, sludge, filth, corpses, and rats, as long as the fighting lasted. Shock and rage increased when, in 1915, German Zeppelin air raids over Britain made dangerous the one place—the home—where people had always presumed themselves to be safe. Even among the victors, the end of the war on November 11, 1918, was greeted somberly, with heartfelt relief. By the end of the war, almost ten million had lost their lives.

### 1916 DIVIDE AND RULE

IN 1916, WHEN THE British encouraged the Arabs in Palestine to revolt against their Ottoman Turkish masters—a revolt, that succeeded brilliantly—the Arabs came to believe that a measure of independence would be their reward. In 1917, in the Balfour Declaration, the British gave a broad hint to the Jews that Palestine, their ancient ancestral home, would again be theirs instead. The result was that Palestine, which became a British mandate from the League of Nations after World War I, was the scene of vicious rivalry and hatred—outbreaks of fighting and raiding that the British tried, but ultimately failed, to bring under control. Worse still, both Jew and Arab came to believe that the British were favoring the opposing side, fueling anti-British sentiment on both sides.

*British Prime Minister David Lloyd George, with his wife and daughter.*

## 1920s NO HOME FIT FOR HEROES

THE "HOME FIT FOR HEROES," promised by British prime minister David Lloyd George (1863–1945), proved a myth. Many "heroes" returned home to unemployment. Some sold matches in the streets, displaying their medals to encourage custom. Domestic servants who had hoped to escape it, were forced back into service. In defeated Germany, rampant inflation and crippling reparations imposed by the victors led to mass poverty and destitution. The rescue promised by the Nazi leader Adolf Hitler, who came to power in 1933, seemed a tempting way out, with assurances of full employment and socialist benefits.

Too late, the Germans realized the price: total submission to Nazi rule and for some—liberals, homosexuals, Jews, and Gypsies—imprisonment or death.

## 1920s THE ROARING TWENTIES

AFTER THE WAR, some young men and women blanked out their grief for lost friends and relatives with thrills and pleasure. There were wild parties and new, provocative dances, such as the "Black Bottom." Cars crammed with noisy young people headed for nightclubs, from which many did not emerge until dawn. Young women in particular claimed new freedoms: they cut their hair short and wore "indecently" short skirts (above the knee in 1926) or drank and smoked—

*Typical 1920s' costumes; women like this were known as "flappers."*

things that would never have been permitted them only a short while before. The so-called "Roaring Twenties" was a crazy time, but not one in which the mass of people could share; their reaction to the war was despair.

## 1929 THE WALL STREET CRASH

THE EARLY POST-WAR period was boom time in the United States. War industries, turning over to civilian production, poured out goods for an eager consumer market. Rich dividends were promised to investors, some of whom (the smaller ones) invested their entire savings in stocks and shares. They felt certain of making a profit. Instead, they faced ruin. The boom was a bubble

*Despair on the streets after the Wall Street Crash.*

that had to burst. Signs that the U.S. economy was not as healthy as investors believed began to appear. Stock values began to fall. Then, on October 24, 1929, the pressure became so great that the New York Stock Exchange crashed. Investors besieged banks, clamoring to withdraw their money, but for many it was too late. They had lost everything.

## 1930s HOLOCAUST

PREJUDICE, PERSECUTION, and pogroms had stalked Jews for many centuries, but nothing compared to the Nazis' systematic attempt to exterminate them as a race during World War II. All over occupied Europe, Jews were rounded up, crammed into cattle trucks and transported to extermination camps, which the Nazis had set up in Poland and Germany. The Nazis had also constructed gas chambers where the Jews were taken, supposedly to take showers, but were then shut in and gassed to death *en masse*. Later, their bodies were burned in ovens. Some six million were wiped out in this horrific fashion. Jews, however, were not the only victims of Nazi "ethnic cleansing": Gypsies, also regarded by the Nazis as a blight on society, received the same sadistic treatment and four million died.

## 1940 CONQUERORS AND CONQUERED

BETWEEN APRIL AND JUNE 1940, Nazi Germany overran Norway, Denmark, France, Belgium, and the Netherlands, and, in 1941, parts of Russia. Poland had already been conquered in 1939. These countries were now forced to live under foreign, and often retributive, domination as the Nazi conquest brought curfews, shortages, and savage punishments for disobedience. This produced several reactions. Most people simply tried to survive as best they could and keep out of trouble. Others risked everything to form resistance movements, and were not always helped by their compatriots who thought it best to keep their heads down. Some collaborated with the Germans, seeking safety by fraternizing with the winning side. Their punishment after the war was savage.

## RATIONING

BECAUSE OF ITS island location, rationing was essential in wartime Britain. Luxuries, and certain foodstuffs, especially oranges and bananas from distant countries, and for a time chocolate, were unobtainable. Essentials—butter, eggs, meat, fish, and clothing—were strictly apportioned out through ration books containing coupons. It was a well-considered system; in fact, it provided some Britons with better nutrition than they had had in peacetime, when poor families relied too much on carbohydrates and not enough on vital proteins. The radio and newspapers carried regular hints on how to make the most of the rations, but there were, of course, black marketeers; many were unwilling to buy from them. Others, who told the police about blackmarketing activities, could be ostracized.

*Dig for Victory poster, circa 1940.*

*French citizens lining up to join Resistance movement.*

## 1941 RESISTING THE NAZIS

IN THE NAZI-OCCUPIED countries, those who chose resistance not only risked their lives every day, but assumed the tremendous nervous strain of a clandestine existence. Some were simply patriots, determined to eject the hated invader from their land. Others had their own agendas, such as the Communists in Yugoslavia or the supporters of the "Free French" general Charles de Gaulle (1890–1970), who hoped for political power after the war. Whatever their motivations, resistance fighters lived a life of constant suspense, constant watchfulness, and always the danger of betrayal. They knew what capture could mean—torture, imprisonment, and death—and that all their willpower would be needed not to yield the information that the Nazis tried to force out of them.

## 1947 ORIGINS OF COLONIAL INDEPENDENCE

THE EFFECTS OF independence in many former colonial territories laid bare the effects of imperialism. Native cultures had necessarily been suppressed during the long decades of colonial rule. When independence revived them, the spectacle was sometimes alarming. For example, in Africa, where Ghana (the former Gold Coast) was the first imperial possession to be granted independence, in 1957, the leaders of countries accepted Britain's "gift" of a democratic, parliamentary system. Before long however, their tendency toward rule by one "strong man," a characteristic of their precolonial days, reasserted itself. Tribalism was also now expressed in damaging civil wars. This greatly exacerbated the basic poverty of newly independent countries and sank them into a dispair from which many have not yet recovered.

## 1947 THE SEEDS OF FREEDOM

THE QUEST FOR FREEDOM seemed to be in the air once World War II was over. As imperial powers, the French and the Dutch had suffered severe loss of face during the war, and Britain, although a major victor, had been impoverished by its efforts. The new Labor government, elected in Britain in 1945, believed also that colonial rule should come to an end. In 1947, with the independence of India and the creation of Pakistan for the Muslims, a long process of decolonization began. Other lessons had gone home elsewhere. During the War, African Americans had made their own considerable contribution and suffered their own losses. The segregated regiments in which army GIs had served now seemed iniquitous, and African Americans baulked at returning to their previous, downtrodden status.

## 1948 APARTHEID

SOUTH AFRICA officially imposed apartheid, the separation of races into categories—white, black African, mixed race, and, later, Asian—in 1948. The Boers, the white South Africans of Dutch descent, believed they were the superior race and had, in fact, found justification for that in the Bible. Their thinking, of course, ran counter to the more liberal ways of thought gaining ground in the West during the 1960s, but South Africa's comparative isolation enabled them to sustain it. The liberalizing influences put pressure on South Africa nonetheless. In the West, a campaign of sanctions and censure began to make apartheid untenable. Over 30 years passed and much suffering took place before it succeeded in ending apartheid.

*Nelson Mandela (born 1918), whose campaign eventually overthrew the apartheid regime in South Africa.*

## 1949 THE STATE OF ISRAEL

IN 1944 AND 1945, as the Allied forces closed in on Nazi Germany, the ghastly revelations of the newly liberated

*Victims of the "Final Solution," Jews from the concentration camp Bergen-Belsen.*

### 1954 THE WORLD OPENS UP

TELEVISION, invented in 1925 by John Logie Baird, was the first medium to open up a window on the world after it became widely available by about 1954. Through television, life can be observed going on in distant places, even beneath the sea. Jumbo jets can carry 300 people or more to the other side of the world in a few hours. Computer users can make instant links, letters that would take days or weeks to travel by post, appear instantly as faxes. E-mails flash onto computer screens at the click of a mouse. These capabilities are so familiar in this new millennium that they have lost much of their wonder, yet barely 50 years ago they were not yet possible.

concentration camps, with their skeletal, dehumanized survivors, shocked and appalled the world. This gave a powerful impetus to the aspirations of Jews in Palestine who believed that, without a country of their own, this "Holocaust" could happen again. Once the British, exasperated by the savage Arab-Jewish rivalries, returned the Palestine mandate to the new United Nations, a vote was taken there in 1947 to create the State of Israel. The new state was immediately challenged by the surrounding Arab countries and a bitter war ensued. By 1948, Israel prevailed and the State of Israel was formed, but Arab-Israeli hatred survived scarring the region ever since.

*A television receiver made in the 1950s.*

## 1960s AGAINST WAR

IT HAD ALWAYS been the fate of young men to fight and die in society's wars. This principle could be maintained as long as war was considered glorious and patriotic, but the young generation, born during or just after World War II, sought to break what they saw as a pernicious mold.

Pacifism was nothing new at this time, but the scale of it was. The Korean War (1950–53) and the fighting in French Indochina, Greece, and Malaya suggested that nothing had changed. However, vociferous, often violent protests and demonstrations took place, as the young challenged the establishment's presumption that yet another generation would let itself be decimated by war. With this, other establishment values came under equally heavy fire.

society. Young men grew their hair long. Young women wore revealing miniskirts. They lived together before marriage, experimented with drugs, embraced mystical religions, such as Zen Buddhism, and gathered at rock festivals to listen to their own brand of popular music. Some, such as the "Flower

*Large crowd of people, including those sitting on top of cars and buses, during the Woodstock Music Festival, August 1969.*

## 1960s GIVE PEACE A CHANCE

THE MASS SOCIAL REVOLT of the young, which left their elders feeling thoroughly beleaguered, seemed to involve everything pugnaciously different from the principles of existing

Children," went so far as to create an "alternative society" with some of the same elements. It included a philosophy, which sprang from their idea that if only everyone would "give peace a chance" (as one of their songs went), then the world would be a wonderful place.

## 1960s SPURNING THE GLOBAL VILLAGE

THE MATERIALISTIC LIFE, with its emphasis on consumerism, was spurned by unconventional "hippies" who adhered to their principles of "flower power," peace, and an unsophisticated life. The hippie subculture was originally a youth culture that began in the early 1960s in the United States and quickly spread to other countries throughout the Western world. Even today, a great deal about the 1960s lives on through the small communities of hippies who still persist—the hallucinogenic drugs, the long hair, the transcendental meditation, but also a strong sense of community, the desire for a peaceful coexistence, and a belief in love as the magic elixir for a good and happy life. Realizing, even so, that most of the world does not seek to run on these lines, hippies tended to live in tight, sometimes remote communities or, in their more recent "New Age Traveler" persona, they move from place to place like gypsies.

## 1960s BAN THE BOMB!

PROTEST SOON became the virtual symbol of the 1960s, with rallies, marches, demonstrations, and clashes with the police. The Nuclear Age, which followed the atomic bombing of Japan in 1945, produced rowdy, vociferous demonstrations in Britain, France, and Germany, demanding that governments eschew atomic weapons. The war in Vietnam, too, roused fury at what young Americans, British, and French saw as an immoral conflict. Some Americans went to Canada to avoid being drafted into the war and were dubbed cowards by some, but heroes by others. In the United States, Martin Luther King Jr. (1929–68) used peaceful, but determined methods to promote African American equality. Malcolm Little (Malcolm X, 1926–65) preferred more violent ways to achieve the same object. Both their lives were to end violently in assassination.

*Martin Luther King Jr. (1929–68), advanced peaceful methods in the fight for African American equality.*

## 1960s WOMEN'S LIBERATION

THE CENTURIES-OLD subordination of women to men could basically be regarded in two ways: women were either nurturers of children, performing society's most vital single task, or victims of male oppression, which denied them their ambitions and talents. The women's liberation movement took the latter view and the clamor began for equality with men, abortion "on demand," access to education and training, as well as to jobs formerly reserved for men, even access to men's clubs and other "bastions" of male domination. There was, naturally enough, resistance—and not just from men, either. Concerns were voiced that if women abandoned their traditional role, or even supplemented it with the new roles they demanded, the fabric of society could suffer.

## 1969 SPACE EXPLORATION AND ITS BENEFITS

FOR CENTURIES HUMANKIND had been struggling to unravel the mysteries of space. The first moon landing in 1969 was one of the greatest breakthroughs in space exploration. Space is not simply a playground for scientists or the source of exciting television transmissions. Benefits for humanity can come from

*An astronaut from the Space Shuttle* Challenger *"walks" in space.*

space exploration. Medical research could gain much from the germfree conditions to be found in space. Minerals brought back from the moon could lead to new drugs. The experiences of astronauts, in particular weightlessness, may lead to new understandings of the human body and its capabilities. The Hubble Space Telescope, launched in 1990, is able to make its observations without the interference from the atmosphere that sometimes complicates the work of the earth-based astronomers. This makes possible closer observations of the stars, including the sun, and greater understanding of their functions and of the sun's effects on the earth and its life.

## 1970s ISLAM VS. THE WEST

ISLAM AND CHRISTIANITY were rivals, often savage rivals, almost from the moment Islam was founded in AD 624. The Western world, which was largely the product of Christianity, has now taken over as Islam's modern challenger, and one which fundamentalist Muslims in particular regard as an evil to be expunged. Several Muslim countries, such as Iran and Algeria, have sought to close themselves off from "pernicious" Western influences, although still dealing with the West for political or trade purposes. Their rivalry is, however, a fruitful ground for Muslim terrorist groups who have used modern weaponry, especially bombs, to make their presence known. This has often resulted in scenes of destruction and carnage, made all the more impactive by graphic television coverage. Since the 1970s, terrorism has been widespread in many countries, and has become a characteristic of modern religious conflict.

## 1990s REMAINING PROBLEMS

ON THE BRINK of the third millennium, the world is not without its serious problems—war, urban crime, economic difficulties, poverty, and family breakdown. There is, however, a distinct internationalism at work in the search for some solutions. Scientists and governments have come together to tackle AIDS, HIV, and drug abuse, all of them international problems. International aid has many times gone to the rescue of famine sufferers in Ethiopia, the Sudan, and many other places. Multinational forces have policed trouble spots, such as the civil-war-torn former Yugoslavia. Environmentalists fight to preserve the earth and its life, activists to save endangered species. Among ordinary people, television no sooner shows terrible scenes of suffering and deprivation from anywhere in the world than donations flow in to mitigate them.

*The World Trade Center billows smoke after hijacked airliners crashed into it on September 11, 2001.*

## 2000s A DECADE OF NATURAL DISASTERS

WHILE NATURAL disasters are nothing new, the start of this new millennium seems to have more than its fair share. It began with the 2004 Indian Ocean earthquake that occurred on December 26, off the west coast of Sumatra, Indonesia. The earthquake triggered a series of devastating tsunamis along the coasts of most landmasses bordering the Indian Ocean, killing over 230,000 people in 14 countries, and inundating coastal communities with waves up to 100 feet (30 m) high. It was one of the deadliest natural disasters in recorded history. Indonesia was the hardest hit, followed by Sri Lanka and Thailand. Hurricane Katrina in the 2005 Atlantic hurricane season, was the costliest natural disaster, as well as one of the five deadliest hurricanes, in American history. At least 1,836 people lost their lives in the actual hurricane and in the subsequent floods, making it the country's deadliest hurricane since 1929; total property damage was estimated at 81 billion dollars. Haiti suffered a shattering earthquake (Richter magnitude 7.0) on January 12, 2010. By January 24, at least 52 aftershocks measuring 4.5 or greater had been recorded. An estimated three million people were affected by the quake; the Haitian government reported that an estimated 230,000 people had died, 300,000 had been injured, and 1,000,000 made homeless. They also estimated that 250,000 homes and 30,000 shops and offices had collapsed or were severely damaged.

## 2009 GLOBAL FLU PANDEMIC

INFLUENZA A (H1N1) VIRUS is a subtype of the influenza A virus and was the most common cause of human flu in 2009. Some strains of H1N1 are prevalent in humans and cause a small fraction of all flulike illness and a small percentage of all seasonal flu casualties. Other strains of H1N1 are endemic in pigs (swine flu) and in birds (avian flu). In June 2009, the World Health Organization declared the new strain of swine-origin H1N1 as a pandemic. This new strain spread worldwide and caused

*A view after the tsunami swept through Banda Aceh on January 1, 2005, in Sumatra, Indonesia.*

*Thousands of people wait in line to receive an H1N1 flu vaccination during a clinic, December 22, 2009, in San Francisco.*

about 17,000 deaths by the start of 2010. In the wake of the 1918 Spanish flu pandemic, which is estimated to have killed between 50 to 100 million people (or 3-6 percent of the world's population at the time), worries persist as to how well the world could react should this new strain of H1N1, or any other pandemic, become more serious.

## 2010 POLAND MOURNS

THE 2010 POLISH AIR Force Tu-154 crash occurred on April 10, 2010, near the city of Smolensk, Russia, killing all 95 people on board. These included the Polish president Lech Kaczynski and his wife. Also killed were Poland's deputy foreign minister, Polish government officials, 12 members of the Polish parliament, senior members of the Polish clergy, senior Polish military officers, the president of the National Bank of Poland, and relatives of victims of the Katyn massacre. They were on their way from Warsaw to attend an event marking the 70th anniversary of the Katyn massacre. The cause of the crash is still under investigation.

## 2010s WORLD POPULATION GROWTH SLOWS

IN 2009, IT WAS estimated the world population would reach seven billion in 2011; current estimates by the U.S. Census Bureau put the population at 6,860,100,000. Despite many wars, diseases, and global disasters, the world population has experienced continuous growth since the end of the bubonic plague around 1400. The highest rates of growth—increases above 1.8 percent per year—were seen during the 1950s, 1960s, and 1970s. The growth rate peaked at 2.2 percent in 1963, and declined to 1.1 percent by 2009. Annual births have reduced to 140 million since their peak at 173 million in the late 1990s, and are expected to remain constant, while deaths number 57 million per year and are expected to increase to 90 million per year by 2050. Current forecasts show a steady decline in the population growth rate, with the population expected to reach between 8 and 10.5 billion between the year 2040 and 2050.

# Exploration and Empires

*Norwegian explorer Fridtjof Nansen (1861–1930).*

### 1909 REACHING THE NORTH POLE

NORWEGIAN SCIENTIST Fridtjof Nansen (1861–1930) was a principal polar explorer who completed the first expedition to the Greenland ice cap (1888–89). He then designed a ship capable of withstanding the pressure exerted by ice and embarked on an expedition across the Arctic basin in 1893 by drifting with the ice instead of ramming it. After realizing that the ship was not drifting toward the north pole, he set off with a companion to reach it on specially designed sleds but was forced to turn back 230 miles (370 km) from their objective. In 1909, American Robert Peary (1856–1920) claimed to have reached the north pole with Inuits on sleds. The Japanese adventurer Naomi Uemura made the first solo trek to the north pole (1978).

### 1910 THE SOUTH POLE

ANTARCTICA WAS the last continent to be explored. In 1908, Ernest Henry Shackleton's (1874–1922) British expedition set out on a 800-mile (1,300-km) trek to the south pole but food shortages forced them to turn back 100 miles (160 km) from their objective. The "race" to the south pole began in 1910 between a Norwegian team led by Roald Amundsen (1872–1928) and a British one

*Irish Antarctic explorer Ernest Henry Shackleton.*

led by Robert Scott (1868–1912). Using Inuit survival skills, dog sleds, and fur clothing, the Norwegians advanced faster than the mixture of horses, dogs, and motorized sleds used by Scott. Amundsen took seven weeks to reach the pole in December 1911. Scott's team arrived in January 1912, but the entire team perished on the return journey.

## 1919 POST WORLD WAR I UNREST: AMRITSAR

DURING WORLD WAR I, the imperial empires maintained the cooperation of their colonial subjects, but the period after the war exposed the fragility of their imperial control. Efforts to satisfy Arab aspirations in the Middle East led to Britain establishing the kingdoms of Iraq (declared independence 1932) and Transjordan. Similar promises made to the Jews for a "Nation Home" in Palestine created more complications and violence. The Indian independence movement proved a serious threat to British rule, with growing demands for Indian representation in central government. The 1919 Amritsar massacre of 400 Indians hardened nationalist campaigners and emergency powers were subsequently introduced to repress protests amid growing violence.

## 1920s ANTARCTIC EXPLORATION

IN 1929, RICHARD BYRD (1888–1957) flew over the south pole, Roald Amundsen became the first man to reach both the north and south poles, after flying over the North Pole in 1926, and American Lincoln Ellsworth (1880–1951) made the first flight across Antarctica (1935). Many nations have laid claims to Antarctica but conflict has been averted by international treaties that encourage conservation and cooperation in research. The potential to extract minerals from Antarctica may still generate rivalry over the continent.

*Rear Admiral Richard Evelyn Byrd (1888–1957), with his plane, the "Floyd Bennett," after an expedition to Antarctica.*

## 1930s THE GREATER EAST ASIA COPROSPERITY SPHERE

JAPAN'S INVASIONS were initially perceived as liberating nations from European colonists. Semi-independent governments were appointed, except in the "inferior" Southeast Asia region. Japan often failed to mobilize occupied areas and faced disorder and hostility instead of cooperation. Local nationalists were often given responsibilities but they used this collaboration to bolster their movements. Japanese barbarity was commonplace with forced labor, massacres, and human-rights violations. This was first displayed during the Manchuria invasion (1931), and the invasion of China (1937), where 250,000 people died in Nanking alone. China responded by resisting Japan and 15 million Chinese died.

## 1930s GANDHI AND THE INDIAN STRUGGLE

THE 1935 GOVERNMENT of India Act granted limited self-government and progressively pledged to transfer power. Such vague promises failed to satisfy the Indian National Congress. Nationalist leader Mohandas Gandhi (1869–1948), also known as Mahatma, led a campaign of *satyagraha*: passive civil disobedience

*Indian leader Mohandas Gandhi in London to attend the Round Table Conference on Indian constitutional reform.*

and the boycotting of European goods. In 1931, the British imprisoned Gandhi but failed to suppress the momentum for change. In the immediate postwar period, war-weary imperial powers were often unable to restore colonial control fully. Civil unrest in India and a naval mutiny (1946) forced Britain to accelerate moves toward independence. In elections, Indian Muslims in the north voted overwhelmingly for the Muslim League, which demanded a separate state. In August 1947, the country was partitioned into the independent India (mainly Hindu) and the newly created Pakistan (mainly Muslim).

## 1935 THE "NEW ROME"

ITALY'S EMPIRE, forged by the infamous Benito Mussolini (1883–1945), was a small and short-lived creation. It began with the invasion of Ethiopia in 1935, followed by Albania in 1939, and British Somaliland in 1940. Sections of France, Yugoslavia, and Greece also came under her control. Italy, however, lacked the capability and the commitment to retain her conquests. Britain repulsed her attack on Egypt (1940–41), then recaptured East Africa (1941). Public support for Fascist imperialism and the war was short-lived. Before Mussolini fell from power (1943), the empire was already strained by deteriorating relations with Germany in the occupied regions they shared, especially over the treatment of Jews.

## 1936 MILITARISM IN JAPAN

JAPAN HAD SEEN the rise of militaristic and imperialistic movements since 1918. Since Japan's emergence from isolationism in the nineteenth century to become modern and industrialized, the nation had developed into a leading military and economic force within Asia.

It had already gained territory from China (1894–95) and Russia (1899–1902) through military conquests. After World War I, it gained former German islands and Chinese outposts. Overseas expansion became a key policy in the period between the world wars, with Japan invading Manchuria (1931). After the military took power (1936), they began attacking China (1937). Japan's aim was for a "Greater East Asia Coprosperity Sphere," in theory, a mutually beneficial trading network; but, in reality, it was a framework to secure raw materials for Japan and markets for Japan's exports.

*Japanese troops entering Manchuria in the wake of the so-called Mukden Incident during the Sino-Japanese War.*

263

## 1939 OCCUPIED POPULATIONS

THE EFFECTS UPON Nazi-occupied populations were traumatic. Intellectual freedoms were constrained by Nazi doctrine, cultural and religious expression was replaced by the Nazi identity, politics was repressed by propaganda, information was censored, and freedom of movement limited. Economic dislocation impoverished populations and food production was directed to Germany. As conditions deteriorated and transport systems faltered, the rationing of populations reached critical levels. One of the most terrifying manifestations of the New Order was the Nazi attempt to achieve racial supremacy. The Nazis aimed to create a demographic transformation in Europe by gathering the German race. This involved enslaving the Slavs and destroying the Jews. Unlike the barbarism of former conquerors, Nazi violence was not random, but systematic, and millions were killed with bureaucratic efficiency.

## 1940s THE NAZIS PLUNDER EUROPE

GERMANY HAD ANTICIPATED a rapid victory and economic planning focused upon restructuring her empire for the postwar era. The prolonged war, however, presented Germany with pressing needs. Economic squads swarmed into conquered lands to seize raw materials, gold, machinery, and anything else of value. Germany assumed control of fuel, materials, currency, and prices. Occupation costs were imposed on countries, with France paying 10.9 percent of her national income in 1940 and 36.6 percent by 1943. German labor shortages were made up for by prisoners of war, and "voluntary"

*Norwegian Fascist traitor Vidkun Quisling (right) giving Nazi salute to an unidentified soldier.*

*German prisoners after the Battle of Stalingrad in 1943.*

or forced foreign workers that were compelled to work in Germany. By 1944, some 2 million prisoners of war and 7.5 million adults and children from across German-occupied Europe were working in Germany.

## 1945 BEYOND WORLD WAR II

THE FASCIST EMPIRES of Germany and Italy had collapsed by 1945 at the end of World War II. A total of 60 million people had died during this time. The human and material cost of these regimes was unprecedented, and they opened the eyes of the world to the dangers of such political cults. Their rise, domination, and collapse had far-reaching repercussions for the shape of the postwar world, the prewar colonial powers, and the ascendancy of new power blocs. In this short period, the world view of persecution, basic human rights, and warfare itself had changed forever.

## 1946 OPERATION HIGHJUMP

ADMIRAL RICHARD BYRD (1888–1957) returned to Antarctica in 1946 to lead the largest expedition ever mounted to that inhospitable continent. Operation Highjump involved a fleet of 13 ships and 4,700 men. Highjump charted a large extent of the coastline of the ice pack covering the pole. Expeditions such as these were considered highly prestigious in the ideological war between the United States and the Soviet Union. The scientists involved, however, preferred activities such as the International Geophysical Year (1957–58). Some 12 nations participated in this, involved in projects such as the causes of earthquakes, oceanography, meteorology, and the crossing of the Antarctic.

*George C. Marshall testifying at Senate Appropriations Committee's hearing and defending European Recovery Program against proposed cuts.*

the European Recovery Program), giving financial aid to the governments of Western Europe, erasing trade barriers and setting up institutions to coordinate economies. This aid, and other assistance to procapitalist parties, helped defeat the Communists in elections in 1948.

### 1947 THE DIVISION OF EUROPE

THE SOVIET LEADER Joseph Stalin (1879–1953) feared U.S. military power, especially the monopoly of atomic weapons. When Winston Churchill (1874–1965) made his notorious "Iron Curtain" speech in February 1946, the suspicious Stalin denounced it as "a dangerous act." In 1947–48, the Communists seized power in eastern Europe, including the now divided East Germany, all under the domination of the Soviet Union. At the same time, the Soviets gave considerable financial support to the Communist parties of France and Italy. In that year, the United States launched the Marshall Plan (officially

### 1948 COLLAPSING EMPIRES

WORLD WAR II saw the first steps toward the collapse of colonial rule, as European powers became embroiled in a global conflict that exposed deep cracks in the foundations of imperialism. The omnipotence of colonial powers was shattered by the conquests of their homelands or of their colonies. Bargaining for support, Britain offered India postwar independence in return for Indian help during the war. The Indian National Congress demanded independence immediately and, in an about-turn, an Indian National Army even fought with the Japanese against Britain. Resistance groups who campaigned against occupation planned to fight both the Axis powers and the imperialists.

### 1948 GLOBAL COLD WAR

THE BEGINNING OF the Cold War is normally associated with the Berlin Blockade of 1948. At the beginning of 1942, the Communists triumphed in China, while in August, the Soviet Union detonated an atomic bomb, ending the atomic monopoly of the United States. Suddenly, the Communist bloc had been transformed into a genuine global rival to the United States. In 1950, the Communists of North Korea invaded South Korea which was backed by the United States. The United Nations, founded to end such conflicts, intervened when the Soviet Union boycotted a crucial Security Council meeting, and so was not able to use its veto against an american proposal to name North Korea as the aggressor. Hundreds of thousands of American and allied troops invaded Korea under the flag of the United Nations. The war lasted until 1953.

### 1950s THE DOMINO ERA

COMMUNISTS WERE frequently involved in the highest councils of independence movements, which, therefore, became suspect in the eyes of the United States. The worst offenders from this perspective were the Indochinese Communists led by Ho Chi Minh (1890–1969). When the French finally agreed to the independence of Indochina, the United States supported an anti-Communist regime in its own state in the south. The Vietnamese War continued because political leaders in the United States had adopted a strategy of containment. Friendly governments were established in various states bordering the Communist bloc, and linked by means of military alliances, such as the Baghdad Pact of 1955 between Turkey, Iraq, Iran, and Pakistan. The strategy was publicized under the less aggressive name of the "Domino theory."

*Troops in Berlin at the beginning of the Cold War in 1948.*

267

*A rally in Trafalgar Square, London, in protest against the British government's action in the Suez Crisis.*

## 1956 THE SUEZ CRISIS

WITH LITTLE COLONIAL reform in Africa, independence campaigns arose. The first major incident, which exposed imperial vulnerability, was the Kenyan Mau-Mau guerrilla war (1952–56). Nations like Britain became increasingly aware that decolonization would not disrupt overseas economic interests, but would relieve them of imperial defense and administration. The 1956 Suez Crisis, where France and Britain had to make a humiliating withdrawal from Egypt under American pressure, undermined the credibility of the colonial powers and revealed their declining global status. A major review of Britain's imperial position resulted in Ghana becoming the first independent nation in Africa (1957). By 1964, British prime minister Harold Macmillan (1894–1986) spoke of a "wind of change" as decolonization spread through Africa and the Caribbean.

## 1956 FIGHTING AND FREEDOM IN AFRICA

IN 1956, FRANCE left Morocco and Tunisia, but Algerian independence was opposed by the one million Algerians

*Crowds in Algiers celebrating their country's Independence Day in the city center.*

of French descent (*colons*), who rejected the idea of an Arab Muslim state. In 1954, a nationalist Arab rebellion sparked a bitter civil conflict. To halt any withdrawal, French army officers sympathetic to the *colons* revolted (1958) and a new premier, Charles de Gaulle (1890–1970), was appointed. De Gaulle withdrew from the colonies of Guinea (1958), Cameroon, Congo, Gabon, Chad, and the Central African Republic (1960). Algeria finally gained independence in 1962. In Southern Rhodesia, the ruling white minority declared independence in 1965. White-dominated South Africa adopted a racist apartheid policy in 1948 and amid opposition from the British Commonwealth, became a republic (1948).

*Cuban rebel leaders Fidel Castro (center) and Camilo Cienfuego enter Havana after the victory over the forces of Cuban dictator Fulgencio Batista.*

## 1957 THE HIGH WATERMARK OF COMMUNISM

IN OCTOBER 1957, the Soviet Union's considerable investment of resources into rocket technology paid off with the launch of an unmanned satellite, called Sputnik, into space. Politicians and military leaders in the United States were alarmed. The United States had, in 1955, openly declared its intention of launching a space satellite in 1958 as part of International Geophysical Year. The Soviets had kept quiet and beaten the United States to it. The advantage the Soviets had in rocket technology enabled them to repeat the feat of beating the United States in what had been christened "the Space Race." In 1959, a Cuban civil war ended with the victory of Fidel Castro (born 1927), a man who openly welcomed the support of Cuba's Communists to his regime.

## 1960s THE SPACE AGE

ENTERING SPACE was first achieved by American Robert Goddard's (1882–1945) liquid fuel rocket (1926). In 1957, the first satellite was launched by the Soviet Union. The first manned space flight carried Russian Yuri Gagarin (1934–68) in 1961. John Glenn became the first American to orbit the earth in 1962. Russian Valentina Tereshkova (born 1937) was the first woman astronaut (1963) and Russian Alexei Leonov made the first space walk (1965). Space exploration was entangled with superpower rivalry and became a showpiece for technical superiority. One of the greatest missions was the "race" to the moon. In July 1969, the United States won when Neil Armstrong (born 1930), Buzz Aldrin (born 1930), and Michael Collins (born 1930) landed on the moon.

*Russian astronaut Yuri Gagarin (1934–68) became the first man in space in 1961.*

## 1960 THE SUBMERSIBLE RECORD

IN 1930, AMERICAN INVENTOR William Beebe (1877–1962) designed a spherical diving machine capable of withstanding water pressure at deep levels. In 1948, Swiss scientist Auguste Piccard (1884–1962) designed a submersible that could dive and surface without assistance from a ship. In 1960, a submersible made a record-breaking descent 7 miles (11 km) into the Mariana Trench in the Pacific Ocean, the world's deepest recorded place. In 1943, Frenchmen Jacques Cousteau and Emile Gaynon designed the first aqualung: cylinders containing compressed air fed to divers through a mouthpiece. This invention opened a new era in exploration because divers could now descend to 200 feet (60 m) without being constrained by heavy suits or air cables.

## 1975 THE UNITED STATES AND THE SOVIET UNION

SO MUCH OF the Soviet Union's resources were devoted to military expenditure that it was distorting economic development. After the victory of North Vietnam in 1975, the United States began to reject Soviet overtures to reduce tension between the superpowers. In 1979, when an internal political dispute threatened the stability of a Soviet-sponsored regime in Afghanistan, the Red Army invaded. This intervention allowed the United States to sponsor a guerrilla movement of Islamic militants. By 1985, when Mikhail Gorbachev (born 1931) emerged as party leader, the event signaled an end to old policies. Once the threat of military intervention was lifted, the Communist bloc fell apart. Non-Communists formed a government in Poland in 1989, and in 1991, the Soviet Union itself began to fall into disintegration.

*The launch of the Space Shuttle* Columbus *in 1982.*

### 1977 SPACE EXPLORATION: VOYAGERS

HUMAN SPACE TRAVEL still involves considerable obstacles. Prolonged weightlessness causes physical problems. Protective clothing must be worn at all times outside the spacecraft because of extreme temperatures and radioactivity. Space debris from previous explorations is now posing a threat as a collision with fast-moving fragments can damage craft. Space probes capable of breaking free of gravity are a major part of exploration. They have the capability to send back pictures and signals from distant destinations. Launched in 1977, Voyagers 1 and 2 have made some spectacular discoveries during flights to Jupiter, Saturn, Uranus, and Neptune.

### 1990s–2000s PROFITS OR PROPHETS?

DURING THE 1990s, it seemed old-style military imperialism was vanishing, but the United States involvement in Afghanistan (2001) and Iraq (2003) brought echoes of earlier history. In the modern global economy, commercial empire building has proved more successful. The flow of money between financial centers can bring national economies to their knees, while the impact of "cultural" imperialism can be seen everywhere, with familiar logos, brands, and fast foods ousting local styles. The challenge to consumer imperialism and to democratic liberal thinking seems to come from religious conservatism, for example, from Islamic fundamentalists.

271

## 2001 WORLD'S FIRST SPACE TOURIST

DENNIS ANTHONY TITO (born 1940) is an American multimillionaire, and the first space tourist to pay for his own ticket. In mid-2001, he spent nearly eight days in orbit on the International Space Station. In a project first arranged by MirCorp, Tito was accepted by the Russian Federal Space Agency as a candidate. Before the launch, Tito met criticism from NASA, which considered space tourism inappropriate. Through an arrangement with the space tourism company Space Adventures Ltd. Tito joined Soyuz TM-32 on April 28, 2001, spending 7 days, 22 hours, 4 minutes in space and orbiting the earth 128 times. Tito performed several scientific experiments in orbit that he said would be useful for his company and business. Tito paid a reported 20 million dollars for his trip.

*Chinese astronaut Yang Liwei waves before emerging from the Shenzhou V capsule in Inner Mongolia, October 16, 2003.*

## 2003 CHINA'S FIRST MANNED SPACE MISSION

ON OCTOBER 15, 2003, Yang Liwei became China's first man in space in their spacecraft Shenzhou. Unmanned test flights first began in January 2001, and China since became only the third country to attempt and successfully achieve human space flight independently. The Shenzhou was developed to become the foundation of China's manned spaceflight program. Its name can be loosely translated to mean "Divine Craft" but can also mean "Vessel of the Gods", "Divine Mechanism", and is also a play on a name for China. The Shenzhou is equipped with its own propulsion, solar power, and control systems, which allows independent flight. In March 2005, an asteroid became named 8256 Shenzhou in honor of the spacecraft.

## 2005 PROBE REACHES SATURN'S MOON

THE HUYGENS probe, a mission by the European Space Agency, was an entry probe carried to Saturn's moon Titan as part of the Cassini-Huygens mission. The combined Cassini-Huygens spacecraft was launched on October 15, 1997. Huygens separated from the Cassini orbiter on December 25, 2004, and landed on Titan on January 14, 2005, near the Xanadu region. It touched down on land, although the possibility that it would touch down in an ocean was also taken into account in its design. Although it was never officially designated a lander, the probe continued to send data for about 90 minutes after reaching Titan's surface.

## 2008 INDIA REACHES THE MOON

THE MOON IMPACT Probe was developed by the Indian Space Research Organization (ISRO), India's national space agency. It was a lunar probe that was released by ISRO's *Chandrayaan-1* orbiter, which in turn was launched, on October 22, 2008, aboard an adapted version of ISRO's Polar Satellite Launch Vehicle. The probe separated from the moon-orbiting *Chandrayaan*-1 on November 14, 2008 at 8:06 p.m., and landed, as planned, on the lunar south pole after a controlled descent. The probe struck the moon's surface on November 14, 2008, releasing underground debris that could be analyzed by the orbiter for presence of water.

*A series of images, captured by Cassini on October 6, 2004, were composed into the largest, most detailed, global natural-color view of Saturn and its rings ever made.*

# Trade and Industry

### 1903 THE MOTOR VEHICLE

THE AUTOMOBILE industry is the world's largest industry, employing about one-tenth of all manufacturing workers. Automobile manufacture began in France, in about 1890, at first in small workshops producing one car at a time. About ten years later, automobile factories appeared in the United States. In the early days, the European makers built all the necessary parts themselves, whereas the Americans assembled parts they bought in from other firms. Henry Ford (1863–1947) founded the Ford Motor Company in Detroit in 1903 and five years later invented the famous

*Motoring pioneer Henry Ford (1863–1947), one of the first producers of mass-produced cars.*

*The Model T Ford, the first car made on an assembly line.*

Model T Ford, which was made on an assembly line using standard, mass-produced parts. In the same year (1908), William Durant founded the General Motors Corporation, also in Detroit.

### 1914 THE INVENTION OF INVENTION

THE PROCESS OF INVENTION underwent an important change from 1914 onward. Before then, most inventions had been made by individuals working to their own brief and from their own passion or inspiration. The inventors often had heart-wrenching difficulty in persuading others of the value of their work, let alone in getting the invention put into production. World War I changed this. From then on, manufacturers and managers analyzed where there were bottlenecks or inefficiencies, identified what kinds of machine or weapon or process were needed, and then commissioned experts to come up with ideas that met the specifications. Invention was, thus, deliberate instead of accidental, and was controlled by technological advance. The rate of invention accelerated greatly and the link between theory and practice became infinitely more direct.

## 1918 JAPANESE INDUSTRIAL ETHOS AND DEVELOPMENT

AFTER WORLD WAR I, when Japan was eager to industrialize in order to become militarily strong, cheap labor, efficient new machinery, and active government participation brought striking success. Japanese samurai traditions persisted, with minor adaptations. Profit was never an end in itself but was secondary to honor and prestige. The old warrior virtues of courage, endurance, and loyalty translated smoothly into managerial skills. The relationships

between samurai and peasant also carried over into the workplace: managers commanded, workers obeyed, and, in return for absolute loyalty, were looked after for life. Similarly, the practice of "putting out"—hiring outworkers and purchasing their finished products at decent prices—was a system of benevolent patronage. The economic miracle in Japan was not, therefore, the product of modern, democratic ideas.

*Samurai traditions continued in Japan into the 20th century.*

## 1920s HYPERINFLATION IN GERMANY

INFLATION IS THE RATE of increase of prices. Inflation makes people's savings worthless and makes the whole economy less efficient. To keep inflation under control, governments now work with trade unions and businesses to limit wage and price rises. Extremely high inflation, normally interpreted as more than 1,000 percent a year, is called "hyperinflation." This happened in Germany in 1922–23. Workers had to be paid twice a day! In Europe in the sixteenth century, prices rose about 400 percent after silver discovered in Peru brought an abundance of bullion to Europe. Later, inflation hit developing countries hard, partly because of the dramatic oil-price increase of 1973–74 and poor harvests worldwide.

*A crowd of depositors outside the American Union Bank in New York, having failed to withdraw their savings before the bank collapsed.*

## 1930s THE GREAT DEPRESSION

THE GREAT DEPRESSION was a worldwide economic slump that began in 1929 with the Wall Street Crash. The Crash was caused by excessive investment in the domestic market that pushed prices up to unsustainable levels, whereupon shareholders switched to selling and prices plummeted. On "Black Tuesday," October 29, 1929, 16 million shares were traded and 10 billion dollars were wiped off share values. The Crash caused large-scale bankruptcies and unemployment rose by nearly two million within six months. Elsewhere in the world, banks, unable to pay depositors, were forced to close. A shortage of cash meant that less money was available for investment in industry or in farm products. In the United States, drought and dust storms devastated parts of the Midwest and southwest, causing the so-called Dust Bowl.

## 1930s THE DEMISE OF THE GOLD STANDARD

THE GOLD STANDARD is a system under which money may be converted, on demand, into gold. It was a system that was widely adopted in the second half of the nineteenth century, principally to make international transactions easier to settle and to stabilize foreign-exchange rates and domestic money supply. Great Britain was the first country to go on the gold standard (1816) followed by the United States (1873). Most countries abandoned it again in the 1930s, in the wake of the Great Depression. This was because they believed that their exports would be boosted if they devalued their currencies in terms of foreign exchange. Once this practice had become widespread, however, no country was left with any competitive advantage. By the late 1970s, gold had become more of a commodity than a standard and no major currency could be redeemed as gold.

### 1933 THE NEW DEAL

IN 1933, PRESIDENT, Franklin D. Roosevelt (1882–1945), inaugurated a "New Deal" in response to the Great Depression that had been afflicting the country and devastating the national and global economies since the Wall Street Crash in 1929. Immediate measures included the provision of employment on public works, government loans to farmers at low rates of interest, and a restriction of agricultural output to raise prices. Other reforms included old-age and unemployment insurance, measures to prevent forced ("sweated") and child labor, protection of employees' rights to organize protests against unfair employment practices, and assistance with slum clearance. The New Deal was successful in that it reduced unemployment from 17 million to 8 million. Interestingly, the Supreme Court in 1935–36 declared many of the provisions of the New Deal unconstitutional. A major New Deal project was the Tennessee Valley scheme that harnessed the Tennessee River to provide cheap electricity and protection from floods.

*President Franklin D. Roosevelt (1882–1945).*

## 1944 ORGANIC FARMING

LADY EVE BALFOUR (1899–1990) headed a movement biological, regenerative, or sustainable farming. Not only a talented jazz trombonist and pilot, Lady Balfour was an assiduous agricultural researcher and in 1944 published *The Living Soil*. Two years later she helped form the Soil Association. Organic farming as much as possible excludes the use of synthetically produced fertilizers, pesticides, feed additives, and growth regulators. Preferred farming methods, therefore, include crop rotation, the use of green and animal manures, and biological pest and weed control. Organic farming methods are sometimes the only option in underdeveloped and developing areas. In developed countries, organic farming is gaining ground, often as a reaction against intensive or factory farming or scares about food safety.

*Scientific advances in agriculture have had profound effects worldwide.*

## 1945 TECHNOLOGICAL ADVANCE

THE MOST SPECTACULAR technological developments from 1945 onward were in the military field, but a greater number occurred in other areas. Chemical fertilizers, insecticides, herbicides, seed selection, and animal breeding changed agriculture completely. New drugs were developed, which went into production on an unprecedented scale. Television found its way into millions of homes. Although these advances brought advantages, they also tended to widen the gap between rich and poor nations. The former had the resources and skilled manpower to pursue research; the latter often suffered a "brain drain." Scientists and innovators also attained a not wholly enviable status as "ivory-tower" eggheads, remote from the rest of society.

## 1947 GATT AND WTO

THE GENERAL AGREEMENT on Tariffs and Trade (GATT) was signed in Geneva in 1947 by representatives of

23 non-Communist nations. By 1988, there were 96 members. GATT created an international forum dedicated to the expansion of multilateral trade and the settlement of trade disputes. Members agreed to treat all other members equally, following the most-favored-nation policy. In theory, this represented a desire to abolish all nontariff barriers to trade. The eighth round of trade negotiations, the Uruguay Round, continued from 1986 to 1996, and the final agreements resulted in the creation of the World Trade Organization (WTO), which superseded GATT. The WTO incorporates the original principles of GATT but extends them to include trade in services, intellectual property rights, and investment and, since February 1997, the liberalization of the telecommunications trade.

## 1950s THE NUCLEAR AND SPACE RACES

IN 1945, ONLY the United States possessed atomic bombs. By 1949, Soviet scientists, working partly on information collected by spies, were able to duplicate the technology and detonated their first atomic bomb. The government then started work on the H-bomb, a more powerful type of nuclear warhead, in which energy is derived from hydrogen fusion. The Soviets were only a few months behind; both nations exploded their first hydrogen warheads in 1953–54. The next goal was to develop rockets capable of delivering nuclear warheads, which both had achieved by the early 1960s. Into the 1970s, the armaments race demanded a very considerable part of their national resources. A by-product was the exploration of space. Since rockets could carry warheads, they could also launch artificial satellites into orbit around the earth.

*This picture taken in 1970 shows a French nuclear test at Mururoa, French Polynesia.*

*Drake's Well in Pennsylvania, where oil was first struck in 1859.*

## 1959 THE PETROLEUM INDUSTRY

WORLD OIL OUTPUT attained about one billion tons for the first time as the petroleum industry celebrated its first centenary in 1959. The industry began with Drake's well at Titusville, Pennsylvania, which was the world's leading producer almost unbrokenly until the 1960s. Its feverish attempts to search for oil had included the digging of more than a million wells. Of the top ten producers in 1989, the first four, measured in terms of years of reserves, were in the Persian Gulf area. Oil offers tremendous advantages over most other forms of energy: it is a liquid and, thus, easier to handle than coal, for example; it has a higher calorific value than coal, weight for weight; and it can be refined for different purposes.

## 1960s CHANGES IN ENERGY PRODUCTION

IN THE HUNDRED YEARS after 1860, world energy production increased about 30 times. Most of that increase occurred in countries with high levels of economic development. Energy supplies are regarded as either primary or secondary. Primary consists of new increments of energy, whereas secondary energy is primary energy that has been rendered into a more convenient and usable form. Primary energy resources are of either the perpetual or the accumulated type. The former come from solar radiation and exist in enormous quantities accordingly, but they are difficult and expensive to harness because the energy is dissipated almost as fast as the earth receives it. Hydroelectric, tidal, and solar energy are examples. Accumulated resources consist of fossil fuels, such as coal and oil.

## 1960s GREEN REVOLUTION

FIRST USED used in the 1960s, the green revolution is the term used to describe the effort to increase and diversify crop yields in developing countries. American agricultural scientist Norman E. Borlaug is often considered the founder of the Green Revolution. Many countries have taken steps to implement Borlaug's

*Wind turbines in a farmer's cornfield.*

program for achieving agricultural efficiency. Paradoxically, it stresses the need to: abandon local, traditional strains of plants and animal breeds in favor of new strains and breeds; conduct research to enable new procedures to be adapted to local conditions; and obtain long-term support from government to apply and extend knowledge and achieve changes in the infrastructure in order to stabilize the numbers of people in a society and enhance the quality of their lives.

## 1960s THE COMPUTER INDUSTRY

IT WAS NOT until the 1940s that the computer industry even existed and its products were not widely used until the 1960s. The computer industry is now one of the fastest growing industries in the world. The largest companies making machines include IBM (which has set the standard, especially for home computers), Hewlett Packard, Apple, and Acorn. Other companies make the components used to build computers. Computer hardware is sometimes now made in developing countries, where the labor is inexpensive. Components such as silicon chips are still made in industrial countries, such as the United States and Japan. The software-operating systems that computers use are written by computer programmers. The largest software company is Microsoft Corporation, which provides millions of computer-operating systems worldwide. Computers continue to become faster and more efficient with larger memories and more power.

*The first computer, from 1944; over the next five decades, the computer industry would advance beyond recognition.*

## 1965 THE RISE OF INTERNATIONAL TRADE

INTERNATIONAL TRADE has grown greatly as a proportion of total economic activity in the twentieth century. Protectionist interests within regional trading communities, such as Mercosur (Latin America), may cause them to restrict trade with countries outside their own circle, but equally the regional groupings can serve as first steps toward reaching broader trade agreements. World trade increased fivefold between 1965 and 1976 and almost doubled again by 1985.

## 1979–2002 TOWARD A SINGLE CURRENCY

THE EUROPEAN MONETARY SYSTEM (EMS) came into force in 1979, with the aim of establishing monetary stability within the European Community, which became the European Union (EU) from the 1993 Maastricht Treaty. The aim was to correct fluctuations in exchange rates, and a standard monetary unit, the European Currency Unit (ECU), was created. The Exchange Rate Mechanism set up within the EMS was a stepping stone toward monetary union, established in January 1999, and followed in 2002 by the introduction in all but three EU member states of the new euro currency. Euros replaced familiar coins and notes (French franc, Italian lira, German deutsche mark, etc). Critics feared loss of national autonomy over monetary policy; Britain remained outside the euro zone, pending a referendum on membership.

## 1980s ROBOTS

NOT ONLY HAS the computer changed people's personal and business lives, it has also changed manufacturing. In many factories, robots perform simple tasks faster and more accurately than people. When computers are used to design, make, and assemble product parts, this is called computer-integrated manufacturing (CIM). Computers control robots, which can be adapted to do new tasks simply by changing the computer

*Robots at work in a car factory.*

program. The use of robots makes smaller factories possible: robots take up little space and are flexible. A robot can make a small number of a particular product and then switch to making a different one. Factories can, thus, produce a wider range of low-cost products.

### 1980s GOVERNMENT SERVICE

IN MOST ECONOMIES, the State has usually been the largest employer. Some developing countries in the early days of independence developed a very large civil service. This was because employment by the State was regarded as a reward to individuals for having helped the nation achieve self-determination or prosperity. When the planned economies, especially in the then Soviet Union and eastern Europe, collapsed in the late 1980s, they took with them their inflated bureaucracies. Capitalist states also recognized the need for a reduction in government role in economies.

### 1990 TOURISM BUSINESS

TOURISM HAS BECOME a gigantic business since the 1960s. As people became more affluent, they could spend more on vacations. Many developing countries have promoted themselves as tourist destinations in order to earn

*People spend more on vacations as they become more affluent.*

foreign currency, which they can use to pay for the imports they need. The Gambia, in West Africa, is one country in which tourism has become a major sector of the economy. In 1965, it received just 20 visitors. In 1990, there were 114,000. The gains and losses in the tourism industry can be quite complex. The profits from hotels and other tourist services may go to foreign owners, although taxes paid to the host government represent a gain. Some of the goods and materials provided for tourists, such as food and drink, may be imported, at the expense of support for local agriculture and manufacture. On the other hand, the business provides jobs for local people.

*Container ship in the port of Genoa, Italy.*

## 1990s INDUSTRY VS. MANUFACTURING

THE WORD "INDUSTRY" is often used interchangeably with "manufacturing." Manufacturing is the making of goods by taking raw materials and applying skills and machines to them. Until the mid-twentieth century, more people worked in manufacturing than in any other form of work. Now, with the advent of automation and more advanced machinery, including computer-assisted processes, no more than 30 percent of people work in manufacturing. Industry in its widest sense includes manufacturing and the provision of services, mining, extraction and semiprocessing, and trade. A distinction may be made between heavy and light industry. Heavy industry includes such basic industries as coalmining, shipbuilding, and steelmaking, requiring heavy equipment. Light industry refers to the processing in smaller factories of such goods as electronics components and glass.

## 1990s SUPPLY AND DEMAND

THE PRICE OF A COMMODITY tends to depend on supply, that is, the amount available for sale, and demand, the amount that consumers want to buy. The higher the price of a commodity, the more of it suppliers will want to sell. Supply, therefore, generally increases as the price increases. On the other hand, rising prices will eventually discourage buyers. In a free market, a balance is usually achieved between supply and demand by pitching prices at the right level. Governments are responsible for printing money. It might be supposed that if they simply print more, everyone will be richer. In fact, if the money supply increases, people are increasingly eager to buy more goods and services. The higher demand then leads to higher prices (inflation).

## 1998 CRISIS IN THE GLOBAL ECONOMY

IN THE LATE 1990s an economic crisis occurred in Southeast Asia and spread across the world. In July and August 1998 alone, four trillion dollars were wiped off the value of shares worldwide. Commodity prices, including oil and grain prices, collapsed to their lowest level in real terms since the 1930s. The Asian "miracle" burst as a result of massive speculation against fixed currencies. For example, Singapore had pegged its dollar to the United States since the early 1970s and had succeeded in attracting huge flows of inward investment. China's devaluation of its currency in 1994 was a last straw. Just as other Asian economies were moving into a boom, their fixed link to the dollar was making exports uncompetitive. Inflation rose. One by one, countries were forced off the dollar peg, currencies plunged, and stock markets crashed. Leading economists suggested exchange controls as the least damaging way out of the crisis.

## 2000s THE POLITICS OF SCARCITY

SURPLUS WAS A KEY FEATURE of the world economy in the 50 years after World War II. Now, scarcity is more prevalent, with oil prices, for example, rising sharply in 2004 as demand from China surged. Uncertainly about security, especially in oil-rich Saudi Arabia and Iraq, also affected the oil market. China's growing economy has stimulated consumer demand from its one billion-plus population, and demand is also growing fast in other Asian states such as India, Indonesia, and South Korea. Asia is more agriculturally vulnerable, particularly as it depends heavily on grain imports from the United States. Fast-growing populations put even greater pressure on food supplies, especially in parts of Africa hit by drought or civil war.

*Muslim workers pray outside a factory in Jakarta, Indonesia, during the emerging markets collapse of 1998 and the currency, the rupiah, lost a lot of its value.*

## 1990–2000s RESPONDING TO WAR AND OIL LOW PRICES

LEADING UP TO the 1990–91 Gulf War, Iraqi president Saddam Hussein promoted the Organization of Petroleum Exporting Countries (OPEC) to push up oil prices in an effort to assist Iraq and other member states to service debts. However, the division of OPEC countries caused by the Iraq-Iran War and the Iraq invasion of Kuwait marked a low in OPEC's solidarity. Once supply disruption fears that accompanied these conflicts relented, oil prices began to slide dramatically. After oil prices dropped to around 15 dollars a barrel in the late 1990s, concerted diplomacy, attributed to Venezuelan President Hugo Chávez, achieved a coordinated scaling back of oil production in 1998. In 2000, Chávez hosted the first summit of heads of state of OPEC in 25 years. The next year, however, the 9/11 attacks against the United States, the subsequent invasion of Afghanistan, and the 2003 invasion of Iraq prompted a huge surge in oil prices to levels far higher than those targeted by OPEC. In November 2007, global oil prices reacted strongly as OPEC members spoke about potentially converting their cash reserves to the Euro and away from the U.S. dollar. On October 10, 2008, oil began trading below 85 dollars.

*Venezuelan president Hugo Chávez, sign a 20-point Caracas Declaration adopted at the end of a two-day OPEC summit.*

## 2007–10 GLOBAL FINANCIAL CRISIS

THE FINANCIAL CRISIS that began in 2007 was triggered by a liquidity shortfall in the U.S. banking system caused by the overvaluation of assets. It resulted in the collapse of large financial institutions, the bailout of financial institutions by national governments, and a decline in global stock market values. The housing market also suffered, resulting in numerous evictions and foreclosures. It is considered by many economists to be the worst financial crisis since the 1930s' Great Depression. It contributed to the failure of key businesses, declines in consumer wealth, and a significant decline in economic activity. The collapse of global housing prices, which peaked in the United States in 2006, caused the values of securities tied to them to plummet, damaging financial institutions globally. Economies worldwide slowed during this period as credit tightened and international trade declined. Critics argued that credit-rating agencies and investors failed to accurately price the risk involved with mortgage related financial products, and that governments did not adjust their regulatory practices to address the twenty-first century financial markets.

*Richard Fuld Jr., CEO of Lehman Brothers Holdings, testifies before a House Oversight and Government Reform Committee hearing about the bankruptcy of his company, October 6, 2008.*

## 2008 LEHMAN BROTHERS, FANNIE MAE, AND FREDDIE MAC GO BUST

The real estate and financial crisis that was prompted by a sudden and striking rise in subprime mortgage foreclosures in the United States. Until declaring bankruptcy in 2008, Lehman Brothers Holdings Inc. was one of the world's most important global financial services firms and was a primary dealer in the U.S. Treasury securities market. On September 15, 2008, the firm filed for bankruptcy protection, following an exodus of most of its clients and a devaluation of its assets. The filing marked the largest bankruptcy in American history. A report by a court-appointed examiner in March 2010, pointed toward Lehman executives regularly using accounting tricks to make its finances appear stronger than they were. In the same year, there was a federal takeover of Fannie Mae (Federal National Mortgage Association) and Freddie Mac (Federal Home Loan Mortgage Corporation), when they were placed into conservatorship by the U.S. Treasury in September 2008. This action was one of the most sweeping government interventions in the private financial markets in decades. Between the two organizations, they owned over half of the American mortgage market, valued at over 6 trillion dollars. The result of these closures and many more like them has been a large decline in the capital of many banks and financial institutions, creating a worldwide credit crunch.

# Science and Technology

### 1900s ELECTRIC APPLIANCES

THE INTRODUCTION OF domestic electricity supplies led to an inevitable vogue for electrical "labor-saving" devices for the home. There have been many and various appliances marketed, some of which have become ubiquitous components of the household; others have become obsolete or just didn't take off. The familiar inventions include: iron (1882); kettle (1891); toaster (1893); hair dryer and heater (1899); washing machine (1907); dishwasher (1914); mower (1916); clock (1918); blanket (1927); microwave oven (1947); watch (1957); calculator (1964); and personal organizer (1993). The fact that these devices are so often taken for granted is testament to their usefulness. They are so much a part of our lives that they become very conspicuous by their absence if they break down or if the electricity supply is cut off.

### 1900s GADGETS

THERE HAVE BEEN many useful gadgets introduced during the twentieth century that are not technologically significant, but nonetheless are important for our daily routine in the modern environment. They include: safety razor (1901); lipstick (1915);

*Illustration showing the first Gillette safety razor with replaceable blade.*

electric razor (1931); aerosol canister (1941); ballpoint pen (1944); disposable pen (1953); quartz watch (1960); electric toothbrush (1961); tab-opening beverage can (1962); color Polaroid camera (1963); digital watch (1971); disposable lighter (1973); disposable razor (1974); and disposable camera (1986). The use-once-and-throw-away philosophy is indicative of the ethos of modern society, where new is perceived to be good and old bad. It is generally an optimistic outlook that arose in the 1950s and 1960s and has since created a consumer-led market. It should be pointed out, however, that the recycling of disposed materials has become an intrinsic part of the philosophy over the latter part of the twentieth century.

## 1900s MEDICAL SCANNING

MODERN TECHNOLOGY has provided new ways for scanning the body since the advent of X-rays. Sound waves at frequencies inaudible to humans are used in the ultrasound scanner. The sound waves, emitted by the scanner, penetrate the tissue and bounce back in different ways, according to the density and depth of tissue types. The returning waves are interpreted by the scanner and an image is assembled on a screen. Sound waves with very high power, called ultrasonics, can be used to disintegrate kidney or gallstones. The advantage of using sound waves is that they are a noninvasive and safe way of scanning. X-rays have been further developed in the CAT (Computerized Axial Tomography) scanner. This machine uses X-rays to build up a stereoscopic image of the body by building up layer after layer of cross-sectional images with a scintillator.

*A physician records notes while reviewing CAT (CT) Scans at Falmouth Hospital in Falmouth, Massachusetts.*

## 1900s SYNTHETICS

THE MODERN WORLD uses many synthetic materials, which are the brainchildren of chemical scientists who have been working on them since the turn of the twentieth century, largely thanks to the petrochemicals industry. Synthetic materials, collectively known as plastics, because they can be molded or formed, have become ubiquitous and frequently used in place of other "natural" materials. There have been many different types of plastics developed over the past hundred years. Most are polymeric structures, which means that they have large molecules that are made up of many relatively simple repeated units. Plastics belong in two groups: thermosetting and thermomelting, the latter being recyclable by heating. The first plastics used were celluloid and Bakelite, but by the 1930s, the polymer plastics began to be developed. They include: polyethylene, polypropylene, polystyrene, polyester, polyamides (nylon), polyvinylchloride (PVC or vinyl), acrylics, viscose (rayon), epoxies, acetates, and polytetrafluoroethene (PTFE). Their applications are many and various, for example molded components, synthetic fibers, sheets, resins, adhesives, hardeners, plasticizers, nonstick coatings, and so on.

## 1903 POWERED FLIGHT

JOHN STRINGFELLOW (1799–1883) first proved that powered flight was possible, with a large model airplane powered by a steam engine in 1848. The first manned powered flight came in 1903, when Orville Wright (1871–1948) took to the air in the "Flyer," built by him and his brother Wilbur (1867–1912), and propelled by a gas engine. The Heinkel He 178, built by Hans von Ohain, was the first plane to use a turbojet engine in 1939, which was superseded by the gas-turbinejet engine, first fitted into the Gloster-Whittle E 28/29 in 1941, and invented by Frank Whittle (1907–96). Modified versions of the Whittle engine went on to become the standard power unit for military and commercial jet planes alike. The earliest helicopters were experimented with after 1905, but the first practical design, with the standard layout, only came in 1935.

## 1905 EINSTEIN'S THEORIES OF RELATIVITY

ALBERT EINSTEIN (1879–1955) formulated theories about the nature and structure of the universe that transformed understanding of the way things behave. In 1905, Einstein's *Special Theory of Relativity* was published. In it, he proposed various ideas on the subject of matter, light, space, and time, not least that they are

*Albert Einstein (1879–1955), whose theories of relativity form the basis of modern science.*

all interrelated. He provided complex mathematical formulae to reinforce his ideas and went on to release his *General Theory of Relativity* in 1916 and *Unified Field Theory* in 1953. Einstein's work led to the developments in nuclear fusion and fission.

## 1908 THE MODEL T FORD

IN 1890, THE FRENCH car manufacturers, Panhard, produced the automobile that established the standard layout of most cars to come. At first, automobiles were expensive to own, but by 1908 Henry Ford (1863–1947) started producing his Model T. It was designed to be affordable and by 1927, 15 million had rolled out of his factories. In 1913, Ford introduced the first conveyor-belt assembly line and truly interchangeable parts, which revolutionized the car industry, as well as others. Inspired by Ford, other car manufacturers followed suit, such as Citroën, Peugeot, Renault, Austin, Morris, Fiat, and Volkswagen. Gas-powered truck and buses appeared in the 1890s, but the diesel engine took over in the 1920s and 1930s. Felix Wankels' (1902–88) rotary gas engine was first used in 1967, but the four-stroke cylinder engine has remained popular.

## 1913 CONVEYORS

MEAT-PROCESSING factories in the United States had introduced conveyor cables for moving carcasses by the 1890s. Henry Ford (1863–1947) introduced a conveyor to his assembly line for producing cars in 1913. After that, conveyors became accepted as part of the route to achieving optimum efficiency in all kinds of industries. Many kinds of conveyors have been developed for handling unit and bulk materials, according to different process requirements. They include belt, roller, chain, bucket, and carousel conveyors. Other conveyors have been invented for carrying people themselves. Escalators, elevators, and moving walkways are all conveying machines designed for saving the effort of walking or climbing.

## 1926 ROCKETS AND MISSILES

THE FIRST LIQUID-FUEL rocket was fired in 1926 by Robert Goddard (1882–1945) in the United States. The German Wernher von Braun (1912–77) developed the principle during the 1930s and made the V2 liquid-fuel rocket used by the Nazis, 1943–45. After World War II , he traveled to the United States, where his work led to Saturn rockets, which launched the Apollo missions between 1968–72. Space rockets have since been superseded by space shuttles, and there are current developments using laser technology as the propellant force. Use of both liquid-and solid-fuel rockets has carried on evolving in the realm of weaponry. Today, sophisticated guided missile systems are state of the art.

*Rocket technology greatly advanced throughout the 20th century, leading to developments in missile weapons.*

### 1926 TELEVISION

THE PRINCIPLE that led to the invention of the television was discovered in 1873. It was found that selenium, a nonmetallic element, was photoconductive. This meant that electrons fired at it would illuminate the surface and that electrical impulses could be made into images by illuminating dots with varying brightness. It was John Logie Baird who first demonstrated "black-and-white" television in 1926. Only two years later, he was able to demonstrate full-color television. In 1908, Campbell Swinton suggested the use of a cathode-ray tube as a transmitter and receiver for electrical information. It had been developed in the late 1800s—Rontgen discovered X-rays while using one—and provided a clear path for electrons because it contained a vacuum. By 1934, the cathode-ray tube had been perfected and was adopted for the production of televisions. In 1929, Germany became the first country to make regular television broadcasts.

### 1933 ELECTROSCOPES

ALTHOUGH THE OPTICAL telescope and microscope still give useful service, the twentieth century has given us electronic means for "looking" at things in more detail. In 1932, astronomer Karl Jansky (1905–50) detected the presence of

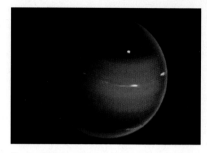

*The planet Neptune, taken from Voyager 2.*

"radio noise" coming from outer space. This led to the development of radio telescopes, with the realization that radio waves could tell scientists a lot more detail about the universe. Radio waves have a much lower frequency than those of light, so a radio telescope is in the shape of a large dish to catch enough information. The first scanning electron microscope was developed by Max Knoll and Ernst Ruska, between 1928 and 1933, in Berlin. It detects electrons that are bounced off the surface of objects being scanned, and creates a visual image on a screen. It can magnify up to 200,000 times. The scanning tunneling microscope can achieve up to 100 million magnifications and works by allowing electrons to jump from a tungsten scanning tip onto the subject, measuring the distance each time to create an image.

## 1934 NUCLEAR TECHNOLOGY

HAVING COME UP with the formula $E=mc^2$, Einstein had shown that matter is lost in the form of heat and radiation by nuclear reactions. Nuclear fission is the splitting apart of nuclei by neutrons in a chain reaction. It was first achieved by Italian scientist Enrico Fermi in 1934. Robert Oppenheimer (1904–1967) led a team that developed the first fission atomic bomb, tested in New Mexico in 1945. By 1952, the hydrogen bomb, a new type of weapon, had been tested. It was a fusion atomic bomb, which joined the nuclei of hydrogen atoms to make helium atoms—a process that would release a lot of heat, thus, called a thermonuclear weapon. Hydrogen bombs also create spare neutrons as part of their exhaust, which give off high levels of radiation. This fact is exploited in the neutron bomb, or ERW (Enhanced Radiation Weapon). The first nuclear power-station experiments were carried out by Fermi in 1942, and the first working nuclear reactor was set up in Russia in 1954. Nuclear power has also been used to run submarines and warships since 1959.

## 1935 RADAR AND SONAR

RADAR, AN ACRONYM of "radio direction and ranging," was invented by Robert Watson-Watt (1892–1973) in 1935 as a way of locating enemy aircraft. It works by emitting radio waves at regular intervals, which bounce back from solid objects if the object is within range. A receiver translated the returning radio waves into a visual dot on a screen, which showed its location. Radar is a vital means for tracking the movements of commercial and domestic air traffic. SONAR is an acronym for "sound navigation and ranging." It works in a similar way to radar, except that it uses ultrasonic waves—because radio waves will not travel through water. Sonar serves the equivalent purpose to radar but in a marine environment. It was invented by Frenchman Paul Langevin (1872–1946) in 1914 for detecting German U-Boats.

*The first nuclear power stations were built in the 1940s.*

## 1936 CIRCUIT BOARDS AND MICROPROCESSORS

IN 1936, AN AUSTRIAN named Paul Eisler, living in England, decided that it would be a good idea to incorporate all the loose workings of his homemade radio onto a board. Having invented the circuit board, he attempted for some years to sell the idea of printed circuit boards to electronics companies. He had no luck initially and had been passed around from place to place. It was the necessity, in warfare, that eventually created a need for the rapid reproduction of electronic circuits, which were used to control the proximity fuses for the antiaircraft shells fired at Nazi V1 "doodlebugs" in 1944. After the war, the printed circuit board was embraced in the United States, and it revolutionized the new and now burgeoning electronics industry. By the 1950s, the country was developing miniature circuit boards using silicon as a semiconductor. These became known as silicon chips, and could comprise many thousands of components all scaled down into a microprocessor. Circuit boards for larger components are still used in conjunction with silicon chips, which are mounted onto them.

## 1945 MICROWAVES

MICROWAVES ARE BEAMS of short wave, or high frequency, electromagnetic radiation or infrared light. They can carry a lot of energy with them and, as a result, have been employed in a variety of ways by many different technologies. Uses include the now familiar household microwave oven, radar, radio broadcasting, and lasers. Percy LeBaron Spencer invented the first microwave oven in 1945, which was marketed as the Radar Range by Raytheon in 1947. He discovered the potential of microwaves when they mysteriously

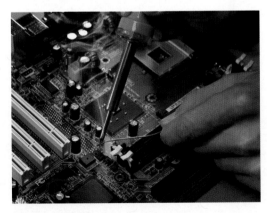

*Soldering a circuit board.*

*Early lasers used ruby crystals to create light. Today, many other materials are used.*

melted a chocolate bar he had in his pocket during an experiment. LASER is an acronym for "light amplification by stimulated emission of radiation." The first laser beam was produced by Theodore Maiman of California in 1960, using a ruby crystal to create the now well-known red pinpoint path of light. Since then, many solids, liquids, and gases have been used as laser materials and lasers have found many uses.

Communication signaling, cutting, drilling and welding, satellite tracking, weaponry, medical and biological research, surgery, and even entertainment have all benefited from laser technology. The laser used for reading information on RAMS and CDs is a blue short-wave laser developed in 1988 by Japan. IBM introduced microlasers for computer circuitry switching in 1989.

### 1950s DIGITAL CODING

THE TERM "DIGITAL" means to be made up of numbers, as digital information is indeed a numerical code. The numbers used are usually binary, which means just two numbers, which run in sequences: 1 and 0 are used, representing "on" and "off" in effect. Different sequences comprise each piece of data, which is deciphered using a microprocessor within the machine using the digital information. Digital has become the prime means for the coding, storage, transmission, processing, and reconstructing of information. It was adopted readily by industries concerned with computer, audio, and visual information as early as the 1950s, because it offered the advantage of virtually eliminating any degradation or distortion of signals during transmission, storage, and processing.

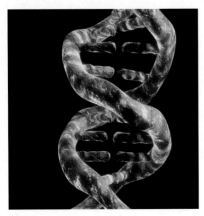

*A length of DNA, showing a double helix.*

### 1953 DNA UNRAVELED

AFTER DARWIN AND WALLACE had hit on the process by which evolution occurs, it came to others to reveal the mechanism and the components within. Gregor Mendel (1822–84) performed experiments, using successive generations of pea plants, which demonstrated how particulate inheritance is controlled by dominant and recessive genes. When the value of his work was recognized in the early 1900s, it encouraged scientists to tread further ground. By the 1940s, it was realized that genes must be components of DNA (deoxyribonucleic acid). The race was on to describe how DNA was structured and, therefore, how genes controlled characteristics and duplicated themselves. In 1953, James Watson (born 1928) and Francis Crick (1916–2004) announced their discovery that DNA must be a double helix, with connecting rungs. Each rung was a base pair of cytosine-guanine or adenine-thymine, thus forming a double-binary code. A different code was carried by each gene comprising the DNA strand, and was used to control the production of amino acids in constructing proteins. What was more, the DNA could "unzip" itself and attract the necessary chemicals to become two identical strands.

### 1957 SATELLITES AND PROBES

SATELLITES HAVE BEEN orbiting the earth since Sputnik I was launched by Russia in 1957. Thousands have been sent into orbit over the years, by various countries, for a wide variety of uses. Many satellites are used to observe or scan the earth for geological information: some are spy satellites, others track the weather, still more are there to make astronomical observations. Communications satellites receive and transmit information from one place to another on the earth's surface, and are usually in geostationary orbits. The first probe was the Russian Luna 3, which sent back pictures of the dark side of the moon in 1959. A number of probes have since been sent on voyages of astronomical discovery. They have supplied a great deal of valuable information about the other planets in our solar system.

### 1961 ROBOTICS

THE FIRST INDUSTRIAL application of a robotic machine came in 1961. General Motors (GM) introduced the Unimation 1900 into their car assembly line. By 1980, GM had a "seeing" robot, which was able to select and separate components by recognition. Since then, many programmable, computer-controlled and remote-controlled robots have been developed, and their applications have been very varied. Most robots are used to complete tasks more effectively than humans, usually because the job is boring or laborious, which may lead to problems with concentration. Some robots, however, have proved very useful in situations that are too dangerous, or simply impossible, for humans to function in. Good examples of these are bomb- disposal robots and roving robots used on the surface of other planets. There are also nanorobots being developed and sophisticated robotic prosthetics.

### 1969 MEN ON THE MOON

THE FIRST HUMAN in space was Russian cosmonaut Yuri Gagarin (1934–68), who completed a single orbit of the earth aboard Vostok I in 1961. In 1969, the first person set foot on the moon. Neil Armstrong (born 1930), accompanied by Edwin "Buzz" Aldrin (born 1930) and Michael Collins (born 1930), landed on the moon in the *Apollo 11* module. The first reusable space craft was the NASA Space Shuttle *Columbia*, first launched in 1981. The first permanently manned space station was Mir, established by the Russians in 1986. The experiences of cosmonauts and astronauts, living for long periods in space stations, have been carefully researched as part of the preparation for planned missions to Mars in the twenty-first century, which will take several months of travel.

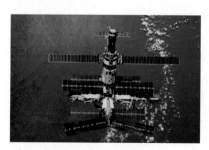

*Mir Space Station launched on February 19, 1986.*

### 1973 GENETIC MANIPULATION

AFTER IT WAS discovered how DNA and their genes work, scientists set about trying to alter the genes of species to achieve new characteristics. Gene splicing, the insertion of pieces of new DNA into an existing DNA strand, was invented in 1973 by American scientists Stanley Cohen and Herbert Boyer. This has enabled scientists to produce transgenic species, so-called because they have had foreign genes introduced. Transgenic or genetically engineered species can possess desired characteristics that make them economically more viable through resistance to disease and pests, higher yields, and so on; or they may be used to produce valuable chemicals, medicines, or hormones for medical use. Genetically manipulated foods became available in 1994 and developments have continued apace. Cloning of species has also been developed so that the desired characteristics are maintained, instead of being diluted by the natural evolutionary process. However, cloning does have the inherent danger of removing the survival mechanism, which is genetic variety.

### 1984 E-MAIL AND INTERNET

THE TECHNICAL FOUNDATIONS for the Internet and the World Wide Web (WWW) were developed as a project, funded by the Advanced Research Project Agency (ARPA), to build an electrically run communications network able to withstand damage by nuclear warfare. Work began in 1984 and, with extra funding from the United States National Science Foundation, was able to link up American universities via five supercomputing centers. By the early 1990s, the service became cheap enough for domestic use. Sending and receiving e-mail (electronic mail), searching for information on the Internet, and advertising on Web sites became a familiar feature of modern life by the end of the twentieth century.

*Dolly, the first cloned sheep, at the Roslin Institute in Scotland.*

*Computer technology saw incredible advance during the last decade of the twentieth century.*

### 1990s PERIPHERAL DEVICES

THE COMPUTER PROCESSOR has become a multifunctional "nerve center" for information and communication technology, in both the workplace and home. There are various essential accessories, known as peripheral devices, which plug into the processor and enable the effective use of it. Peripherals include: monitors, keyboards, scanners, printers, mice, modems, microphones, videophones, speakers, floppy disks, and CD-Rom units. Together with the processor, the peripherals make up the ICT (Information and Communication Technology) kit, which can be assembled according to the specific requirements of the individual user. The memory size of the processor itself can be increased by the insertion of extra silicon chips.

### 1990s NANOTECHNOLOGY

THE INVENTION OF the scanning tunneling microscope (STM) has led to a new technology being possible—nanotechnology. Using a process similar to that used in making microchips, the STM is used to etch or sculpt silicon into minute shapes, which are the components of tiny machines. They are so small that the STM is actually building them, using single atoms or molecules. Tiny electric motors have been made that can rotate at several thousand revolutions per second, yet they are less than one-tenth of a millimeter in size. The uses for such small machines and devices are potentially very varied. It has been suggested that nanomachines could be injected into the body to perform tasks such as fighting pathogens, delivering medicines, or cleaning arteries. Others might be used to operate flying microrobots for reconnaissance work, spying, or hunting down crop pests.

## 1990–2000 HUMAN GENOME PROJECT

THE HUMAN GENOME PROJECT (HGP) was an international scientific research project with the objective to determine the sequence of chemical base pairs, which make up DNA, and map the approximately 23,000 protein-coding genes (far fewer than were expected prior to sequencing) of the human genome. The project first began in 1990 and was headed by James D. Watson at the National Institute of Health. A complete working draft of the genome was released in 2003. Most of the government-sponsored sequencing was performed in universities and research centers from nine countries around the world. The mapping of human genes is an important step in the development of medicines and other aspects of health care.

## 2000 DIGITAL CAMERAS OVERTAKE FILM

DIGITAL CAMERAS TAKE still photographs, video, or both, and most twenty-first-century cameras are digital. Digital cameras can do things film cameras cannot: display images on a screen immediately after they are recorded, store thousands of images on a single small memory device, record video with sound, and delete images to free storage

*The digital camera can produce high-resolution digital images, record sound, and capture video as well as still photographs.*

space. The optical system works the same as in film cameras. The diaphragm and shutter admit the correct amount of light to the imager, just as with film, but the image pick-up device is electronic instead of chemical. Today, digital cameras are incorporated into many devices ranging from PDAs (personal digital assistants) to cell phones; they can even be found as a reversing aid in some vehicles. In less than ten years, the current high-quality images and the convenience of digital cameras have made them more popular than film cameras by far.

## 2000s INTERNET AND CELL PHONES GO GLOBAL

WHILE DIGITAL TECHNOLOGY has been in mainstream usage since the 1980s and 1990s, it was only in the twenty-first century that Internet and cell phone usage really took off. Despite concerns about stress and antisocial behavior from overusing the Internet and worries about microwave radiation from cell phones causing brain tumors, as of 2009, 4.6 billion people, or over two-thirds of the global population, were using cell phones and over 1.73 billion people were using the Internet to send 90 trillion e-mails in that year.

## 2010 FACEBOOK BECOMES A CULTURE

FACEBOOK WAS LAUNCHED in February 2004. By July 2010, it had more than 500 million active users worldwide. Users can network among people and send them messages, update personal profiles, and tell friends about themselves. Users can also join networks organized by workplaces, schools, or colleges. The Web site allows anyone to become members. Facebook has met with some political storms. It has been blocked from time to time in several countries. It has also been banned at many offices to stop employees from wasting time. Privacy has also been an issue, and it has been compromised several times. It has also been involved in hot debate over the sale of fans and friends to other organizations.

*Facebook is a social networking Web site launched in February 2004 that is operated and privately owned by Facebook, Inc. founded by Mark Zuckerberg.*

# Religions, Belief, and Thought

### 1900s CHRISTIANITY IN THE THIRD WORLD

CRITICISM OF COLONIALISM and the brutality of missionaries date back to the time of Bartolomé de Las Casas (1474–1566), a Spanish Dominican missionary who defended the rights of indigenous peoples in Latin America. Franz Fanon's (1925–61) book about colonialism in Algeria, *The Wretched of the Earth*, was one source of the modern Liberation Theology movement. Liberation Theology sees Christ as the friend of the poor, who lived among them and died for them. It stresses biblical opposition to the pursuit of wealth and biblical teachings on justice. Archbishop Oscar Romero (1917–80), who was assassinated by the El Salvador government for speaking out for the poor, is their leading martyr. Theologians include the Catholics Leonardo Boff (born 1938) of Brazil, Gustavo Gutierrez (born 1928) of Peru, Juan Luis Segundo (born 1925–1996) of Uruguay, and Jon Sobrino (born 1938) of El Salvador; and the Protestants José Míguez Bonino (born 1924) of Argentina and Rubem Alves (born 1933) of Brazil.

*From the earliest days of exploration, native peoples were forced to accept the religion of new settlers.*

### 1900s THE REDISCOVERY OF HOLISM

MATHEMATICIAN Ludwig von Bertalanffy, ecologist Aldo Leopold, and statesman Jan Smuts are three diverse sources of systems theory and ecological science. The study of complex systems, such as computer programs, ecological systems, human communities, and the human body, has led scientists to the realization

*Sigmund Freud (1856–1939), the inventor of psychoanalysis.*

## 1900s THE DISCOVERY OF THE UNCONSCIOUS

THE INTRODUCTION OF the concept of the unconscious mind has had a major impact upon the way mental illness and behavior problems are treated, even today. Psychology has, however, come in for much criticism from philosophers. This is because most of psychology's theories cannot be proven. Because of the vagueness and lack of evidence offered in psychology, the field has also been frequently criticized—Freud reduces the cause of all psychological problems to sex, Adler to the will to power, and Skinner to past programming—all of which contradict one another.

## 1900s THE DISESTABLISHMENT OF CONFUCIANISM

THE YEAR 1912 marked the overthrow of the Qing dynasty's last emperor, two year-old Puyi. Confucianism, which put great emphasis upon loyalty to the emperor, was seen as a threat to the new establishment and its revolutionary leader, Sun Yat-Sen. Later, after Mao Zedong's successful revolution in 1949, Confucian teachings were considered elitist and reactionary. The people's Republic of China established the concept of the State run for the welfare of its great population.

that it is impossible to try to understand these structures by analyzing each of its components. In the absence of this detailed knowledge, it is still possible to predict the behavior of these systems with statistical models and general principles of systems theory. Complex systems are self-organizing and naturally maintain themselves unless severely disrupted. This understanding provides a basis for an approach to medicine centered upon allowing the body to heal itself, and an approach to sociology based upon allowing communities to develop naturally an approach to agriculture, which is based upon allowing nature to maximize its own productivity.

## 1913 BEHAVIORISM

BEHAVIORISTS TEACH that psychology should only study physical behavior—how humans or animals respond to a stimulus—and not speculate about feelings, emotions, or the unconscious. Established in 1913 by J.B. Watson, behaviorism was popularized by B.F. Skinner (1904–90). In his book *Walden II*, he advocated that a better society should be created by programming people to modify their behavior. In his *Beyond Freedom and Dignity* (1971), he denies that humans have free will or responsibility for their behavior.

## 1930 THE BIRTH OF JACQUES DERRIDA

JACQUES DERRIDA (1930–2004) was born in Algeria. His thought developed as a response to that of Heidegger. He felt that metaphysical philosophy was without meaning, that it had reached the end of its history, and that the only true philosophy concerned the nature of being. The question he asks is, "What can we say about Being without resorting to any metaphysical assumptions?" He tries to answer this by deconstructing philosophical statements on this matter and showing their limitations, contradictions, and false assumptions.

## 1932 & 1949 ALDOUS HUXLEY AND GEORGE ORWELL

THE SCENARIOS PORTRAYED in the books *Brave New World* (1932) and *1984* (1949), are dystopias—not visions of an ideal world but rather their opposite. In *1984*, George Orwell (1903–50) illustrates an authoritarian Communist world similar to Stalin's Soviet Union—a world in which everything is controlled by "Big Brother" and his Thought Police for the benefit of the masses. In *Brave New World*, by contrast, Aldous Huxley (1894–1963) describes a world where the arts of the salesman are used by the government, where people are genetically engineered and psychologically normalized to fit into society, where brainwashing and

*Aldous Huxley (1894–1963), author of* Brave New World.

subliminal advertising are used to keep people consuming and to prevent them thinking—the possible future of the consumer society.

### 1934 SIR KARL POPPER'S LOGIC

VIENNESE PHILOSOPHER Karl Popper (1902–94) argued that it is never possible to have certain knowledge. In his *Logic of Scientific Discovery* (1934), he shows that no scientific hypothesis can ever be proved—it can only be falsified. Indeed, if it could never be falsified, it would not be a scientific theory. Therefore, he proposed, every good scientific theory is simply a model that has yet to be disproved. His opposition to the concept of certainty led him, in his *The Open Society and its Enemies* (1945), to criticize authoritarian models of society, such as those proposed by Plato and Karl Marx.

### 1941 THE HOLOCAUST AND THE FOUNDATION OF THE STATE OF ISRAEL

ANTI-SEMITISM, which had declined since the fifteenth century, began to return to France, Germany, and eastern Europe in the late nineteenth century. From 1941, Nazi Germany embarked upon the rounding up and systematic murder of all the Jews in German-controlled Europe.

*Israeli children, orphaned during World War II, dance the hora, a popular dance among the socialist Zionists in a kibbutz in the early days of the state of Israel.*

By the end of World War II in 1945, no less than six million Jews had died in gas chambers. In 1948, Britain, following its victory in the war, was obliged to offer its colonial Palestinian territory as a Jewish homeland. This return to the "promised land," after 2,000 years of exile and the fact that it closely followed the horrors of the Holocaust, was the cause of a determination to succeed among the world's Jewish population. Their hope and enthusiasm have helped them build a modern nation in just a few decades, but it also encouraged a nationalism that has led to the oppression of the Palestinians and conflict with their Arab neighbors.

*French writer and philosopher Jean-Paul Sartre (1905–80).*

## 1943 JEAN-PAUL SARTRE AND EXISTENTIALISM

"EXISTENCE PRECEDES ESSENCE" and "man makes himself." These phrases encapsulate the atheist existentialism of French philosopher Jean-Paul Sartre (1905–80). In the absence of a God who created us with a purpose, he pointed out, we arrive in the world with nothing but our own existence. This problem is explored in his *Being and Nothingness* (1943). We have no choice but to decide for ourselves who we are—we must invent our own essence. The self is not an entity but a project, not something that has being but something that is forever becoming. Whoever defines themselves by their current role in life (for example,

"I am a waiter") lives in "bad faith." It is a philosophy that gives each of us an enormous responsibility but also complete freedom.

## 1949 ALDO LEOPOLD: THE ECOSYSTEM

ALDO LEOPOLD (1887–1948) worked as a conservationist for the U.S. Forest Service. His posthumously published work, *A Sand County Almanac* (1949), introduces the concept of the ecosystem as an interacting web of living organisms that works together in its own natural balance. To manage an ecosystem, it is necessary to "think like a mountain" and obtain an overview of the whole system. His "Land Ethic" is based on the moral maxim that "a thing is right when it tends to preserve the integrity, stability, and beauty of the biotic community. It is wrong when it tends otherwise."

## 1949 MAO ZEDONG AND COMMUNISM IN CHINA

THE COMMUNIST LEADER Mao Zedong(1893–1976) was chairman of the Communist Party of China and the principal founder of the People's Republic of China. Mao helped found the Chinese Communist Party in Shanghai in 1921. In 1927, a military campaign was launched against the Communists, who retreated to rural areas, where they gained the support of the peasants. After Nationalist forces surrounded them in 1934, the Red Army retreated 6,000 miles (9,650 km) to the northwest in the Long March. In 1949, the Communists gained ground and declared the People's Republic. Chairman Mao promoted rural development, equality, and the pursuit of economic self-reliance in the villages. His *Little Red Book* became famous around the world.

*Buddhist practices were ruthlessly suppressed in the Far East during the 1950s.*

## 1950s THE DESTRUCTION AND REVIVAL OF BUDDHISM

COMMUNIST REVOLUTION in China, Vietnam, Laos, and Cambodia led to the abolition of Buddhism and the destruction of temples. In Cambodia, only eight monks survived. In Sri Lanka, colonialism nearly killed the tradition. A new Buddhism concerned with peace and community building has emerged. The Sarvodaya movement in Sri Lanka involves almost every village; in Cambodia, Maha Ghosananda leads huge peace walks across regions sown with landmines; in Vietnam, Thich Nhat Hanh, now exiled, founded *Tiep Hien*, the Order of Interbeing; and in Thailand, Sulak Sivaraksa challenges the government's Westernization policy.

*Mao's writings and thoughts are set out in his Little Red Book.*

## 1950s THE WEST TURNS EAST

THE AMERICAN "BEAT" poets of the 1950s, including Allen Ginsberg, Jack Kerouac, and Gary Snyder, drew upon Buddhism as a philosophy for rejecting the materialism and "work ethic" of the Western world. Their example inspired the countercultural hippie movement of the 1960s. The Beatles became followers of the Maharishi and thousands of young people traveled to India or began to follow Eastern teachers—Hindu, Buddhist, and Sufi. Within ten years, Eastern practices, such as meditation and yoga, became almost universally available to the public.

*Scottish psychiatrist R.D. Laing (1927–89).*

## 1960s R.D. LAING AND ANTIPSYCHIATRY

R.D. LAING (1927–89) was one of the most radical critics of psychiatric practice. In his books, *The Divided Self* (1960) and *Sanity, Madness and the Family* (1964), he rejected the orthodox view that schizophrenia is simply an illness and saw it instead as normal response to an impossible social situation. He, therefore, favored group therapies and attacked chemical therapies and electric-shock treatments. He also viewed madness not as a sign of mental decline, but as a phase through which the mind passed while healing itself. This led him to see the therapist as a companion on a journey through madness.

## 1971 B.F. SKINNER AND BEHAVIORISM

BEHAVIORISM IS A school of psychology based on empirical science. Originating around 1913 by J.B. Watson, and outlined in his book *Behaviorism* (1925), behaviorists believe that the only valid form of psychology is the study of how animals and humans physically respond to stimuli. B.F. Skinner (1904–90) states the position in its purest form in his *Beyond Freedom and Dignity* (1971), in which he presents the mind as an automatic machine and rejects the idea of free will. He concludes, controversially, that our minds should be scientifically programmed by psychologists to ensure socially beneficial behavior.

## 1973 POSTINDUSTRIALISM AND THE REDEFINITION OF WORK

AMERICAN SOCIOLOGIST Daniel Bell (born 1919) argues that the original Protestant work ethic underlying capitalism will collapse as a result of the huge productive capacity of modern technology. This is argued in his books, *The Cultural Contradictions of Capitalism* (1976), *The End of Ideology* (1960), and *The Coming of Post-Industrial Society* (1973). Modern capitalism requires consumers in pursuit of leisure and so is moving us toward a world where work is no longer seen as a virtue. Professor Charles Handy (born 1932) points in a similar direction, predicting the end of the full-time, nine-to-five job and forecasting instead that people will increasingly work parttime on a freelance basis.

## 1973 SMALL IS BEAUTIFUL

E.F. SCHUMACHER'S *Small is Beautiful: A Study of Economics as if People Mattered* was published in 1973. He challenged the vast institutions that were emerging in both capitalist and communist countries and called for small communities, decentralization, and technology on a human scale. Excessive size was, he believed, the cause of the world's woes including unemployment, poor working conditions, inequality, and a decline in freedom. In particular, he was keen to help poor countries develop without suffering the problems of gigantism and, to this end, he helped develop "Intermediate Technologies," machines that could be owned and used on a village scale—an approach that has been widely adopted in developing countries.

*German-born economist Ernst Friedrich Schumacher.*

### 1975 MICHEL FOUCAULT

FRENCH PHILOSOPHER Michel Foucault (1926–84) sought to understand the origin and nature of institutional controls over how we see ourselves. In his *Discipline and Punish* (1975) and his *Madness and Civilization* (1961), he explored the origins and development of concepts and normality by looking at the history of punishment and of asylums. State concepts of normality are internalized and determine how we see ourselves. The "work of freedom" is to step outside these definitions and to create ourselves.

### 1976 GENETIC DETERMINISM

PROFESSOR RICHARD DAWKINS (born 1941) argues in *The Selfish Gene* (1976) that the process underlying life and evolution is the survival and replication of the fittest gene. Derived directly from Darwin's theory of the survival of the fittest organism, Dawkins argues that plants and animals, as well as their nests, burrows, and even ideas, are merely the machines that genes use to survive. Although accused of reductionism by his opponents, his theories have taken a new twist. He argues that any basic unit that self-replicates, whether a gene, a process, or an idea, is capable of evolution through natural selection. This means that not only would individual animals evolve, but so would artifacts, cultures, and religions, communities and ecosystems. He argues that "God" is merely an idea that uses a whole range of effective techniques to survive—but a potential weakness of this argument is that it could be applied to any idea, including his own.

### 1979 JAMES LOVELOCK AND THE GAIA HYPOTHESIS

THE GAIA HYPOTHESIS, as outlined in biochemist James Lovelock's (born 1919) *Gaia* (1979), is a hypothesis that the earth, its soil, oceans, atmosphere, and biosphere constitutes a self-regulating system that can be thought of as living. He has often been accused, by scientists, of arguing that the earth is conscious, but this view, common among many of his

*Gaia sees the world as a self-regulating system that can be thought of as living.*

supporters, forms no part of the theory. His studies of atmospheric chemistry, which led him to discover the hole in the ozone layer and the wide distribution of pesticides, have also provided much evidence for the theory.

*The Iranian-backed Hezbollah militiamen, the largest of the Shi'ite Islamic fundamentalist parties in Lebanon.*

### 1980 THE RESURGENCE OF ISLAM

THE ISLAMIC REVIVAL that has shaken Iran, Afghanistan, Algeria, and most of the Muslim world since 1980 has several aspects that are hard to disentangle. It is both a spiritual revival, although most of the mystic sects have been subjected to harsh oppression, and a militant response to the economic and intellectual dominance of the West. The Islamic Revolution in Iran, led by Ayatollah Khomeini, marked the start of the movement, which inspired the Taliban regime in Afghanistan, the Hezbollah in Palestine, and terrorist groups in many other nations. It is probably too early to tell whether the intellectuals, whose main concerns are cultural and spiritual, will gain the upper hand or whether the fundamentalists will instigate increasingly violent attacks on secular societies.

### 1992 SUSTAINABILITY: THE RIO DECLARATION

IT WAS AT the largest meeting of heads of governments, held in Rio de Janeiro, Brazil, in 1992, that the Rio Declaration on Environment and Development was agreed upon—169 nations signed the document. While the agreement is important for this reason, many have pointed out that it is worded to avoid committing any nation to taking real action. It has also been questioned whether its support for accelerated economic growth can be reconciled with its advocacy of "sustainability."

## 2003 POINCARÉ CONJECTURE IS SOLVED

IN 2000, THE CLAY Mathematics Institute announced the Millennium Prize Problems, and in 2003 the Poincaré conjecture was solved by Grigori Perelman (who declined to accept any awards). Perelman is a Jewish Russian mathematician who has made landmark contributions to mathematics. In particular, he proved Thurston's geometrization conjecture. This solves in the affirmative the Poincaré conjecture, posed in 1904, which was viewed as one of the most important and difficult open problems in topology until it was solved. On December 22, 2006, the journal *Science* recognized Perelman's proof of the Poincaré conjecture as the scientific "Breakthrough of the Year," the first such recognition in the area of mathematics.

## 2005 KYOTO PROTOCOL

ALTHOUGH THE Kyoto Protocol was initially adopted on December 11, 1997 in Kyoto, Japan, it only entered into force on February 16, 2005. As of November 2009, 187 states have signed and ratified the protocol. Under it, 37 industrialized countries commit themselves to a reduction of the four main greenhouse gases—carbon dioxide, methane, nitrous oxide, and sulfur hexafluoride—and two groups of gases, hydrofluorocarbons and perfluorocarbons produced by them. All member countries gave general commitments to reduction. The countries agreed to reduce their collective greenhouse gas emissions by 5.2 percent from the 1990 level. Emission limits do not include emissions by international aviation and shipping, but are in addition to the industrial gases, chlorofluorocarbons (CFCs), which are dealt with under the 1987 Montreal Protocol on Substances that Deplete the Ozone Layer.

*The general view of the commemorative symposium of the Kyoto Protocol hosted by the Ministry of the Environment of Japan.*

## 2005 CHANGING OF THE POPE, SCANDAL IN THE CHURCH

THE PAPAL CONCLAVE of 2005 was convened as a result of the death of Pope John Paul II on April 2, 2005. After his death, the cardinals met and set a date to elect John Paul's successor. The conclave began on April 18, 2005 and ended on the following day after four ballots. Eligible members of the College of Cardinals of the Roman Catholic Church met and elected Cardinal Joseph Ratzinger as the new Pope. After accepting his election, Ratzinger took the name Pope Benedict XVI. This came in the wake of a sexual-abuse scandal in the Boston archdiocese in Massachusetts. In early 2002, *Boston Globe* coverage of a series of criminal prosecutions of five Roman Catholic priests thrust the issue of sexual abuse of minors by priests into the national limelight. The coverage of these cases encouraged other victims to come forward with their allegations of abuse, which resulted in more lawsuits, criminal cases, and the resignation of several priests, bishops, and cardinals.

## 2006 YUNUS RECEIVES NOBEL PEACE PRIZE

In 2006, a Bangladeshi banker, economist, and founder of Grameen Bank, Muhammad Yunus (born 1940)

*Nobel Peace laureate Muhammad Yunus poses for a picture with the Nobel medal and diploma at Oslo Town Hall.*

and his bank were jointly awarded the Nobel Peace Prize, "for their efforts to create economic and social development from below." Yunus was previously a professor of economics, where he developed the concepts of microcredit and microfinance. These loans are given to entrepreneurs too poor to qualify for traditional bank loans. Yunus himself has received several other national and international honors. He is the author of *Banker to the Poor* and one of the founding members of Global Elders.

# Picture Credits

All images courtesy of Getty Images who are grateful to the following photographers and images libraries:

**3D4Medical.com/Getty Images**: 296.

**AFP/Getty Images**: 42, 133, 216, 230, 236, 245, 252, 257, 269, 272, 279, 286, 305, 311, 312, 313.

**Altrendo/Getty Images**: 30.

**Archive Photos/Getty Images**: 34(r), 63, 82, 95(t), 110, 116(b), 124, 137, 148, 169, 175, 193, 206, 209, 222, 224, 225(t), 224, 261, 274(t), 280, 288.

**Bloomberg/Getty Images**: 233, 289.

**Brand X Pictures/Getty Image**: 72.

**Comstock Images/Getty Image**: 218-219, 271.

**De Agostini Picture Library/Getty Image**: 23, 34(l), 59, 71, 81, 99(t), 212, 246, 275.

**Digital Vision/Getty Images**: 32.

**Dorling Kindersley/Getty Images**: 28(b), 60.

**Gallo Images/Getty Images**: 10-11, 52.

**Getty Images**: 99(b), 152, 167, 176, 177, 232, 243, 244, 253(t), 255, 258, 259, 276, 285, 291, 298, 299, 301.

**Hulton Archive/Getty Images**: 33, 35, 40-41, 45, 47, 48(b), 48(t), 49, 50, 55, 56, 67, 69, 83, 85(b), 87, 88, 93, 95(b), 98, 117, 119, 122, 126-127, 144, 156, 161, 162, 163, 165, 171, 178(b), 179, 180, 183, 191, 196, 210(b), 211, 215, 217, 223, 225(b), 227, 234, 238, 242, 248(t), 249, 251, 260(t), 262, 263, 268(b), 268(t), 274(b), 277, 290, 303, 304, 308, 309.

**Iconica/Getty Images**: 294.

**National Geographic/Getty Images**: 20, 21, 228(b), 240, 295.

**Nick Hewetson/Getty Images**: 92.

**Photodisc/Getty Images**: 284, 297.

**Photographer's Choice/Getty Images**: 281(t)

**Photonica/Getty Images**: 307(t).

**Popperfoto/Getty Images**: 13(t), 19, 26, 46, 128, 131, 146, 210(t), 220, 221, 235, 260(b), 270.

**Robert Harding World Imagery/Getty Images**: 78, 140, 302.

**Roger Viollet/Getty Images**: 86, 237, 239 ,306.

**SSPL/Getty Images**: 24, 62, 66, 113, 149, 150, 151(b), 164, 172, 173, 174, 178(t), 185, 204, 207, 212(t), 250, 253(b), 273, 281(b), 300.

**Stone/Getty Images**: 31.

**SuperStock/Getty Images**: 53, 158, 160, 188.

**Taxi/Getty Images**: 22, 282, 293.

**The Bridgeman Art Library/Getty Images**: 12, 14, 15, 16, 18, 25, 28(t), 29, 39, 43, 54, 57, 58, 61, 64, 73, 74-75, 76 77, 80, 84 85(t), 90, 91, 94, 96, 100-101, 102, 103(b), 103(t), 104(b), 104(t), 105, 106, 107, 108, 109, 111, 114, 115, 118, 120, 121, 123, 125, 129, 130, 134(b), 135, 136, 141, 142, 145, 147, 151(t), 153, 154-155, 157, 159, 166, 168, 181, 182, 184(t), 186-187, 189, 190, 192, 194, 195, 197, 199, 200, 201, 202, 205, 208, 248(b).

**The Image Bank/Getty Images**: 37, 70, 138, 278, 307(b), 310.

**Time & Life Pictures/Getty Images**: 13(b), 17, 36, 38, 44, 65, 68, 79, 112, 116(t), 132, 134(t), 139, 170, 184(b), 198, 203, 213, 214, 228(t), 229, 231, 247, 254, 256, 264, 265, 266, 267, 283, 292.

**Washington Post/Getty Images**: 287.

t = top, b = bottom, l = left, r = right

Every effort has been made to trace the copyright holders of the pictures used and we apologize in advance for any omissions. We would be pleased to insert the appropriate acknowledgment in any subsequent edition of this publication.

# Index

315